Women at work

Women at work
Psychological and organizational perspectives

edited by
Jenny Firth-Cozens and Michael A. West

Open University Press
Milton Keynes · Philadelphia

Open University Press
Celtic Court
22 Ballmoor
Buckingham MK18 1XW

and
1900 Frost Road, Suite 101
Bristol, PA 19007, USA

First Published 1991

British Library Cataloguing in Publication Data

Women at work: psychological and organizational
    perspectives.
    1. Great Britain. Women. Employment. Equality of opportunity
    I. Firth-Cozens, Jenny   II. West, Michael A.
    331.41330941

    ISBN 0-335-09253-5
    ISBN 0-335-09252-7 (pbk)

Library of Congress Cataloging-in-Publication Data

Women at work: psychological and organizational perspectives/edited by
    Jenny Firth-Cozens and Michael A. West.
        p.   cm.
     ISBN 0-335-09253-5   ISBN 0-335-09252-7 (pbk.)
     1. Women – Employment – Psychological aspects.   2. Sex role in the work
    environment.   3. Organizational change.   I. Firth-Cozens, Jenny.   II. West,
    Michael, 1951–
     HD6053.W6383   1990
     331.4 – dc20   90–33854 CIP

Typeset by Rowland Phototypesetting Limited
Bury St Edmunds, Suffolk
Printed in Great Britain by Biddles Limited
Guildford and King's Lynn

Contents

List of contributors

Marilyn Aitkenhead Department of Management Studies, University of Technology, Loughborough

Beverly Alban-Metcalfe Nuffield Centre for Health Service Studies, University of Leeds

Rosalind S. Bramwell School of Management, University of Manchester Institute of Science and Technology

Catherine Cassell Department of Communication Studies, Sheffield City Polytechnic

Nina L. Colwill Faculty of Management, University of Manitoba

Marilyn J. Davidson School of Management, University of Manchester Institute of Science and Technology

Jenny Firth-Cozens Department of Psychology, University of Leeds

Jacqueline Bates Gaston Department of Occupational Psychology, University of Ulster at Jordanstown

Daphne F. Jackson Faculty of Science, University of Surrey

Sonia Liff Department of Management Studies, University of Technology, Loughborough

Peggy Newton Now at Manchester University, but this chapter written while in the Department of Behavioural Sciences, Huddersfield Polytechnic

Kate Osborne Psychologist and teacher

Louise Ricklander Freelance Psychologist, Lidingö, Sweden

Sandra M. Simpson Department of Psychology, University of Nottingham

Janet E. Stockdale Department of Social Psychology, London School of Economics and Political Science

Susan Vinnicombe Cranfield School of Management, Cranfield Institute of Technology

Janette Webb Department of Business Studies, University of Edinburgh

Michael A. West MRC/ESRC Social and Applied Psychology Unit, University of Sheffield

Preface

The experience of women in the world of work is a topic of unparalleled importance in the field of organizational psychology, and yet few books have appeared either in the European academic or business spheres, addressing the area. Women represent more than half of the world's population and their representation in organizations is swiftly increasing. At the same time the experiences of women in organizations are very different from those of men. In the past, researchers have either tended to assume a commonality – that what is true of the experience of men at work will be true for women – or have used only male subjects. It is only more recently that women's experience has also been examined. Even then they are often compared with men, using the research methods and asking research questions relevant to the latter. There is, however, a growing movement towards examining the experiences of women in organizations in their own right, in order that a fuller, more accurate picture can be painted. This book is part of that movement and the contributions of the authors combine to form a picture of women's experience both generally and in particular areas of work.

The book examines the area from a predominantly psychological perspective, using paradigms and methods largely drawn from work and organizational psychology (though some chapters present more personal accounts). It also tends to focus mostly on women in administrative, professional and white-collar areas since this is where the bulk of recent research on women within work and organizational psychology has been carried out. But even this is very recent and there is much more to be done before the male imbalance of research in work and organizational psychology is righted.

The book is divided into three parts. The first presents underlying gender issues of psychology, psychoanalysis and politics; the second considers the problems faced by women simply because they are female; and the third considers the implications of these in relation to specific occupations.

Most chapters follow a pattern of presenting an overview of research, describing new research findings, considering the practical implications, and proposing changes in individual and organizational behaviours. They examine the likely trends in the future and, most clearly and sometimes painfully, depict the widespread discrimination and harassment of women in the work-place. In the final chapter we offer our reactions to the contents and our views, as a woman and as a man, of how change might come about. But clearly much remains to be done. We see the book therefore as just one beginning of the examination of the experience of women from the perspectives of work and organizational psychology. We see its success as best determined by whether it brings about an increase in the awareness or improvement in the experiences of any individual, group or organization, or in the research methods used in relation to women in the world of work.

Jenny Firth-Cozens
Michael A. West

Part I
General issues

1 | Women's work . . . is never done

Kate Osborne

Women's work, whether inside the home or outside in the world of paid employment, has traditionally involved caring for others. Women working as housewives, mothers, cleaners, secretaries, nurses, teachers or social workers all share similar tasks. In all of these cases, whether for the family, in a service industry, or in one of the helping professions, such work demands a large measure of emotional input as well as practical skills and specialized knowledge. By definition, servicing is both highly repetitive and never-ending. No sooner is one pile of letters typed, one batch of nappies washed, or one set of meals prepared when the whole process has to start again. Caring for other people often means that the carer has to put the needs of others before her own. It is difficult for women with small children to have time for themselves, and similarly many women in paid work are expected to stay after hours to meet the demands of boss or institution. In addition, women's emotional giving is often eroticized, so that women are expected to service men sexually as part of their work (see Stockdale, Chapter 5). Most importantly, women's work is poorly rewarded, both financially and in terms of the status and power adhering to such services. Housework and mothering are unpaid and considered to be 'non-work' if performed for the woman's own family. Despite attempts at legislation for equal opportunities and pay, women still have lower average incomes than men.

There is also another sense in which women's work is never done: it is never, or hardly ever, done by men. As Janette Webb points out (Chapter 2), jobs themselves are gendered, and in those cases where men have entered 'female' professions, such as primary teaching or nursing, they quickly adopt managerial positions and limit their involvement with service delivery. Domestic responsibilities for housework and child-care are still largely the domain of women, and even when women also work outside the home their male partners only marginally increase the 'help' they give, leading to women's doubt – or treble – shift involving paid work, housework and responsibility for children (see Alban-Metcalfe and West, Chapter 12). Basic necessities for working women such as work-place nurseries are infrequently available and have until recently been penalized by a tax system that regards them as being 'perks', less warranted even than the possession of a company car. Women are therefore often constrained to seek jobs which allow them flexible time in order to fulfil these obligations. These constraints prevent women from having adequate job protection, applying for promotion or re-training, or taking jobs involving travelling and unsocial hours. As we shall see later, the fact that young women are considered to be potential carers of their own families limits their educational choices and career options. These restrictions all have far-reaching effects on women's income, choice of work and career development.

In examining why work is such a potentially more complex issue for women than for men, three aspects of women's psychology will be considered which can be seen to contribute to the dilemma of women's position in the work-force. For it is no longer adequate to view women as being simply passive victims of a sexist society whose structures, institutions and legislation mitigate against women's fuller social participation. All of these factors still operate, but we must also consider how women's development within a patriarchal culture, and the adult identities formed within this context, perpetuate a notion of womanhood that limit the changes made possible by social reforms. First, I shall consider the internal psychodynamics of women's servicing, looking at the way in which women's early experiences of being nurtured and nurturing others shape their future development. Second, I shall look at some of the more frequently postulated aspects of women's psychology as they relate to the demands of the work-place. Finally I shall consider the dilemma of productive versus reproductive work, and analyse the effects of women's mothering on their occupational profile.

In order to do this, I shall where possible rely on sources of information that are woman-centered, rather than use data which have been collected in such a way that women's experiences are misrepresented. As Stanley and Wise (1983) have argued, conventional research in psychology has either ignored women completely, assuming that results pertinent to men can be generalized to women, or objectified women by imposing on them unrealistic and irrelevant test situations which produce spurious information. These traditions have distorted women's experiences, and feminist scholars are now attempting to re-examine fundamental aspects of women's lives in ways which more accurately represent their experiences. Stanley and Wise describe several possible methodologies with which to extract more meaningful and personal information, particularly the analysis of women's own accounts of their experiences, for example in the form of conversations, diaries, letters, auto-biographical accounts and oral reports. Interviews have been used by sociologists to examine women's experiences of central issues such as housework (Oakley 1974), child-birth (Oakley 1980) and the care of young children (Boulton 1983). Women's descriptions of their lives which emerge during individual or group therapy are a more intimate and privileged form of interview, providing greater detail (see for example Krzowski and Land 1988). In all of these cases, particular care has to be taken to protect the identity of the women involved, and the confidential nature of the information they provide. Also, research conducted as it invariably is by a privileged, educated elite samples but a small section of women's experiences. Black, handicapped and minority women are all under-represented in the available literature, and this account will inevitably be constrained by the selectiveness of existing documentation.

The psychodynamics of women's nurturing

There is much debate concerning the extent to which it is legitimate to focus on supposed sex-differences as explanations of women's current position in society. Whereas some argue that a fuller knowledge of women's particular experiences and abilities will allow for a revalorization of women's special qualities and provide a basis for affirmative action (e.g. Gilligan 1982), others fear that generalizations about women will ghettoize them and lead to a form of determinism which is characteristic of much sociobiology (e.g. Segal 1987). Most of the recent work within a psychodynamic perspective assumes the former position and it is within this framework that I shall consider the arguments of a feminist psychoanalysis which are relevant to an understanding of women's psychology.

Early psychodynamic formulations concerning women's servicing of others were dominated by descriptions of women's tendency to put the needs and desires of others before their own well-being, which was seen as being masochistic. In developing his theory of female masochism, Freud (1924) wrote about women's pervasive sense of guilt, which he claimed was largely unconscious, about not doing enough for others, or not being good enough. But whereas Deutsch (1944) viewed this as an inevitable, even innate, aspect of women's psychology, Horney (1967) pointed out the realities of most women's economic and social dependence on men, who have for the most part greater physical strength and power over them. The knowledge that they can be physically intimidated makes it more likely, she argued, that women are used to putting up with being mistreated and to deny their own feelings. Rather than accepting a biological determinism, Horney showed how biological factors prepare women to accept the masochistic role which is often imposed on them by a patriarchal culture. In reconsidering this issue, Caplan (1984) has argued that what women actually *do* when they are described as being masochistic can be seen to be prosocial, loving and nurturant actions, and that such altruism should instead be positively construed rather than pathologized.

Attempts to understand the origins of women's caring for others, whether this be seen as a neurotic compulsion or a positive aspect of their personality, have focused on the early experiences of being cared for. Melanie Klein's observations of the mother–child relationship (see for example Klein 1937) and the extension of these theories by Winnicott (1965) and others within an object-relations approach have been studied by feminist theorists and therapists trying to unravel the long-term effects on women's psychology of their early experiences of being mothered. In her influential book *The Reproduction of Mothering*, sociologist Nancy Chodorow (1978) has reconsidered many psychotherapeutic case histories and produced an account of the development of women's caring. Her central thesis is that the nurturance that children receive (whether by biological mothers or their female substitutes such as child-minders, nannies, nursery nurses and so on) has differential effects on male and female psychology. Little boys, she claims, experiencing their mother's loving pride on having produced a son, grow up to expect care and nurturance to be automatically provided for them by women. In identifying with their fathers, as they reach adulthood they seek to replace their mother's caring for that provided by other women: from their sisters, lovers, wives or secretaries. On the other hand, little girls are often in a more ambivalent position. Not only do they generally receive less of their mother's care, since preference tends to be shown to the males in the household, but also they are often expected from an early age to help take care of others, particularly younger siblings, and even to look after their own mothers. In being 'mother's little helper', Chodorow argues, girls internalize the role of caring which affects the way they relate to other people, their educational achievement and overall adult personality.

In a similar vein, Dinnerstein (1978) has described the effects of women's mothering, in particular the unconscious ways in which women pass on notions of masculinity and femininity. Whereas many women are consciously attempting to resist sex-stereotyping in the rearing of their children (see Grabrucker 1988), it is clear that not only the surrounding culture but also the mother's struggle with her own notions of femininity make this a complex task.

A further dimension to women's psychology has been analysed by Miller (1976). In particular she examines the psychological effects of women's oppression, arguing that like all oppressed groups, women develop emotional mechanisms to cope with their relative powerlessness. These include a heightened awareness of other people's emotional states and a resultant blurring of the boundaries between self and others. Hence women tend to become the emotional specialists in relationships, mediating between children and father, siblings with each other, and carrying over this role into their relationships outside the family. Women, she argues, are more likely than men to define themselves in terms of their relationships with others, and experience separateness as a form of rejection and denial of themselves.

In helping women to examine the nature of their own early experiences of being mothered, Eichenbaum and Orbach (1982) find a history of complex psychodynamics in which women often feel that they lacked the affection and intimacy that they needed, while at the same time were constrained by over-concern about their safety and developing femaleness. Rather than being mother-blaming, as previous theories have tended to be, feminist psychoanalysis puts into context the realities of the mothers' position. For motherhood is still women's principal career, and women are expected to succeed at it with limited preparation or support.

The solution to this impasse, of women continually doing the caretaking both inside and outside the home while men are busy organizing, exploiting and ultimately destroying the world around them, is seen by Chodorow and others to depend on men's greater involvement in nurturing. Only when men become more involved in the care of their own families (and, we can add, looking after the wider society) will psychological changes occur at a fundamental level. If men were to share in the responsibilities for children, girls could experience care from men as well as women, relieving them from the ties of their identification with their mothers, and their mothers' identification with them. Similarly, boys could experience caring from men, rather than being restricted to the rough and tumble play, or indifference, which forms their usual relationships with their fathers. By encouraging men into child-care, Olivier (1989) argues, the boy's fear of the powerful mother, which develops into adult misogyny, and the girl's fear of rejection, which develops into adult insatiability for love, will be counterbalanced. Yet, as Rossi (1981) has pointed out, this begs the question of how such caring fathers are going to be produced. How do we break into the vicious circle to obtain a generation of men who want or are able to participate in the care of young children? Are men really prepared to make way for women in the public sphere if they are no longer restricted to mothering others? The relative unavailability of part-time work, job-sharing, parental leave and other formulae to enable both parents to share the care of their children imposes economic constraints on top of the psychological barriers to men's fuller participation in child-care. Instead, divorce and separation increase the likelihood that the father's emotional absence will be compounded by his physical absence.

A feminist psychoanalysis, then, suggests that men's neglect of their children, and women's resultant over-responsibility for child-care, have profound effects on the adult personality. Whereas men grow up to perpetuate their early struggles against emotional intimacy and take for granted that they will be cared for, women continue their search for affection and connection with others by providing the care. Within marriage, men can continue to be mothered by their wives, who provide for them the physical and emotional care they experienced when little. But there is no one available to mother women, who, if they find the time, have to be contented with mothering themselves. This dynamic continues into women's working lives, where as we shall see women's psychology leads them to construe their work differently from men.

Women's psychology and the demands of the work-place

For the majority of working women, the jobs they do will be an extension of the caring they provide at home. One benefit of working outside the home, however, is that at least their work is recognized and they are paid for doing it (however inadequately), even if when they go home they have to start all over again. Whereas women's nurturing skills make them solicited for certain jobs, particularly those that men dislike such as looking after small children, the sick and the elderly, or doing monotonous and repetitive industrial tasks, these very same capabilities are presumed to negate women from managerial and decision-making positions. Women are therefore often excluded from participation in planning how their jobs are performed. Increasingly, profits are expected to be shown at the expense of adequate provision of services. Even in education and health services, as teachers and nurses are making clear, a male pattern of accountability is dominating the provision of caring. Attempts to stem the tide and introduce more women-centred attitudes, for example in the areas of maternity and gynaecological practice, have resulted in women being reprimanded for confronting male authority (see Savage 1986).

When at work, women find themselves in environments largely dominated by masculine values; by individualism and competitiveness rather than connectedness, and by a denial of affect rather than emotional sensitivity. Many women react to this by experiencing anxieties about their abilities, showing a lack of confidence, and having a sense of emotional splitting where they are unable to be their real selves at work. There have been many attempts to explain why women, who despite contributing in ever greater numbers to the work-force, continue to occupy lower-status positions. One much-quoted study is Horner's (1968) assessment of women's achievement motivation. She attempted to provide explanations for the findings that despite apparent increases in educational and career openings for women, they still seem to show a reluctance to match men in competitive situations. Horner's concept of the 'fear of success' was based on measures of achievement-related imagery to a hypothetical story about a woman's success at medical school. Horner argued that the anticipation of success is anxiety-provoking for women, in that it makes them appear less desirable to men. In order to seem to be more feminine, many women, she claimed, disguise their abilities and withdraw from competitive situations. Horner noted that such women pay a high price for this, in that they showed evidence of feelings of frustration, hostility, bitterness and confusion. More profoundly, psychoanalytic accounts (for example Olivier 1989) have suggested that women have a fear of succeeding where their own mothers failed, particularly those whose mothers gave up promising careers to care for their children. A fear of overtaking their own mothers, and a sense of guilt when they are successful, has been seen to hold many women back. Although women often identify with these descriptions, subsequent research has generated alternative interpretations. Paludi (1984), using more detailed interviews than Horner, found that a fear of success, where it exists, may well be a cultural rather than an intrapsychic phenomenon, being highly dependent on the situational context in both women and men.

Studies of women's decision-making strategies, especially those concerning moral judgements, have lead to a similar controversy. Gilligan (1982) has made use of Chodorow's (1978) arguments, outlined earlier, to explain why women and men respond differently to moral dilemmas. Women, she states, being more oriented towards attachment with others and personal relationships, are more likely to develop moral sensibilities that reflect a concern for care. Men, on the other hand, are said to be more oriented towards individual achievement and find it difficult to establish intimate relationships. Their moral judgements are therefore more likely to reflect a concern for justice and for the objective rather than subjective resolution of a dilemma. Gilligan has criticized developmental theorists, arguing that their findings of women's so-called 'immature' judgements compared with those of men are based on a misunderstanding and devaluation of women's reasoning. Using a real-life crisis situation, that of making a decision concerning whether or not to terminate an unplanned pregnancy, Gilligan has argued that women reason from the basis of a concern for others, rather than from abstract principles. But as Colby and Damon (1983) point out, Gilligan did not question any men involved in this moral dilemma (for example the partners of those women facing a possible abortion) so it is not clear if they would have reasoned differently. What we do know is that it is generally men, in the form of doctors and politicians, who place global restrictions on women's abortion rights. The stereotype continues that women make poor leaders because they tend to favour consideration for the subjective rather than objective factors. There is, however, a growing realization that female caring attitudes are as important to good management and leadership as the ability to be rational and objective.

An area where women themselves often describe difficulties in their working lives concerns situations where they need to assert themselves and face potential conflicts. As we have seen, women are used to being mediators on behalf of others, but lacking a clear sense of their own identity often find it difficult to define and defend themselves. Problems frequently arise when confronted with those in positions of power over them (for example when unrealistic demands are made by a superior), or in situations where the woman's own legitimate authority is in question (for example a teacher trying to control a disruptive class). So common are these experiences that assertiveness training groups (see e.g. Dickson 1982) have helped many women to confront the conflicts they feel about having to individuate and define themselves when they might more habitually merge with the demands of others. But as Sayers (1986) has pointed out, merely attempting to modify women's actions does nothing to alter the fundamental dynamic. Rather than fitting themselves into the constraints of traditional jobs, women are now demanding that paid work itself be differently structured.

Such restructuring is nowhere more important than for women with responsibilities for children. The conflicts between women's mothering and other work are so crucial that we will consider this issue in detail.

Women, work and motherhood

Women's child-bearing abilities can be seen to have a profound effect on their working lives (see Jackson, Chapter 8). Even those who decide that they are not going to have children are invariably treated by employers during their reproductive years as if they will inevitably do so. Earlier, the education and training of girls is affected by the assumption that they will eventually become mothers and leave the work-force. For the majority of women who do have children, their childbearing years tend to coincide with a period in their working lives when they could be moving into positions of responsibility. Those who take extended time off to care for their children find that others (usually men) have been promoted in their place. Joshi (1987) has calculated the high financial cost of motherhood to British women, who take on average seven years off work if they have two children, and then return for many years on a part-time basis.

Women seek to combine motherhood and work outside the home for many different reasons. For those who are single parents, or whose partners are unemployed or poorly paid, their own earnings are a vital contribution to the family income. In the absence of adequate child benefits, many mothers have no choice but to continue in paid work, where available. By contrast, middle-class women with partners whose incomes are larger do have a choice between caring for their children or continuing in paid work, although for many women the choice is effectively made for them in the absence of child-care provisions before the age of 5 and employment with flexible hours.

Contemporary feminism has often uncritically accepted the evaluation placed by society at large on working outside the home. Apart from notable exceptions, such as the 'Wages for Housework' pressure group, and more recently theorists such as Alice Rossi (1981), women have been encouraged to adopt a 'do-both' strategy, combining paid work with having children. Women's desires to be the primary carer of their own children are often seen as a form of 'false consciousness', an internalization of the outside pressures of partners, parents and experts for women to mother. The fact that it is other women who are usually employed (for low wages) to perform the child-care is rarely challenged. Women who stay at home are often described as opting out of participation in the 'real' world (e.g. Wilson 1989). Even 'expert' advice itself seems to turn full circle from blaming working mothers for children's developmental problems to arguing that women who invest all their energy on their children are unable to let them grow up (see Scarr and Dunn 1987). Certainly, in a period where family virtues are cynically manipulated by governments aiming to encourage women's reduced participation in the work-force and unpaid labour at home, women are having to fight hard to defend their employment rights.

One significant factor often ignored by those who argue for or against work outside the home for mothers is each woman's individual needs and reactions in response to motherhood. As recent accounts have shown (e.g. Gieve 1989), women vary enormously in the extent to which they can tolerate intimate contact with their babies. Whereas some feel trapped and de-personified by the thought of being confined to the house with responsibility for one or more highly dependent infants, others enjoy the intimacy provided by close contact with their children. Interviews and therapeutic work with women during pregnancy and after childbirth have shown the differences in women's reactions to motherhood. Raphael-Leff (1985) has argued that whereas some women fear a loss of autonomy and resist the merging involved in infant care, others become involved in their bodily changes, developing what Winnicott (1982) has called a 'primary maternal preoccupation' during the course of their pregnancy such that they often want to withdraw from stressful external situations. Such feelings are often continued into the baby's infancy such that any prolonged separation from the baby is avoided. For the first type of woman, work outside the home clearly is psychologically beneficial, whereas for the second type enforced early return to work is extremely stressful. Ideally, then, a flexible system is required in which women could choose between paid parental leave (for themselves or for their partners) and quality child-care to cover periods when they are away from home. At present, neither option is available for the majority of women. In Britain, child-care provisions and facilities for paid parental leave compare very unfavourably with many of our European neighbours. In France, for example, pro-natalist policies have generated greater maternity and child benefits, including allowances for single parents and women with three or more children to receive a small wage enabling them to care for their children at home for up to three years. In addition, state-subsidized crèches and nursery schools are widely available, with nearly all 3-year-olds and the majority of 2-year-olds obtaining free nursery school places. Such schools are usually attached to primary schools and are open from 9 am to 5 pm, with before- and after-school play provisions.

A move towards more flexible working arrangements, along with improved child-care, would benefit both women and men. Rather than having a two-tiered society consisting of those in full-time employment and an under-class of permanently unemployed, there would be a shorter working week for all. Above all, children would benefit from having the possibility of the greater availability of both parents. As Ernst (1987) has pointed out, the 'maternal preoccupation' which Winnicott saw as diminishing after a few months of motherhood, currently remains as a central aspect of women's lives. Most mothers find it impossible, for both emotional and practical reasons, to work 'like a man' and ignore their families during a long conventional working day. Indeed, as Gilligan (1982) has argued, many women do not want to separate work and care in the traditional way.

A true valorization of women's psychological potential cannot exist without a concomitant re-evaluation of the financial worth of caring for others. It is here that a feminist psychodynamic account must join with a wider appraisal of the value attributed to those who do servicing and reproductive work. Only when women are free to choose when and to whom they offer their care, will it be offered from a psychologically healthy rather than a repetitive position. This demands more than that men learn how to care, which is a minimal requirement, but that they are also prepared to share their financial and working privileges.

References

Boulton, M. (1983) *On Being a Mother*, London: Tavistock.

Caplan, P. (1984) The myth of women's masochism, *American Psychologist*, 39: 130–9.

Chodorow, N. (1978) *The Reproduction of Mothering*, Berkeley, Calif: University of California Press.

Colby, A. and Damon, W. (1983) Listening to a different voice: a review of Gilligan's *In a Different Voice*, *Merrill-Palmer Quarterly*, 29: 473–81.

Deutsch, H. (1944) *The Psychology of Women: vol. 1*, New York: Grune & Stratton.

Dickson, A. (1982) *A Woman in Your Own Right: Assertiveness and You*, London: Quartet Books.

Dinnerstein, D. (1978) *The Rocking of the Cradle*, London: Souvenir Press.

Eichenbaum, L. and Orbach, S. (1982) *Outside In . . . Inside Out*, Harmondsworth: Penguin.

Ernst, S. (1987) Can a daughter be a woman? Women's identity and psychological separation, in S. Ernst and M. Maguire (eds) *Living with the Sphinx*, London: Women's Press.

Freud, S. (1924) The economic problem of masochism, in J. Strachey (ed.) (1961) *Standard Edition of the Complete Psychological Works of Sigmund Freud, vol. 19*, London: Hogarth Press.

Gieve, K. (1989) *Balancing Acts*, London: Virago.

Gilligan, C. (1982) *In a Different Voice*, Cambridge, Mass: Harvard University Press.

Grabrucker, M. (1988) *There's a Good Girl*, London: Women's Press.

Horner, M. (1968) Toward an understanding of achievement-related conflicts in women, *Journal of Social Issues*, 28: 157–76.

Horney, K. (1967) *Feminine Psychology*, New York: Norton.

Joshi, H. (1987) *The Cash Opportunity Costs of Childbearing: An Approach to Estimation using British Data*, London: Centre for Economic Policy Research, discussion paper no 208.

Klein, M. (1937) Love, guilt and reparation, in M. Klein (1975) *Love, Guilt and Reparation and Other Works 1921–1945*, London: Hogarth Press.

Krzowski, S. and Land, P. (eds) (1988) *In Our Experience*, London: Women's Press.

Miller, J. B. (1976) *Toward a New Psychology of Women*, Harmondsworth: Penguin.

Oakley, A. (1974) *Housewife*, London: Allen Lane.

—— (1980) *Women Confined*, Oxford: Martin Robertson.

Olivier, C. (1989) *Jocasta's Children*, London: Routledge.

Paludi, M. (1984) Psychometric properties and underlying assumptions of four objective measures of fear of success, *Sex Roles*, 10: 765–81.

Raphael-Leff, J. (1985) Facilitators and regulators: vulnerability to post-natal disturbance, *Journal of Psychosomatic Obstetrics and Gynaecology*, 4: 151–68.

Rossi, A. (1981) On the reproduction of mothering: a methodological debate, *Signs: Journal of Women in Culture and Society*, 6: 492–500.

Savage, W. (1986) *A Savage Enquiry*, London: Virago.

Sayers, J. (1986) *Sexual Contradictions*, London: Tavistock.

Scarr, S. and Dunn, J. (1987) *Mothercare/Othercare*, Harmondsworth: Penguin.

Segal, L. (1987) *Is the Future Female?*, London: Virago.

Stanley, L. and Wise, S. (1983) *Breaking Out*, London: Routledge & Kegan Paul.

Wilson, E. (1989) *Hallucinations*, London: Hutchinson Radius.

Winnicott, D. (1965) *The Maturational Processes and the Facilitating Environment*, London: Hogarth Press.

—— (1982) Primary maternal preoccupation, in D. Winnicott, *Through Paediatrics to Psychoanalysis*, London: Hogarth Press.

2 | The gender relations of assessment

Janette Webb

In Britain the use of tests in selection to measure candidates' interests, abilities and personality is growing steadily, due to the need expressed by employers to make more effective, objective decisions about job applicants and employees. . . . The injection of objective information . . . makes it harder for stereotyped notions about any candidates, but women in particular, to interfere with selection decisions.

(Pearn *et al*. 1987: 1)

The evidence from attribution theory, and that regarding our implicit theories . . . indicate that the assumption of objective observation and inference is a chimera. All of the procedures involved in selection require the selector to form judgements regarding applicants' characteristics.

(Herriot 1984: 23)

Despite the rigorous and systematic nature of the organisational search for suitable candidates, and the sophistication of the techniques they employ – including psychological tests of various systematically delineated and operationalised dimensions and traits – the salient qualities . . . derive not from some objective assessment of the skills and knowledge required by a particular job, but from a concern to pick people who have the 'proper' or appropriate attitudes . . . and will thus 'fit into' the ongoing organisational culture and be amenable to organisational control.

(Salaman and Thompson 1980: 253)

The premise of this chapter is that the activities of assessment and selection are irreducibly social and subjective. In order to analyse the inequalities experienced by women in organizations, the processes of assessment have to be understood in terms of the power-based relations of gender. I aim to challenge the assertion of scientific occupational psychology, that standardized, validated assessment techniques can, and do, guarantee fair treatment for women. I shall argue that only when psychology requires the theorizing of social categories such as gender, race, age and social class, shall we be able to produce a valid analysis of assessment and selection. Such an account would recognize the importance of making explicit use of subjective knowledge and judgement in assessments, and would be the basis for a more adequate procedural methodology of 'fair treatment'.

The occupational psychology of assessment

The 'fitting the man to the job – fitting the job to the man' (FMJ–FJM) model is a familiar one for most psychologists educated in Britain: it is a formulation devised by Alec Roger, first professor of occupational psychology at Birkbeck College, London, to describe occupational assessment, training and appraisal (FMJ) and work design and ergonomics (FJM). In broad terms, the characterization still holds. Job and individual are assumed to exist independently of each other and to be relatively unchanging. Consequently the characteristics of both can be measured and matched to achieve an efficient fit between task requirements and individual abilities.

Psychometric tests form the basic technology of the selection system, the purpose being to devise tests able to predict the person's future job performance (predictive validity). The use of carefully constructed, standardized and validated tests, it is argued, provides more objective, reliable information about job candidates than does the interview or other forms based on discussion and observation.

When used in conjunction with other information about candidates (such as that derived from application forms) and a standard job analysis, specifying performance requirements for each job, then candidates will be treated fairly; job outcomes and achievements will reflect the relative merits of the individuals concerned, regardless of sex, class, ethnic origin, or other social characteristics.

This functionalist model of assessment is in line with the dominant liberal model of equal opportunity (EO), which is common to North America and western Europe. It is based on a political philosophy which treats equality as founded in free market competition between individuals for a share of scarce symbolic and material goods. The labour market outcomes of women and men are assumed to be determined by such factors as inherent differences in skills and abilities, choices by individuals about investment in training and education, and mobility/flexibility of labour supply. Liberal EO policy attributes the gross inequalities between women and men to distortions in the rational, efficient workings of the free market, which can be corrected by top-down introduction of standardized bureaucratic controls, formalizing recruitment, training and promotion procedures. Formalizing procedures is assumed to force employers to open up the competition for jobs to atypical candidates and to assess subsequent applicants on their individual merits, rather than on the basis of stereotyped beliefs about, for example, married women, young women or mothers. In theory the employer is supposed to assess the individual's suitability for the job, according to functionally specific, job-related technical criteria, which are supposed to be separable from assessments of the individual's acceptability.

Many of the texts and manuals of occupational and personnel psychology implicitly adopt this model of the labour market and, by promoting the notion that standard, formalized assessment defines fair treatment, the profession might be described as seeking to correct the distortions of the free market, by designing the tools and techniques of 'objective' assessment.

The use of psychometric tests

What are some of these tools? Pearn *et al.* reviewed seven examples of currently available tests or test batteries, representative of the main categories of tests in use in Britain, 'from an EO point of view' (1987: 11). These covered verbal, numerical and abstract reasoning, mechanical abilities, and personality-trait questionnaires. Pearn *et al.* also reviewed the reported use made by eight public and private sector employers of a range of tests, again covering the above attributes. It is difficult to get an accurate picture of the range of tests in use, the extensiveness of their use and the weight given to results. Sneath *et al.* (1976), for example, surveyed 281 UK companies and found that 72 per cent used tests, of which half had tried to assess their validity, with 5 per cent using statistical validation methods.

It is even more difficult to obtain information on the actual conditions of test use: even the Pearn *et al.* study uses *reported* practice by those managers who are likely to have a vested interest in creating a favourable impression. Their selection of case studies seems also to be biased towards employers who would be expected to set standards of good practice in test use and interpretation. They are large employers likely to be concerned about public reputation: the Civil Service Commission, MSC, EITB, a motor manufacturer, an energy company, a building society, an insurance company and a local authority. We should expect to find *best* practice in such cases – large employers, investing heavily (particularly at graduate level) in staff, employing psychologists or trained personnel managers to construct assessment procedures.

What picture of best practice emerges? Basically test scores formed part of the material which underlies a more or less complicated series of social judgements and evaluations of job applicants. No one used test scores to *determine* job offers. The Civil Service is probably the organization adhering most closely to the ideal bureaucratic model: at executive officer entry grade, for example, the test process is carefully devised, administered and scored. The tests are used as a pre-selection measure, with a qualifying score set each year depending on the expected level of vacancies. The three tests used are designed to assess: first, ability to make inferences from numerical information; second, verbal aptitude; and third, ability to deal with administrative problems. Candidates' scores on each of the tests are standardized against the average scores achieved in previous years by candidates of the same age and sex.

The Civil Service Commission has invested heavily in development and analysis of the test procedures, because of their use as a basis for excluding the majority of applicants from further consideration (something like 70 per cent, where ages ranged from 17 to 57). In particular, the Commission was concerned that the test scores were unevenly distributed between different age groups and between men and women. A larger percentage of men were passing the test and the 20–28-year-olds also performed better than the younger or older groups. In the early 1980s further detailed examination of these unequal results by age and sex, combined with the lack of evidence of actual differences in job performance of men and women executive officers of different ages, led to the decision to correct test scores for the effects of age and sex. It was also realized that educational level affected test scores: they were measuring not only aptitude but also attainment. The Commission has further conducted a series of concurrent and predictive validity studies and is generally satisfied that, given adaptations to the tests themselves and the interpretation of scores, the test battery is the best available means for assessing candidates' potential for generalist jobs of the executive officer grade, given the massive scale of the recruitment scheme. Tests are less widely used in the recruitment of the many specialist grades and occupational groups which the Commission covers, where 'more attention is paid to the kind of specific attribute that is most readily assessed at interview' (Pearn *et al.* 1987: 49).

The general points which should be made about this test procedure are, first, its scale: in 1985 applications totalled 17,653 men and 14,434 women, of whom 7,137 men and 5,331 women were interviewed; 2,342 men and 2,198 women were appointed. The test procedure is initially a massive sorting operation. It is an *administrative* solution to the 'problem' of open competition for relatively desirable posts, in a period of relative job shortage. The tests provide a standard means of excluding a large proportion of the applicant population in a 'seen to be fair' way.

Second, there had been a massive investment in the process: the cost of recruiting at the highest level of administrative trainee is reckoned to be one year's administrative grade salary.

Third, careful adjustments have been made to the test structures and interpretation of scores to create equitable treatment for women and men and different age groups. The 'objectivity' of testing is thus a socially constructed objectivity: carefully managed and manipulated, to produce the desired results. This would seem to undermine any claims to the 'neutrality' of tests *per se* and provide good evidence that test construction and test norms can be devised to produce any desired range of results, according to the dimensions of interest.

Fourth, what cannot be shown is what proportion of the 70 per cent rejected at the test stage could have performed the job satisfactorily anyway. In other words, is the cost of the procedure actually justifiable in terms of selecting those who are going to be the most able executive officers, and rejecting all others, or is it primarily justified because it is a publicly acceptable way of sifting out large numbers of candidates? More acceptable in our society, for example, than using a criterion such as 'deservedness' for the job of public servant? In terms of gender relations, Civil Service Commission practice shows that, with determination and investment of resources, a test procedure can be devised to lead to men and women being invited to interview in rough proportion to the numbers applying. The result has, however, been achieved by building back into the test process the notion of social category membership, as opposed to the idea of individuals being effectively interchangeable, and differentiated primarily by ability of which pure measures can be attained by testing. In effect the Commission is saying that test measurements discriminate between men and women, but this is not reflected in lower standards of job performance by women. Therefore the test results will be interpreted according to social category membership. Not only does this undermine the purist model of matching measured individual ability to job specifications, but also it is very unlikely that most organizations would be so systematic or make the high level of investment in checking and monitoring necessary to produce such a sophisticated use of test results which does more than take them at face value as factual indicators of the differential ability of men and women.

Probably the most extreme comparator with the Civil Service Commission considered by Pearn *et al.* is the case of a local authority's use of tests for assessing clerical trainee applicants. The local authority had a reasonably developed equal opportunity policy, covering recruitment and selection, training, staff development, maternity leave, and so on. Tests were not in common use as part of selection, but had been introduced for the recruitment of apprentices and trainee clerical staff. All eligible applicants (that is, those aged under 20, residing in the area and unemployed at the time of application) were interviewed and tested, using Saville and Holdsworth's Personnel Test Battery, including Verbal Usage, Numerical Computation, Checking and Classification. The resulting test scores were, however, used only for 'marginal' candidates where selectors are uncertain whether to accept or reject the applicant. In 1989 eleven women and nine men were recruited, though in fact men scored higher than women on each of the tests. Despite the commitment of this local authority to the formal approach to equal opportunity, they had not in fact followed the prescribed procedures for selection, even in relation to this limited sample. Relatively little formal job analysis had been conducted, therefore making it impossible to say that the tests used were relevant to the jobs which trainees would be doing. Furthermore, it was practically impossible to conduct the type of job analysis recommended by the textbook model, because jobs varied from year to year and content differed significantly. They had not collected, at the time of the study, validation data to show whether test scores predicted job performance. Nor had they actually compared male and female test results, but relied on selectors' overall impressions of how men and women were doing (Pearn *et al.* 1987). Although the intentions were honourable in the local authority case, actual practice demonstrated two important points. First, the psychometric model of matching an individual to a job is again undermined: the 'job' as such varied from year to year and this, I would argue, is relatively common, certainly in the non-manual, clerical and administrative areas, even if broadly the same reasoning and verbal capacities are required for acceptable performance. Second, selectors were guided heavily by their 'impressions' of candidates' abilities to the extent of 'mis-reading' the actual pattern of test results. Their judgement continued to be given most weight.

The most significant general point illustrated by this case, however, is the tendency of employers to look for selection tests *because* they believe that the results are 'scientific' assessments of candidates and therefore carry absolute authority: testing is treated as a guarantee of 'fairness', absolving the employer from further responsibility for any actual differences in recruitment between men and women. When combined with expediency – if you can find a test which discriminates between applicants, which is cheap to use, and which fits in with received notions of fairness, then use it – this approach is likely to perpetuate existing patterns of male/female recruitment into different jobs, with unequal prospects of training and promotion. This is particularly the case since many of the tests are standardized against all male, or mostly male, samples; or no data on the composition of the sample are given in the test manual.

The central problem with the psychometric approach is thus the unrealistically technical view of the processes of selection and the failure to recognize and incorporate an analysis of social relations of assessment at any level. Pearn *et al.*'s careful appraisal of the use of tests in large, socially concerned employers, likely to provide examples of best practice, demonstrates the irreducibly social character of assessment. The difficulties of 'enforcing' the liberal model of fair assessment reside precisely in the attempt to disconnect selection decisions from the everyday processes of judgement and social evaluation. Assessors are required not to use their acquired knowledge of how to 'judge' and discriminate between people. It might be expected that the result of such an artificial, imposed requirement would be to give a spurious fairness to procedures, while assessors find ways round the test and assessment methodology, in order to make sure that their judgement of the candidates is still represented in the outcome.

On the one hand Pearn *et al.*, as advocates of the liberal model of equal opportunity, urge employers to 'reduce subjectivity', which is equated with bias; on the other hand, their findings and recommendations demonstrate unequivocally the need to *interpret* test scores and to use discretion (albeit in a publicly accountable way) in the weighting to be given to test results in comparison with other 'evidence' from interviews, curricula vitae (CVs), discussion groups and in-tray exercises.

The case studies reveal only too well the social context of test use: some employers used a test because other organizations were known to use it; the value of the test was taken on trust; test norms were not necessarily equally appropriate to men and women; tests may become outdated with the *meaning* of items changing over time; test use was not always consistent; some organizations did not monitor the effects of testing or have a clear justification for using particular tests: 'in one case it appeared that tests were being interpreted in a way that confirmed stereotypes that the recruiters already had about men and women' (Pearn *et al.* 1987: 73). Lastly, Pearn *et al.* express concern that employers may place too much faith in test results as a true and fair reflection of individual ability, because they produce numerical scores.

There is still relatively little evidence about the *actual* use (as opposed even to reported use) of tests by UK employers. Pearn *et al.* recommend that the British Psychological Society should encourage research in this area, to offset the risk that testing will be discredited, as happened in the USA in the 1970s, when the civil rights movement challenged the fairness of tests, through litigation, particularly in terms of their discriminating effects on the black and ethnic minority population. Pearn *et al.*'s review, though committed to the notion of testing as fairer than interviewing, nevertheless shows the intractability of the social and subjective in assessment, but continues to insist that the subjective is equated with bias. It thus neatly evades open discussion of how decision-makers' deep-seated convictions about the qualities of men and women as workers, and differential recruitment of men and women into jobs and grades offering unequal prospects of progress, are to be incorporated into an analysis and, having been recognized, how such practices could be overcome. Exhorting managers to 'judge people on their merits', ignoring all they 'know' about the supposed capacities of men and women and the actual functioning of their organization, is like asking someone to ride a bicycle by following the instructions in a rule-book, ignoring all their ordinary know-how.

On test construction

What constitutes an 'individual's abilities' is itself socially defined and normative. The definition of intelligence has shifted over time, hence skills and abilities constituting intelligence have also changed. Over and above the judgement of what should be measured is the judgement of what test items, rating scales or multiple-choice questions can provide an appropriate measure of the desired attribute. The construction of test items can be manipulated so as to favour one group over another. This has long been known in the sphere of intelligence testing: 'whether boys or girls obtain higher IQs depends upon the items included in the test. When no deliberate effort has been made to exclude sex differences from the test, there has generally been a tendency to favour girls' (Anastasi 1958: 459). The IQ debate continues, but there is adequate work to substantiate the argument that the construction of such tests can be manipulated to reproduce, or to undermine, socially approved results for the distribution of intelligence according to class, gender and ethnicity (Gardner 1983; Block 1976; Walker 1981): 'in early versions of the tests, males and females scored differently on certain items (the females scored higher). The tests were modified. . . . Which measures the biological "reality", the test with, or without, the differential scoring items?' (Rose 1976: 119).

The personality questionnaire is an even better known example of the social character of assessments. The most widely used version is probably the 16PF, which is criticized and venerated in about equal proportion. Apart from the assumption behind all such measures that personality is an absolute, unvarying quality possessed by the person, regardless of context, occupational structure, or straightforward social (un)desirability of some characteristics, it is common for personality questionnaires (and the 16PF is no exception) to result in the familiar stereotypes of masculine and feminine: women score as more submissive, men as more dominant and assertive; men as more tough-minded, women as more trusting and less self-assured, and so on. When one thinks about how people fill in such questionnaires, they are likely either to give the answer they think fits the 'type' the employer is looking for (few people would rate themselves as shy and reserved if going for a sales job they actually want, for instance), or to use their social know-how about what women or men are meant to be like, in the abstract, and out of any context they would normally be involved in. Hence most people, as Hollway (1984) points out, have difficulty assigning themselves unequivocally to an either/or category and want to answer: 'it depends . . .'. Responses may be telling the employer about self-presentation, but are not in a literal sense predicting behaviour in particular contexts.

The scoring of tests, particularly those involving ratings, is equally subject to the predilections of the assessors. For example, not only does the sex, ethnicity, etc. of the rater matter, but also when the occupation is typically held by men, women applicants are rated less favourably. The more white men among the raters, the lower were black women rated (Herriot 1984). The current move towards the use of assessment centres, particularly at graduate level, is an important instance of the rating of applicants who are assessed in groups over two or three days, by a group of managers.

University, and other, examinations are another example of candidate assessment by ratings. Spender (1982) asked teachers to mark essays and projects, sometimes telling them that they were by boys and other times that they were by girls: 'whenever teachers have assumed they were marking the work of boys, they have consistently rated it as "better" than when they have thought it was written by girls' (1982: 78). In the university sector, Bradley's (1984) comparison of internal and external examiners' marks on named student projects in four departments showed that external examiners tended to mark women towards the centre (internal marks of first-class down to upper-seconds and thirds up to lower-seconds), whereas men were marked out to the extremes and given more firsts and thirds, thus reproducing conventional expectations that women are steady but middling, while men are either brilliant or stupid.

Test construction, use and interpretation is irreducibly social; test-batteries are at best another 'tool' in the assessment techniques of employers along with the interview, the leaderless group discussion, the intray exercise and CVs; they may have constructed into them assumptions about the different abilities or characteristics of men and women and some employers may be sensitive to such features. At worst, however, tests may be used purely in an expedient way, their 'objectivity' presented as a guarantee of good practice, so long as their results broadly fit in with managers' expectations about masculine and feminine qualities and corresponding appropriate occupations for men and women.

Who gets tested?

The foregoing assumes that it is the norm for an employer to have a deliberate selection and assessment policy, at least an *espoused policy*, even if the actual operation is somewhat divergent. Yet it could be argued that such attempts at system and standardization are in themselves unusual and that only a tiny proportion of the job-seeking population experience anything more than cursory selection. Employers of significant numbers of graduates, skilled technical and clerical/administrative staff are usually those with some formal-ized assessment policies. A smaller number of employers would use psychometric tests as part of selection procedures for some grades of staff. Hence, one fundamental problem with the assertion that the use of psychometric tests makes the competition for jobs fairer to women is that most women never get to a 'starting line' for those jobs allocated by open competition involving both sexes.

Most women work in job categories dominated by women (in health, welfare, education; personal and domestic services; clerical and secretarial); very few women work in occupations with similar proportions of men and women or with a majority of men (see e.g. Dex 1985). Those that do tend to be in the better-paid jobs. Most women are not, in fact, competing in the same segments of the labour market as men, but are competing for jobs with other women. Equal opportunity policies which concentrate on formalizing and standardizing assessment are therefore, at best, beneficial only to those women with credentials validated through higher education or vocational training (such as women graduates looking for management or professional careers). Formalized testing and assessment for access to clerical level jobs does not, because of the structure of internal labour markets, guarantee greater mobility for women into managerial and administrative occupations. Indeed where men and women enter a company at similar clerical grades, they typically have different internal rates for access to higher grades, with the ceiling for women being much lower than that for men (Crompton and Jones 1984; Collinson 1988).

The viability of assessments based on suitability requirements

The formal test and assessment approach to selection assumes that technical suitability requirements can be specified for any job; these should then form the basis of discrimination between individual applicants; that is applicants should be assessed on their merits, not on the basis of whether the assessor likes them or not. Most manual and routine non-manual jobs, however, have very low suitability requirements: virtually anyone can do the job or learn to do it very quickly (Jewson and Mason 1986a). Jobs are therefore allocated on the basis of acceptability: will the person 'fit in' easily, be reliable and amenable, and not disrupt established routines? Since such jobs are typically sex-segregated, women and men continue to be allocated according to past conventions. Women continue to be cleaners and catering workers; men are porters and signalmen. In such jobs, cost is a key factor: the employer is not primarily concerned to generate large numbers of applicants for any vacancy, where most people can meet the skill requirements, but to find staff who appear to be reliable, honest, and tolerably compliant. All of these are social judgements routinely discussed as most important by employers in a recruitment context; they are qualities assessed by a range of criteria (usually different ones for men and women) and have little to do with measurements of technical capacity to do the job (Salaman and Thompson 1980; Silverman and Jones 1976). Collinson (1988) reports, for instance, that a family and a mortgage are taken as indicators of stability and reliability in a man, but family commitments are equated with unreliability in women.

The role of informality in recruitment

Much of the effort of psychologists and other personnel consultants concerned with fairness and efficiency in recruitment has centred on perfecting the assessment of individuals, rather than the ways in which job requirements and occupational structures channel and constrain access to the competition and direct the differential evaluation of men and women candidates. This has been broadly in line with an equal opportunity model advocating formalization as the mainstay of new procedures. Formalization is regarded as the major means of controlling selectors' discretion, and hence of limiting the effects of individual prejudice. Such policies do not in practice guarantee the abolition of discretion (Jenkins 1986; Jewson and Mason 1986b; Salaman 1986) and can moreover come to be regarded as ends in themselves, rather than the means to improving women's access to jobs and resources (Webb and Liff 1988).

Where there is a formal policy, there is no guarantee that job requirements will not be designed in such a way as to exclude women applicants – the use of the term 'engineer' for example excludes most women, though the technical content of many of the jobs so titled may be learned relatively easily.

A commitment to formal recruitment practices is unlikely to be sustained in periods of high unemployment. Wood's (1986) research shows that the main effect of a recessionary economy on recruitment was the increasing reliance on informal channels. There was a reluctance to use even open advertising of vacancies, because of the difficulty and expense of processing the increasing applications which advertisements produced. Instead, word-of-mouth and the extended internal labour market were used to secure workers who are already known to be capable, and known by their 'mates' and therefore relatively compliant. The subsequent assessment procedures may still be rigorous, but again women would be shunted into 'women's jobs'.

How managers assess men and women applicants

Even for those jobs with distinguishable suitability requirements, few women are likely to be successful in entering male jobs as a result of introducing a standardized assessment. The reasons for this centre on the evidence that jobs are gendered: that is they are not neutral territory, but come to be seen as possessing masculine or feminine attributes. The process by which such gendering is brought about is examined in Cockburn (1985). It is practically not possible to make an absolute distinction between the job and the job occupant: job requirements are defined in terms of current job holders, including their gender. Hence it becomes inherently more likely that more men than women will appear suitable for jobs conventionally held by men, and women will appear more suitable for jobs conventionally held by women. Treating such specification as technical, rather than socially created will only serve to decrease the likelihood of women gaining access to jobs held by men. The process of creating 'masculine' and 'feminine' people does, of course, have real material consequences: men and women typically have different ranges of skills and competence, as a result of gendered routes through education and training thus reinforcing the segregation of men and women into different occupations. For many managerial jobs the conventional requirements are more likely to be found amongst men than women, thus making men appear more suitable. The gendering of job requirements is discussed further in Webb (1989).

There is however a deep-seated problem to be overcome before employers are willing to re-think job requirements that do not exclude competent women. This is the widespread belief amongst senior managers that women are by nature unsuitable for certain types of work and are in fact incapable of carrying out technical, managerial and leadership roles, while being eminently 'suitable' for monotonous, repetitive, routine occupations or nurturing work. Supposedly standardized job requirements do not stop this process: far from it, as Collinson (1988) shows that standard requirements can be used to legitimize the selectors' preferred choice of job applicant. Indeed employers routinely and confidently discriminated against qualified women applicants where the job was typically held by men. This did not seem to strike them as unfair, much less illegal, despite Collinson's study being sponsored by the Equal Opportunities Commission and having accepted Collinson's presence as observer during the processes of candidate selection. Collinson's study of managers in sixty-four private-sector work-places showed how job-related criteria of stability, flexibility and compatibility were used to justify a preference either for a man or a woman, depending on which sex typically occupied the job. This was achieved by applying what might be described as a job model to men and a sex-role model to women. For example, domestic responsibility was taken as an indicator of stability in a man but unreliability in a woman applying for a 'man's' job. The requirement for flexibility and mobility in banking and insurance jobs were presented as fixed and rigid in the case of women (who were treated as non-mobile by virtue of their gender and therefore as technically unsuitable) but as inessential and negotiable in the case of men. In fact, as Collinson's own survey showed, the more senior the men in the insurance firm concerned, the less likely they were to classify themselves as geographically mobile. In practice it seems the mobility requirement *could* be adapted to the situation of particular staff (but only if they were men).

Such beliefs about the 'natural' differences between men and women and their suitability for different roles in the work-place are not superficial or easily overcome by the introduction of standardized assessment. Nor is there any evidence that change is happening with new generations of entrants to the work-force (Roberts *et al.* 1988).

Organization structure and the social relations of assessment

The argument made here is that gender relations are fundamental to understanding the outcomes of selection and assessment. An occupational psychology concerned with overcoming sex-segregated selection would give greater emphasis to the political character of assessment and would incorporate analysis of the subjective evaluations made by managers of applicants.

The present emphasis of occupational psychology on assessing the individual is characterized by Salaman (1979) as a form of ideology which results when the structure of the work-place is regarded as a natural outcome of neutral principles and pressures and individuals' experience. The individual is meant to be an adaptable resource; individual qualities and abilities are meant to be the cause of success or failure of the business. The concern of senior members is with getting 'the right man for the job'. The focus on the individual obscures analysis of inequality and conflict – and the creation of structured inequality between men and women in the work-place.

In practical terms, occupational psychologists would be more effective in redressing such inequalities by concentrating on the analysis of job requirements and exploring ways of structuring these such that competent women are not excluded at least from applying. Practitioners are then faced, in their analyses of the work-force and personnel policies, with challenging the sex-typing of jobs. Such a task would be principally concerned to develop an alternative approach to policy. This means departing from the present universalistic liberal model and substituting instead policies designed to meet the needs of different groups, within an economic context where employers are primarily concerned to control labour costs and maximize profitability/efficiency.

Lastly, there is a key area of work for academic research, and this is the examination of the structure and functioning of organizations in terms of relations between masculinity and femininity. So far work psychologists have been slow to use the term gender, focusing instead on women or on men and seldom on the relations between them. They have tended to rely on the liberal model of EO, which assumes that women's 'socialization into the feminine role' has resulted in women's 'failure to achieve', and that the solution is for women to convert themselves into honorary men.

If gender is based on a complementarity of masculinity and femininity however, the only way to challenge the exclusion of women from senior jobs and the segregation of women at work is by challenging the rigidity of that division and by dismantling the taken-for-granted practices which perpetuate it. Otherwise new structures are likely to evolve with the old genders firmly in place.

References

Anastasi, A. (1958) *Differential Psychology*, London: Macmillan.

Block, J. H. (1976) Issues, problems and pitfalls in assessing sex differences, *Merrill-Palmer Quarterly*, 22: 283–308.

Bradley, C. (1984) Sex bias in the evaluation of students, *British Journal of Social Psychology*, 23: 147–53.

Cockburn, C. (1985) *Machinery of Dominance*, London : Pluto.

Collinson, D. (1988) *Barriers to Fair Selection*, London: HMSO.

Crompton, R. and Jones, G. (1984) *White Collar Proletariat: Deskilling and Gender in Clerical Work*, London: Macmillan.

Dex, S. (1985) *The Sexual Division of Work*, Brighton: Harvester.

Gardner, H. (1983) *Frames of Mind*, London: Paladin.

Herriot, P. (1984) *Down from the Ivory Tower: Graduates and their Jobs*, Chichester: John Wiley.

Hollway, W. (1984) Fitting work: psychological assessment in organisations, in J. Henriques, W. Hollway, C. Urwin, C. Venn and V. Walkerdine (eds) *Changing the Subject: Psychology, Social Regulation and Subjectivity*, London: Methuen.

Jenkins, R. (1986) *Racism and Recruitment: Managers, Organisations and Equal Opportunity in the Labour Market*, Cambridge University Press.
Jewson, N. and Mason, D. (1986a) Modes of discrimination in the recruitment process: formalisation, fairness and efficiency, *Sociology*, 20: 43–63.
—— (1986b) The theory and practice of equal opportunities policies: liberal and radical approaches, *Sociological Review*, 34: 307–34.
Pearn, M. A., Kandola, R. S. and Mottram, R. D. (1987) *Selection Tests and Sex Bias*, London: HMSO.
Roberts, K., Richardson, D. and Dench, S. (1988) Sex discrimination in youth labour markets and employers' interests, in S. Walby (ed.) *Gender Segregation at Work*, Milton Keynes: Open University Press.
Rose, S. (1976) Scientific racism and ideology: the IQ racket from Galton to Jensen, in S. Rose and H. Rose (eds) *The Political Economy of Science*, London: Macmillan.
Salaman, G. (1979) *Work Organisations: Resistance and Control*, London: Longman.
—— (1986) *Working*, London: Tavistock.
Salaman, G. and Thompson, K. (1980) *Control and Ideology in Organisations*, Milton Keynes: Open University Press.
Sneath, F., Thakur, M. and Medjuck, B. (1976) *Testing People at Work*, Information Report 24, London: IPM.
Spender, D. (1982) *Invisible Women: The Schooling Scandal*, London: Writers and Readers Co-operative.
Walker, B. (1981) Psychology and feminism: if you can't beat them join them, in D. Spender (ed.) *Men's Studies Modified*, Oxford: Pergamon.
Webb, J. (1989) The politics of equal opportunity: job requirements and the evaluation of women's suitability, in S. M. Oliver (ed.) *The Psychology of Women at Work*, Conference Proceedings, Worthing: P-Set.
Webb, J. and Liff, S. (1988) Play the white man: the social construction of fairness and competition in equal opportunity policies, *Sociological Review*, 36: 543–51.
Wood, S. (1986) Personnel management and recruitment, *Personnel Review*, 15, 2: 3–11.

3 | The effectiveness of equal opportunity policies
Marilyn Aitkenhead and Sonia Liff

It would be nice to believe that progress is being made towards equal opportunities and, indeed, there are well-documented cases of organizations where significant changes have been made along these lines. We have had anti-discrimination legislation in Britain for fifteen years, and codes of practice to help organizations interpret this legislation for around five years. Creative equal opportunity initiatives being adopted by organizations cover a wide area and include career-break schemes which usually guarantee re-employment at equivalent levels for people who wish to take time out of the job market to care for dependent relatives; work-place nurseries; women-only training programmes; special holiday entitlement for people from ethnic minority groups; adaptation of application forms and training for interviewers. (For a review of initiatives in relation to women with children see IDS 1989.) While the legislation and equal opportunities initiatives are not of course centred upon women, this chapter will concentrate mainly upon gender issues, though relevant issues relating to ethnicity will also be raised. Within the UK increased impetus for the development of equal opportunities comes from the demographic changes; the number of school leavers has fallen rapidly from the highpoint caused by the 1960s 'baby boom' and is not predicted to begin rising again until the mid-1990s (Department of Employment 1988). Labour market shortages, it is argued, will mean that organizational strategies for survival will need to include policies for recruiting and retaining currently under-represented groups. In particular, some organizations are actively developing policies to recruit and retain women with children, for example, the Midland Bank and the Trustee Savings Bank (TSB). The Equal Opportunities Commission (EOC) has made these labour market changes a central focus of their strategy for improving the position of women over the next few years (EOC 1989).

However, employment indicators are contradictory. On the one hand, women's participation rates continue to rise such that women are now 46 per cent of the work-force (Department of Employment 1989: Table 5.8.1.1.8) and there has been some increase in the number of women entering the professions (EOC 1987). Furthermore, the availability of financial and training schemes has encouraged more women and ethnic minorities to set up their own business (Hakim 1989; Wilson and Stanworth 1988). On the other hand, there is a continuing discrepancy between men's and women's pay; women are still largely confined to the lower levels of organizational hierarchies, and occupational segregation along gender lines is pervasive. The contractual basis for employment of women and men is also very different – for example, women do the majority of part-time jobs, a form of working normally associated with fewer employment rights. In some occupations and training schemes there is a smaller proportion of women than there used to be: for example, the proportion of women who do computing courses has fallen from 25 per cent in 1979 to around 10 per cent in 1989 (Virgo 1989; and see Newton in Chapter 11). It also cannot be assumed that equal opportunity initiatives are widespread. For example, the British Institute of Management (BIM) recently carried out a survey on women managers and discovered that few organizations made adjustments to accommodate high-flying women with children. Of the 800 women who responded, only 11 per cent were offered crèche facilities, and few companies maintained adequate links with female employees who had taken a career break in order to raise a family. Instead, the organizations tended to offer work-sharing and part-time employment. But, since 44 per cent of the married women managers in the survey were the prime earners in their families, clearly policies which will cut their pay are unattractive. Peter Benton, BIM director general, said 'It is time companies sat up and took notice of what is going on around them. They will only have themselves to blame if they fail to heed the warnings and then lose their high flying women managers to more responsive organisations' (BIM 1989). Furthermore, research reveals that prejudices and misconceptions about women and black-people are deeply rooted and widespread (e.g. Collinson and Knights 1985; Jenkins 1986). Thus despite some successes, black people and women in general still predominate in the poorly paid and insecure sectors of labour markets, and still fail to climb organizational hierarchies.

How can we account for this mixture of continuity and change? There are a number of levels at which it is possible to look for an explanation. These most commonly include the individual, social group, organizational and societal levels. For example it is frequently argued that members of certain social groups share characteristics which make them appear less suitable for certain jobs or constrains their ability to accept certain terms or conditions of employment. Similarly that the experiences associated with group membership lead individuals to choose certain occupations in preference to others. From cross-national studies we can see that certain higher levels of social provision of child-care and other domestic support provisions are associated with higher participation rates and/or levels of full-time working for women (Beechey 1989; O'Donnell and Hall 1988). Different forms of legislation and enforcement also seem to be associated with different patterns of distribution within organizations of women and ethnic minorities (Dex and Shaw 1986).

While acknowledging the significance of all these factors, and their interdependence, we will focus our discussion on the organizational level for three main reasons. First, as we have already noted, major changes are currently being initiated at this level. In Britain, in particular, this is in stark contrast to the lack of initiatives at governmental level. Second, we shall argue that organizations play an important role in processes which are often seen as being located at other levels. For example they play a crucial role in the construction of job requirements by which groups and individuals are later judged more or less suitable, and in determining the assessment measures by which such suitability is judged. Third, despite variation in the levels of participation and patterns of jobs undertaken by women and ethnic minorities in various countries, no country has succeeded in overcoming occupational segregation nor in fully breaking the association of these groups with low status, poorly paid work. As Beechey (1989) points out in her comparison of policies in France and Britain relevant to the employment of women, the generous cash benefits to parents and the greater availability of services to children means that more women workers in France are full-time (80 per cent vs 50 per cent). But 'The fact is that French women have work histories which are more like men's but they are none the less disadvantaged in the labour market. The important question is how these differences are to be explained' (Beechey 1989: 374). This suggests that equal opportunities are not just a problem of implementation but, in contrast, that important parts of the process still need to be better understood, particularly at the organizational level.

Crucial to this endeavour, we feel, is consideration of the following issues. First, how do criteria for the evaluation of equal opportunity initiatives come to be identified, and are they understood? Second, is there agreement within and between organizations on what the criteria ought to be? If not, how can such differences be explained and what might be their implications? Third, to what extent can we disentangle the relationship between policy initiatives and concomitant organizational changes? In exploring these issues we adopt an approach which highlights as explanatory concepts interpersonal and group processes involved in the construction of social understandings and policy development (see e.g. Aitkenhead 1988; Jewson and Mason 1986; Webb and Liff 1988).

It is also important to bear in mind another complicating factor, namely that the *aims* (clearly stated or inferred) of policy initiatives may differ (e.g. Aitkenhead 1987). In relation to equal opportunity initiatives, different aims include: tokenism; changed work-force distributions; improved work-force morale; solving organizational problems such as recruitment and retention of key workers. How can such different aims be recognized in the ways policies are evaluated? Our solution is to identify different understandings of equal opportunity and to explore how different criteria might be employed within these contrasting understandings. Though we do attempt to unravel the links between understandings, policy development and policy evaluation we do nevertheless argue that, ultimately, two criteria are overriding in their suitability. First, the degree to which organizational outcomes are suitably distributed. Of course, precisely what outcomes to include in any evaluation are likely to be hotly contested within organizations, but we would argue that outcomes such as pay, promotions, training, benefit packages, hours of work, and those associated with various stages of the recruitment process are generally relevant. Second, the degree to which organizational policies and working environments meet the different needs of different individuals and groups. Again, relevant needs are unlikely to be uncontested, but we would suggest two important ones are the recognition by organizational members as individuals and as policy-makers that different needs exist, are relevant and to some degree can be catered for, and that majority group members recognize and do something to alleviate the strain they often impose on minority group members through a variety of micro-discriminatory practices.

Though as researchers and as working women we feel we can justify the above two criteria, those used by people *within* their organizations are likely to be derived from a socio-political process where the power of different groups and individuals to influence both personal understandings and organizational structures is important.

An illustration of how different conceptions of equal opportunities may be associated with different criteria for judging the effectiveness (or otherwise) of particular policy initiatives comes from Jewson and Mason (1986) in their brilliant analysis of two organizations. In one, a large engineering firm with headquarters in the USA, two different understandings of equal opportunities were identified by the researchers. The first they called the 'liberal' approach, which they defined as resting upon a bureaucratic, procedural model of equal opportunity. According to this model, providing there are fair procedures to ensure that meritocracy prevails (i.e. that the best person gets the job, the most deserving gets promoted, and so on) then equal opportunities necessarily also prevail. Thus the existence of a policy to ensure fair procedures, the setting up of equal opportunity committees, and positive action initiatives are the criteria people adhering to this model use to judge whether or not equal opportunities occur. Contrast this model with one where *outcomes* are the criteria used. These outcomes refer to organizational distributions – for example the proportion of women in management positions; the proportion of black people getting on to skills training courses; the proportion of black people in skilled as opposed to unskilled jobs. This model Jewson and Mason call the 'radical' approach.

It is easy to see that these two models have different implications for the criteria used to judge the effectiveness of equal opportunities policies. In the liberal model criteria relate to procedures, whereas in the radical model they relate to outcomes. What Jewson and Mason found was that these two conceptions were confusedly used by both management and the work-force. On the whole, management used the liberal approach and parts of the work-force the radical. The former felt they were making significant strides towards equal opportunities by the introduction of a policy, and the setting up of a joint negotiating committee. The latter felt that management were just being tokenist because no significant changes in distributions occurred. As an illustration of the problems this confusion provoked, there were *more* complaints of racial discrimination *after* the introduction of the policy than there were before, to the genuine puzzlement and disappointment of management. Clearly, different understandings resulted in different evaluations, and contributed in this case to greater conflict.

Thus within the liberal mode of thought, lack of change from current distributions does not necessarily imply that any procedural changes made are ineffective. Holders of this view are likely to look elsewhere for explanations concerning lack of distributional change. There are two alternative explanations readily available in our culture, namely that people from certain groups do not want certain types of jobs and, second, that people generally achieve the organizational outcomes they deserve. Part of this ideology may be the strongly held, and laudable, view that people should be judged as individuals and not have their social group membership held against them (e.g. Billig *et al*. 1988; Liff 1989; Lovenduski 1989). But this fails to take account of the fact that not everybody starts from the same point so disadvantage will continue (such starting-point inequality of individuals being strongly associated with group membership). It also ignores the fact that gender, ethnicity and other social categorizations are used by people perceiving others to pull into place a whole host of stereotypical judgements about their abilities, interests, willingness and, in particular, how well they will 'fit in' to the organizations as currently constituted. Such stereotyped judgements are undoubtedly discriminatory. Several of them have been elucidated in relation to women by Spencer and Podmore (1987) and in relation to ethnicity by Jenkins (1986). Since these judgements, and their imagined relationship to job performance, are usually only vaguely articulated they can be flexibly used, without any particular demands for logical rigour, when selection decisions are being made. Moreover, holders of the 'liberal' view are primarily concerned with how well individuals will fit in to the existing organization. Its current structure and work-force are taken for granted (Argyris 1982), and often regarded (for the purposes of selection) as unchangeable. The social processes involved in the construction of suitability criteria from job and job-holder characteristics are ignored, and hence there is little to mitigate their more adverse effects.

A further ramification of the liberal ideology is the view that people generally 'get what they deserve' (Lerner and Mathews 1967). If this belief is held, it becomes easy to infer that the lack of women or people from various ethnic groups at the top of organizational hierarchies is because, as individuals, they do not deserve to be there. Policy initiatives to increase the proportion of under-represented groups may therefore actually be regarded as unfair. This reasoning process can also be used to justify exclusion from top jobs on the grounds of group membership. Since there are few people (of a particular type) in certain jobs, and since such people are not there because they do not deserve to be there, it follows that a person's group membership can be used to infer unsuitability. People's reasoning processes may thus provide a great deal of justification for the status quo.

It follows, therefore, that procedural changes may be regarded, in themselves, as a major improvement. There is no necessary link to distributional change. A second way in which procedural changes may be used is, of course, to indicate the good intentions of management. Managers may see them as a cost-effective way of satisfying organizational members, and have little incentive to make real changes. A third possibility, however, is that there may be a group of people who feel, rightly or wrongly, that certain procedural changes will bring about changed distributions. Such people are not content simply to change policies in order to make them fairer: they want changed distributions. They believe that procedural change is an essential prerequisite for distributional change.

Such a belief appears to be being made by the EOC and the Commission for Racial Equality (CRE). The approach these two organizations take is essentially a bureaucratic one, and they go into a great deal of detail on precisely what procedures should be followed. A written equal opportunities policy is recommended and guide-lines are provided for the creation of one. These guide-lines point out a number of selection boundaries within organizations (for example initial interviews, training courses, promotion) and suggest ways of ensuring that those boundaries do not discriminate against members of minority groups, (see e.g. EOC 1985; CRE 1983).

Certainly, as will be elaborated upon later, it is helpful for increasing access if such boundaries are scrutinized and evaluated. The cognitive blindness which lack of scrutiny implies may mean that inequalities are not even noticed, let alone regarded as requiring change. But to achieve change, the bureaucratic approach goes further and assumes that a written equal opportunities policy covering a wide range of organizational selection boundaries is required. Is this assumption justified? It may be that having a written policy is neither necessary nor sufficient to promote change (Aitkenhead 1987). It may be unnecessary because rapid change may occur with very simple procedural changes initiated by a single organizational member 'in the right place at the right time', without any written policy being adopted. For example, Alan Wild of Express Foods was able to bring about the employment of a much higher proportion of black people in secretarial positions simply by observing that most secretaries began as temporary employees and that the employment agencies used operated mainly in white areas. So he asked the existing agencies to send along more black people for interview, and added agencies to the recruitment list operating in areas where there was a higher proportion of black people. Hardly an elaborate, formalized, equal opportunities policy, yet within months the proportion they employed rose dramatically (Wild 1986). In this case, the combination of the following seemed important:

- A powerful member of an organization, who
- noticed inequalities
- wanted to change them
- understood the recruitment process and
- operated in an organization where recruitment was virtually continuous, and that
- there was no shortage of applications from the targeted under-represented group.

As yet, we do not know how common this fortuitous combination of factors is nor how vital is each factor in stimulating change. But if a written policy is not *necessary* for change, is it helpful? The assumption that effective procedures need to be written policies is being challenged in other areas of personnel functioning also, for example, Anderson *et al.* (1987) describe an effective but unwritten appraisal system.

Now, it could be the case that a written and elaborate equal opportunities policy in general serves an educative and information-providing function for an organization's members. It could show up inequalities more clearly and point to organizational boundaries which might be operating as discriminators, enabling changes to take place if there is sufficient commitment, particularly from top management (the CRE and EOC recognize commitment as a crucial factor for the success of policies). What evidence is there that equal opportunities policies do serve these functions? Sadly, very little. Few systematic surveys have been conducted comparing organizations with and without equal opportunities policies in terms of how distributions change, or even examining how familiar key organizational members are with organizational selection boundaries. Case study material, while illuminating, does not readily allow for more general inferences to be made. Stone (1988) reports on a survey of equal opportunities in local authorities. She refers to the usual depressing picture of occupational segregation, whereby women are in the less-well-paid jobs. Though not all local authorities keep comprehensive statistical records, what data are available also reveal that black people are significantly underrepresented compared to local labour markets, and are confined to a narrow range of low-status jobs (see Stone 1988: 5–6).

Gaining the information is one thing, but what then? Do local authorities with equal opportunities policies employ more women and black people in better paid jobs? Is there less occupational segregation, for example? Stone is not optimistic:

> There exists within the local authority context, as in most large organisations, a kind of built-in resistance to change created by traditional power relationships which must work against equal opportunity initiatives, regardless of their structure, level of resources, or policy orientation.
>
> (Stone 1988: 11)

However, she does not compare local authorities with and without equal opportunity policies. Instead, she concentrates exclusively on twenty who have equal opportunity officers. Unfortunately for our purposes, she does not report distributions in a way which enables a generalized comparison to be made. Her report documents in detail some of the strategies used and changes in priority needed to implement changes when operating in a highly political organizational climate. It still leaves open the question of whether, despite the huge difficulties that equal opportunities officers face (see also Hackett 1988), organizations which have equal opportunity policies make more (or more rapid) changes in distributions than do those which have not. Case study material does reveal organizations which have made rapid changes in distributions, but how relevant any written policy is as a push for such changes cannot as yet be properly assessed. There is some survey evidence from the USA (Leonard 1986) that companies which compete for federal contracts, and which therefore come under the USA contract compliance legislation, do have more women and black people in higher organizational positions than those which do not. This is suggestive, but again the necessity of a written policy for producing these changes is open to doubt. Tinkering with aspects of organizational procedure and structure may well be as effective in producing change as attempting to implement a cumbersome policy. Such policies may cause administrative nightmares (Webb and Liff 1988; Jewson and Mason 1986) and these may even lead to their abandonment. Policies may also be undermined if those at the sharp end of implementation are resistant to changes (e.g. Aitkenhead 1988; Salaman 1986).

So far distributions have been discussed as if they refer only to proportions of people holding particular types of jobs. It is reasonable to broaden out the concept of distribution, however, to include a wider set of organizational outcomes which are relevant to an evaluation of equal opportunities, for example salary levels, and even indicators like the proportions going on training courses.

How far is having a formalized set of written policies associated with equal pay for, say, men and women? This question has been investigated by Ghobadian and White (1987; 1988), and they provide strong evidence that the more systematic recruitment procedures are, the more it is likely that men and women's pay levels are equal when like work is compared. However, *placement* procedures (such as having a written job description, applicants negotiating their own point of entry and pay levels), were not linked to equitable pay structures. Neither were their chosen indicators of formality of promotion procedures. They also found that recognition of trade unions was positively linked with pay structures which discriminated less between men and women, as was implementation of a systematic job evaluation scheme.

The Ghobadian and White research clarifies two important issues. First, that formality *per se* is not associated with more equitable pay outcomes. Instead, highly specific aspects of, particularly, recruitment procedures and job evaluation schemes seem to be the crucial factors. Once again, this leaves open the question of how necessarily a written equal opportunities policy contributes to less discrimination. Second, that comparing like work for men and women may reveal equal pay, but how that work is distributed may still be highly segregated along gender lines and thus result in women's mean pay levels being less than those of men. Can such an organization truly be said to be an equal opportunities employer? While 'equal pay for equal work' may be regarded as only a partial indicator of equal opportunities, even when occupational segregation is reduced and more women appear in what were previously men's jobs, there is still the question of how far the needs of different groups are being met. It is clear that most organizational structures have evolved to accommodate white men in the higher positions and women and black people in the lower ones. In most high-powered jobs, the small proportion of women who reach them are much more likely to be single and childless than are the majority who are men.

The reality is that most women still do the majority of household and caring tasks outside work. This takes time and energy. As Blum and Smith put it, 'to what extent does women's movement into . . . managerial positions represent real progress?' (1988: 545). There have so far been few organizations making structural alterations to accommodate women's or men's needs related, for instance, to the care of dependent relatives. There is little social policy in the UK to encourage such accommodations. Even work-place nurseries have been taxed. Organizations may enable women to work part-time, but in doing so the women lose valuable entitlements to benefits such as pensions, and remain concentrated in less-well-paid jobs. As well as the lack of structural changes, women who wish to work in non-traditional jobs face the strain of being doubly different – neither typical women nor typical job-holders.

These considerations raise another set of criteria by which equal opportunities policies may be evaluated; not objective head-counts, but more difficult to assess subjective measures such as degree of satisfaction, degree of role-strain and policy initiatives undertaken by the organization to accommodate to the needs of under-represented groups. As yet, there are few models of what such an accommodating organization would look like. But, in the end, such accommodations must surely be linked with outcomes – women and minority group members achieving a greater share of organizational rewards. Distributions may not be enough by themselves, but ultimately other criteria cannot stand alone either.

So far we have been examining the relationship between three main ways of approaching equal opportunities: producing a written policy; changing distributions; and accommodating structures to the needs of different groups. It has been argued that all are flawed as measures of the effectiveness of equal opportunities initiatives, and that extraneous variables (such as the composition of local labour markets; growth rates of the sector) can exert a profound effect upon the minority group composition of a work-force. It has further been argued that what equal opportunities initiatives take place within organizations depends crucially upon how equal opportunities are understood by its members. It therefore becomes important to understand how different conceptions of equal opportunities get created and maintained within organizations, as well as to elaborate what implications they may have for policy development. A useful series of concepts come from social identity theory (e.g. Tajfel 1981; a useful exposition is in Brown 1986) and related theoretical work by Salaman (1986), and from recent anthropological work on the relationship between individual cognition and organizational procedure (Douglas 1987).

Social identity theory has as its basis the assumption that people's identities become intimately related to social groupings. In order to maintain a positive social identity, we each come to value certain perceived distinguishing characteristics of those groups we are members of (ingroups) relative to those we are not members of (outgroups). Within organizations, group identity becomes fractured along the lines created by the organizational structure. Though, as both Salaman (1986) and Billig (1987) point out, endless exceptions for individuals may be made, when *groups* are the focus for attention individual reactions will be more positive if it is an ingroup than if it is an outgroup. This implies, for the development of equal opportunities, that there will be some psychological resistance to the opening up of opportunities to members of groups seen as outgroups. By definition, many outgroups will consist of those whose members are less well represented within certain organizational positions.

Salaman (1986) illustrates this with an account of the attempt to introduce an equal opportunities policy into the London Fire Brigade, which aimed to recruit more women and black people into firefighting positions. It generated a great deal of resistance, justifications for the status quo, and negative comments about women and black people. The policy had little impact on distributions and, instead, generated defensive psychological reactions which resulted in the organization becoming more closed and less permeable to the very under-represented groups it was created to increase. For example, the inappropriateness of women as firefighters was justified both in terms of women's lack of the physical characteristics needed to do the job, and in terms of how women would destroy the 'family' atmosphere of the service – a clear reference to the comfortable group feeling which ingroup members felt would be destroyed by the introduction of people from outgroups. This group feeling thus was regarded by current organizational members as necessary for the success of the service, and also as dependent upon the group being made up of people like those already members of it, that is white males.

Though people at top management level clearly had a conception that certain groups were under-represented, and introduced the policy in order to change these distributions, it is clear that in this case the work-force had a totally different view. Not only were they resistant to arguments for changed distributions, but also they were resistant to the idea that a policy was needed at all. It is a good example of how top-down policies can be undermined by those at the 'shop-floor' end of the organization. Ultimately, for a policy to be effective, it depends upon people being willing to implement it. For equal opportunities to become more of a reality an important aspect of this willingness is how welcoming current organizational members are to new ones from groups previously considered as outgroups. Even if people from under-represented groups do manage to become employed by an organization, the strain of being an out-group member is often intense. It requires huge amounts of energy just to survive and to prevent one's feelings of competence from being eroded.

Opting out is a choice made by many who suffer from attacks to their identity (e.g. Breakwell 1986). Others who stay suffer in their positions of 'double marginality' (Apfelbaum 1986) whereby individuals uncomfortably have to cope with belonging neither to their usual ingroup (because they are in a job which is unusual for its members) nor fully to the job ingroup (because they are an atypical member of it).

Another response which social identity theory suggests group members may make when their group identity is threatened is to change what is valued. Group identity does not rest upon an invariant set of activities performed by members and defining the group. Rather, it is continually reconstructed out of a flexibly used series of concepts. Cockburn's work (1985) can be understood in these terms. She discovered that as new technology was introduced into organizations, what became regarded as 'men's work' and 'women's work' subtly shifted but that occupational segregation along gender lines was preserved. The activities women performed in relation to the new technology were valued less than those performed by the men. Bielby and Baron (1984) found a similar phenomenon in the USA, Game and Pringle (1984) in Australia. Social identity theory, then, reminds us that the processes of change do not automatically happen simply because a new policy is introduced, and it points us to the group patterning of relationships and value systems derived from the organizational structure. It goes some way towards clarifying the relationship between organizational structure and individual value systems. A person's understandings of equal opportunities and resistance to (or acceptance of) particular policy initiatives are partly created by his or her location in the structure and the group interactional contexts implied by that (see also Cockburn 1989).

But organizational policy, when it is translated into operational procedures, has implications for a person's activities and hence for his or her cognitive world. Simply performing a task means that one is *required* to make certain distinctions, to remember certain things and 'forget' others, to have some thoughts and not others. In her recent book *How Institutions Think*, Douglas (1987) clarifies this relationship. Our thinking, the categories we use in thought, ultimately becomes organizationally defined, and the organizational procedures (both formal and informal) come to confine, create and reflect the cognitive worlds of the organization's members. As Douglas puts it:

> institutions [i.e. organizations] need to be established by a cognitive device. Mutual convenience in multiple transactions does not create enough certainty about the other person's strategies. It does not justify the necessary trust . . . for discourse to be possible at all, the basic categories have to be agreed on . . . nothing else but institutions can define sameness.
>
> (Douglas 1987: 55)

In other words, organizations can exist only provided there is sufficient agreement on the cognitive categories used to permit socially predictable activities to be conducted. The relationship between organizational procedures and individual cognitive worlds is two-way. What this suggests for equal opportunities initiatives to achieve the objectives of their initiators is that, first, certain cognitive distinctions need to be made and, second, that certain activities need to be performed so that these distinctions can be maintained.

Douglas goes on to develop the argument that these agreed upon categories, both enshrined in procedure and created by them, result in it becoming easier to remember some things and to forget others. What is regarded as information, with meaning, becomes highly constrained; it becomes easier to think certain things than others; easier to act in certain ways than others. Discourse analysts in the UK have also emphasized the importance of categorization (e.g. Billig 1987; Potter and Wetherell 1987).

Introduction of a policy requires that is it conceived of in the first place. Such conception, of course, is no guarantee that the policy will be unproblematically implemented (as argued above), but for any policy initiative to occur at least one organizational member (though usually many more) must be able to conceive of a problem and of desirable changes. In the area of equal opportunities, if changed distributions are the ultimate goal, then clearly cognitive distinctions need to be made by key policy-makers between the relevant groups and about how members from each are distributed within the organization. What distributions are noticed becomes an important issue. Obviously, one aim of monitoring is to bring into focus information about distributions so that specific action can take place. Having, in addition, some understanding of how current organizational practices operate as processes of exclusion for people from certain groups, and some ideas about what could be done to make the organization a more welcoming place for people from under-represented groups would be helpful.

More pessimistically it may well be that many key decision-makers assume that equality of opportunity already exists. If they consider themselves already to be equal opportunity employers, they will have little incentive to initiate policies in the area. Why commit scarce resources to where they are not perceived as being needed?

As yet, there has been little research systematically investigating these issues across a number of organizations. In order to clarify how equal opportunities are understood, a telephone survey was conducted by Marilyn Aitkenhead and Cathy Gorham in 1988 whereby a representative of twenty randomly chosen companies from the Times Top 1,000 Index (for 1987) was interviewed in depth (see Aitkenhead 1988).[1] Every fiftieth company on the list was approached, providing it employed more than 3,000 people in the UK. Since we wanted to relate understandings to the development of policies to promote equal opportunities, we decided to direct our initial efforts at those within the organizations who had some responsibility for this task. The switchboard operator was therefore asked to put us in touch with a person in the organiz- ation who had responsibility for equal opportunities. Most of our sample were personnel specialists, and nearly half were women. The issues covered were wide-ranging and the most relevant for our purposes here include:

1 How were equal opportunities conceived of? In particular, what were the group and organizational categories which came into people's minds when asked about equal opportunities?
2 Did they consider themselves to be an equal opportunities employer? If they did, then clearly there would be little incentive for the further development of equal opportunities policies.
3 What factors did they consider might hinder the development of equal opportunities? We were looking here to see how far organizational struc- tures and procedures were considered as hindrances, and how much there was a focus on individuals.
4 How would they assess whether or not an equal opportunity policy was working? Did they have a clear set of criteria which they could articulate?
5 How was equal opportunities represented within the structure? For example, how many had an equal opportunities committee; how many had systematic monitoring procedures the results of which were widely disseminated?

The results were depressing. The main group and organizational categories used are shown in Table 3.1 and 3.2 respectively. It is clear that over half the sample provided no people categories at all. When we asked what the term 'equal opportunities' meant to them, they said things like 'equal opportunities for everyone' or 'no bias'. Table 3.2 shows that our respondents were not

Table 3.1   People categories used

Category	No of respondents
None	12
Sex	5
Marital status	2
Colour/ethnicity/race	5
Creed	1
Disability	2
Age	1

Table 3.2   Organizational categories used

Category	No of respondents
None	13
Recruitment	3
Job specification	3
Promotion	2
Selection	1
Career development	1
Training	1

highly attuned to organizational boundaries when thinking about equal opportunities, and well over half did not mention the organization at all. Thus many respondents were not making the cognitive discriminations required even to enable of the conception that inequalities prevailed. This finding is borne out by another result: when we asked them if they thought their organization was an equal opportunities employer, they nearly all said yes (eighteen out of twenty).

We also asked what resistances they perceived to the development of equal opportunities within their organization, and once again organizational barriers or the needs of different groups hardly featured. About half (nine) could think of none, and of the rest the most common resistance mentioned (by seven) was that of prejudiced individuals. Things like qualification rules, benefits, access to facilities such as a crèche or a bank, working arrangements such as flexible hours, job-sharing or career-break schemes, just did not enter their minds. Moreover, organizational *problems* (such as recruitment shortages) were not connected with equal opportunities policies, even when we asked our respondents about these directly.

When we explored the criteria they would use to assess the effectiveness of equal opportunities policies, many respondents could not think of any! Though this time around half mentioned distributions (the proportion of women and men in various organizational positions, for example) once again most of these respondents made very few distinctions. It would be foolhardy to assume, however, that because half our sample would *examine* distributions implies also that they felt distributions needed change. We asked them what they thought an equal opportunities policy could achieve and most answered in very vague terms indeed – changes in distributions were mentioned by only seven respondents. Even when we asked *specifically* whether distributions should be changed, very few (six) gave an unqualified 'yes'. The rest dissembled, saying things like:

'depends on whether there is any evidence of disadvantage'

'only if suitable for positions'

'never had any problem – people are selected because they are the best candidates'

'can't change policies to suit women'.

The results of the survey clearly indicate that the majority of our respondents had a view of equal opportunities such that

1 they already prevailed
2 they were not conceived of in terms of organizational structures requiring adaptation to suit individual needs
3 distributional changes were regarded as unnecessary
4 criteria for evaluating them, if they existed, were only vaguely conceived of.

These results do not paint an optimistic picture of the present or future development of equal opportunities. Since most respondents felt little needed to be done within their organizations, it is not surprising that little *was* being done. Only eight companies had any form of monitoring, but of these in only one could it be said to be comprehensive. Existing in such an uninformative environment with respect to possible inequalities and organizational boundaries is also not conducive to change. Only three companies had an equal opportunity officer or unit, and another had in addition an equal opportunities committee. Thus sixteen of our twenty companies had no place for developing equal opportunities formally represented within their structure. It seems clear that, within the context of this random sample, the development of effective equal opportunities policies is unlikely to take place.

Conclusions

It has been argued that evaluating the effectiveness of equal opportunity policy is highly problematic for a number of reasons. First, in relation to what aims are we to evaluate the effectiveness of the policy? Policies may be generated for a number of different reasons: to appear to be doing something; to solve some organizational problems such as recruitment shortages; to change distributions. Researchers may feel policies ought to have certain aims – we have argued that changing distributions is not enough by itself, and that organizations should become more accommodating to the needs of particular individuals from under-represented groups – but we accept that there is unlikely to be agreement on what an equal opportunities policy should achieve. Second, different conceptions of equal opportunities mean there are different sets of criteria available for evaluation, and if these are used differently within organizations confusion, disappointment and conflict are likely to result. Third, any changes may be the result of factors which probably have little to do with the policy – turnover levels, growth rates and so on. Disentangling the effects of policy *per se* is therefore well-nigh impossible. We have also argued that written policies may be neither necessary nor sufficient for changes in distributions to occur. As yet, much of the research required to test out assumptions has simply not been done. We do not know whether or not morale, satisfaction and productivity are greater within organizations with an equal opportunities policy, for instance, or whether adopting one ensures a more efficient use of human resources; yet these are outcomes the EOC and CRE state will occur once a policy is introduced. We followed this with a discussion of reasons why organizational changes are likely to be slow at best –

the defensive reactions of ingroups and the ways our cognitive worlds are structured by organizations. Finally, we reported a study which implied that people with a responsibility for the development of equal opportunities perceived their organization as an equal opportunity employer and thus had little incentive to change it. They did not inhabit an information-environment which would reveal to them the degree to which inequalities prevailed.

The implications of existing evidence, the arguments discussed here and our survey results are profoundly depressing for the development of equal opportunities. It seems that women and ethnic minority group members are currently required, and will be required for some time to come, to fit in to organizational contexts where they are disadvantaged.

Note

1 The interviews were conducted by Cathy Gorham and we presented a joint paper on the study at the Psychology of Women at Work International Research Conference, July 1988.

References

Aitkenhead, M. (1987) Assumptions surrounding equal opportunities policies, *Occupational Psychologist*, 3: 42–4.
—— (1988) Perceptions of equal opportunities, in S. Oliver (ed.) *The Psychology of Women at Work*, Worthing: P (SET) Centre.
Anderson, G., Hulme, D. and Young E. (1987) Appraisal without form-filling, *Personnel Management*, February: 44–7.
Apfelbaum, E. (1986) Women in leadership positions, *Social Section Newsletter*, 17: 3–18, British Psychological Society.
Argyris, C. (1982) *Reasoning, Learning and Action*, San Francisco: Jossey-Bass.
Beechey, V. (1989) Women's employment in France and Britain: some problems of comparison, *Work, Employment and Society*, 3, 3: 369–78.
Bielby, W. and Baron, J. (1984) A women's place is with other women: sex segregation within organisations, in B. Reskin (ed.) *Sex Segregation in the Workplace: Trends, Explanations, Remedies*, Washington, DC: National Academy Press.
Billig, M. (1987) *Arguing and Thinking*, Cambridge University Press.
Billig, M., Condor, C., Edwards, D., Game, M., Middleton, D. and Radley, A. (1988) *Ideological Dilemmas*, London: Sage.
BIM (British Institute of Management) (1989) *Survey on Women Managers*, prepared by Tim Rycroft, available from the Representation Unit, BIM, 64–8 Kingsway, London, WC2B 6BL.
Blum, L. and Smith, V. (1988) Women's mobility in the corporation: a critique of the politics of optimism, *Signs*, 13, 528–45.
Breakwell, G. (1986) *Coping with Threatened Identities*, London: Methuen.
Brown, R. (1986) Ethnocentrism and hostility (Ch. 15), in Brown, *Social Psychology*, 2nd edn, New York: Free Press.
Cockburn, C. (1985) *Machinery of Dominance: Women, Men and Technical Know-How*, London: Pluto.
—— (1989) Equal opportunities, the long and short agenda, *Industrial Relations Journal*, 20: 213–25.

Collinson, D. and Knights, D. (1985) Jobs for the boys: recruitment into life insurance sales, *EOC Research Bulletin*, 9: 24–43.

CRE (Commission for Racial Equality) (1983) *Code of Practice*, London: HMSO.

Department of Employment (1988a) New entrants to the labour market in the 1990s, *Employment Gazette*, May: 267–74.

—— (1989) *Employment Gazette*, Oct, Table 5.8.1.1.8.

Douglas, M. (1987) *How Institutions Think*, London: Routledge & Kegan Paul.

Dex, S. and Shaw, L. (1986) *Women at Work: Do Equal Opportunity Policies Matter?*, London: Macmillan.

EOC (Equal Opportunities Commission) (1985) *Code of Practice*, London: HMSO.

—— (1987) *Women and Men in Britain*, London: HMSO.

—— (1989) *From Policy to Practice: An Equal Opportunities Strategy for the 1990s*, Manchester: EOC.

Game, A. and Pringle, R. (1984) *Gender at Work*, London: Pluto.

Ghobadian, A. and White, M. (1987) Factors contributing to the implementation of unbiased job evaluation schemes, *Personnel Review*, 16, 5: 21–5.

Ghobadian, A. and White, M. (1988) Personnel policies, structural characteristics, and equity in job-evaluated payment systems, *Personnel Review*, 17, 5: 29–32.

Hackett, G. (1988) Who'd be an equal opportunity manager?, *Personnel Management*, 20, April: 48–55.

Hakim, C. (1989) New recruits to self-employment in the 1980s, *Employment Gazette*, June: 286–97.

IDS (1989) *Maternity Leave and Childcare*, IDS Study 425, Jan, London: IDS Ltd.

Jenkins, R. (1986) *Racism and Recruitment*, Cambridge University Press.

Jewson, N. and Mason, D. (1986) The theory and practice of equal opportunities: liberal and radical approaches, *Sociological Review*, 324: 307–334.

Leonard, J. (1986) Contract compliance in the USA: an evaluation of import and cost, in *Equal Opportunities Through Contract Compliance*, report by the ILEA Contract Compliance Equal Opportunities Unit, London.

Lerner, M. and Matthews, G. (1967) Reactions to suffering of others under conditions of indirect responsibility, *Journal of Personality and Social Psychology*, 5: 319–25.

Liff, S. (1989) Assessing equal opportunity policies, *Personnel Review*, 18: 27–34.

Lovenduski, J. (1989) Implementing equal opportunities in the 1990s: an overview, *Public Administration*, 67, 1: 7–18.

O'Donnell, C. and Hall, P. (1988) *Getting Equal*, London: Allen & Unwin.

Potter, J. and Wetherell, M. (1987) *Discourse and Social Psychology*, London: Sage.

Salaman, G. (1986) *Working*, Harmondsworth, Penguin.

Spencer, A. and Podmore, D. (eds) (1987) *In a Man's World*, London: Tavistock.

Stone, I. (1988) *Equal Opportunities in Local Authorities*, London: HMSO.

Tajfel, H. (1981) Social stereotypes and social groups, in J. Turner and H. Giles (eds) *Intergroup Behaviour*, New York: John Wiley.

Virgo, P. (ed.) (1989) *Towards an Open and Equal IT Careers Initiative*, Report of the Women into Information Technology Campaign Feasibility Study, London: ICL (available from IT Strategy Services, 2 Eastbourne Avenue, London, W3 6JN).

Webb, J. and Liff, S. (1988) Play the white man: the social construction of fairness and competition in equal opportunity policies, *Sociological Review*, 36: 543–51.

Wild, A. (1986) Realistic expectations of equal opportunities, *Personnel Management*, 18, Oct: 45–50.

Wilson, P. and Stanworth, J. (1988) Growth strategies in small Asian and Caribbean businesses, *Employment Gazette*, Jan: 8–14.

4 | Women's training needs
Nina L. Colwill and Susan Vinnicombe

Sex-segregated training is as established as the division of labour by sex. Until recently, virtually all occupations have been sex-segregated, and the training for these occupations has, by definition, been separated by sex as well. In fact, it is only in recent years, as we have come to hold gender integration of the work-place as an ideal, that the notion of women-only training has been opened to criticism (Fonda 1986).

The idea of women-only management training is not based on the different characteristics and different goals of men and women; for the attitudes, personality characteristics, and organizational behaviours of women and men in the same occupation are far more alike than different (see e.g. Colwill and Pollick 1987; Colwill and Roos 1978; Harlan and Weiss 1980). Rather, the argument for single-gender training for women has been based upon the unique set of problems and issues that women must face in the work-place. The argument is usually based upon a desire to end discrimination, to treat women and men equally, and to minimize rather than to emphasize differences between the sexes. This chapter explores the advantages and disadvantages of women-only training and, having concluded that such training clearly does have a place in management education, examines some of the most effective directions it can take.

The drawbacks of women-only training

Although there has been a call for a 'women's studies' approach in management education (Novarra 1982), that is studying women managers as a topic in its own right, such a trend may be fraught with problems. A women's studies approach, which many people consider to be sexist, can serve to differentiate further between male and female managers, as if they are not managers with more shared than unique problems. A women's studies approach could serve to establish equally powerful male and female camps, and gender integration of the work-place would be postponed yet further. It is more likely, that women, the more recent players in the work-place game, would be even more strongly defined as the outgroup, and would therefore suffer the greater loss.

Men who now support women's full work-place integration, for economic or ethical reasons, or because they believe that male–female work-place relationships enhance the quality of work life, might be given the impression that women would rather 'do it alone, thanks!' Furthermore, a women's studies approach to management training lessens the responsibility of management educators to address the myriad issues involved with 'gender integration' of the work-place, as these problems are considered to be well covered by women-only courses.

One of the major arguments against women-only training lies in its potential for trivialization (Bargh 1986). Women, that which women do, and that which has been restricted to women, have traditionally been accorded lower status than men and all things male-like; and, in many organizations, so has special training for women. Furthermore, women in both Britain (Hammond 1986) and Canada (Colwill and Josephson 1983) do not fare as well as men in obtaining the company-sponsored management training they desire. Management-training resources are scarce resources, and if women's share of them consists primarily of women-only training which the organization considers to be trivial, any benefit that women derive from their special training may be more than offset by the disadvantages.

Another drawback of women-only training is the artificial situation which it creates. Women in management do not interact on a daily basis in the safe situation afforded by single-gender workshops, so the generalizability of the learning is open to criticism. This may be particularly true of assertiveness training, for many women experience assertiveness problems only with men.

Many women who participate in women-only training feel that they are the converted, and that those who have a real need to hear the material are sitting at their desks, oblivious to the issues being discussed in the seminar. In fact, women-only training may actually serve to postpone the day when sex discrimination is faced by men and women together (Bargh 1986). This argument presupposes, of course, that if such training were abolished, gender-integrated classes on sex-role issues in organizations would spring up everywhere, and that they would be well attended by managers of both sexes.

In sum, women-only training has its drawbacks. It is sexist in itself, may reinforce work-place segregation and may separate women from the men from support sex-role liberation. Furthermore, women in management training carries with it the potential for being seen as trivial and artificial. Yet, in spite of these problems and in spite of the fact that such training may constitute preaching to the converted, many people, including ourselves, believe that there are strong arguments to be made for this approach.

The argument for women-only training

Life differs for the average man and the average woman in various ways, many of which exert a profound impact on their working lives. In their personal lives, for instance:

1 Women are more likely than men to have been absent from the work-place

or to have worked part-time in the interest of children or family (Colwill and Erhart 1985).
2 Women are more likely than men to accept the ongoing lion's share of the household and family responsibilities, placing an extra strain on their time, energy and areas of commitment (Colwill and Erhart 1985).
3 Husbands are more likely than wives to be engaged in careers which, by virtue of their greater earning potential, takes precedence over those of their partners, further widening the gap in their earning potential (Frank 1978).

In their work lives:

1 Women are more likely than men to suffer from sex-role stereotyping and sex discrimination, both of which exert negative impacts on their upward mobility (Colwill and Roos 1978).
2 Women rarely have female role models in senior positions in their organizations. Further, the same women may have to serve as role models to other women, thereby increasing their stress (Cooper and Davidson 1982).
3 Many women in male-dominated fields feel that they are operating in an alien world, in which the rules of power and politics require great investments of emotional energy to understand and to practise (Loden 1985), or that they are working alongside men who do not share or empathize with their values (Fonda 1986).

Women's unique issues may rarely be raised in mixed-sex groups because of the fundamental differences between male and female communication patterns. Men tend to dominate mixed-sex groups (Bunker and Seashore 1977), to talk more and to make more suggestions than women do; women spend more of their verbal time yielding, agreeing and praising others (Lockheed and Hall 1976). Men initiate and are the recipients of the majority of verbal interactions. Men interrupt more than women do and women are more likely to be the object of these interruptions (Zimmerman and West 1975). Furthermore, although men express their feelings more openly in mixed-sex groups, women express theirs more easily in all-female contexts. Taken together, these studies clearly indicate that women do not enjoy equal participation with men in any type of mixed-sex training.

Notwithstanding the communication barriers, women may also be reluctant to discuss home and work-place conflicts with men (Fonda 1986), lest they be seen as incapable of coping. Many women-only programmes emphasize such life experiences (Spero 1987). These tend to be gender-related, and to be more easily identified with by members of one's own sex. Working through such conflicts is integral to women's psychological well-being. Women-only programmes are important because they encourage participants to talk about these experiences (Vinnicombe and Colwill 1987).

It is to be hoped that the day is approaching when women in management course trainers have no material to discuss; when power and influence and household responsibilities are equally distributed between women and men; when the salary gap between men and women has closed; and when sexual harassment has ceased to exist. For the time being, however, the need for special courses for female managers is a continuing reality.

The content of women-only training

This training exists primarily because there are certain broad issues that can best be addressed in women-only groups, where women do not have to protect men's feelings. It's not surprising that, whether or not they are specifically written into the course outline, certain issues surface in most of these programmes: power and politics, sexuality, and leadership style.

Organizational power and politics

The basis for most women-in-management courses, however the instructions actually define it, is the concept of organizational power and politics. In fact, it is difficult to imagine how one could study organizational power and politics without addressing the issue of women in management, or how one could study women in management independent of organizational power and politics. Women receive lower salaries than men; they give fewer orders; their placement on the organizational ladder is lower than that of men. To say that the status of women is lower than the status of men is redundant; to say that women have less power than men is to state the obvious. Not quite as obvious, however, are the ways in which the sex-differentiated communications of women and men maintain and enhance sex differences in organizational power (Spinner and Colwill 1982). The whole realm of assertiveness skills represents a practical attempt to address this issue.

The issue of sexuality

Sexuality is a work-place issue, and one that women often find easier to discuss among themselves. Is the office romance ever worth its attendant frustrations? How should one deal with a well-liked colleague who is becoming romantically involved? How does one deal with sexual innuendos from peers? How should a manager deal with sexual innuendos from subordinates? How does one deal with a superior whom one suspects of being capable of sexual assault? These issues are difficult ones for women and men to discuss openly, because they are affected in fundamentally different ways. For example, females are twice as likely as males to be fired when an office romance creates complaints (Collins 1983). The discussion of work-place sexuality is even more sensitive when the topic of sex and aggression arises. Women are the great majority of victims in sexual harassment cases (Licata and Popovich 1987). In recognition of the traumatic effects of sexual aggression on its employees, Dupont has initiated a rape prevention programme, the core of which is an eight-hour women-only rape prevention workshop (Arey 1987).

Sex differences in leadership styles

Research to support the idea of differences in the working styles of male and female managers is hard to come by. The inappropriateness of the profiles commonly used in the leadership area to illuminate gender differences does not help this situation. However, recent research (Vinnicombe 1987) at

Cranfield School of Management using the Myers Briggs Type Indicator (MBTI), which is based on Jung's personality types, has yielded some significant and interesting findings about the differences between male and female working styles. The MBTI classifies people according to their combination of preferences along four dimensions; extraversion/introversion, sensing/intuition, thinking/feeling and judgement/perceptive. The most significant difference between male and female managers is along the sensing/intuition dimension. Women tend to be much more intuitive, 70 per cent of male managers are sensing, whereas 40–60 per cent of women are intuitive; the percentages vary a little according to the professional backgrounds of the women. Women enjoy ambiguous problems, get bored with routine problems, frequently ignore the facts and search for creative approaches. Men tend to be much more sensing, preferring practical problems, systems and methods, are patient with routine details and search for standard problem-solving approaches. There are no good or poor management styles; organizations needs all kinds of different styles. If these results can be generalized, then it suggests that women managers do show important differences in their working styles, compared to the majority of male managers. If these differences are not recognized, appreciated and capitalised upon by organizations, many women managers will be squeezed out of organizational life.

The design of women in management programmes

Women in management programmes are basically of two types: those that restrict their membership to women but address general management topics like accounting, marketing and strategy, and those that primarily address the social-psychological issues facing women in the work-place and that restrict their membership to women. In this section we examine two such programmes: University of New Brunswick's women-only mini-MBA-type programme, and Cranfield School of Management's approach to addressing women's issues with female managers and management students.

In 1983 the University of New Brunswick in Fredericton launched the most comprehensive women-in-management programmes offered anywhere. Several years in preparation, this ten-month mini-MBA-type programme is aimed primarily at university-educated women who are currently employed and who wish to broaden their career prospects. Participants attend monthly three-day sessions in such areas as finance, marketing, organizational behaviour and business strategy. Each month they receive an assignment to be completed in their work-place, and each monthly session begins with a review of the previous month's assignments. Female academics from across Canada combined their expertise to design the programme, which is taught by female professors with interest in women's issues as well as their own substantive areas. While the focus is on the core management topics, the atmosphere is one of shared personal issues and common perspective.

For the past three years Cranfield School of Management has been running a women's personal development programme (a programme run in two one-week modules) for practising managers, and an all-female elective on the MBA programme, which extends over one morning a week for five consecutive weeks. In both of these programmes the female participants work with experienced female tutors in small groups, in an informal, highly interactive manner. The emphasis is working on the personal issues facing the female participants in their work and private lives. Management style, motivation, interpersonal skills, handling politics, managing stress and career counselling are the key topics addressed in the programmes. Throughout, the aim is on being not only positive and constructive, but also confronting. All too often women recognize how discrimination occurs to them in general, but fail to accept how it has specifically occurred to them in their own lives. A prime example is sexual harassment.

Recommendations

Having argued the need for women-only training and suggested some key topic areas to address in such training, we suggest that the following points be borne in mind by anyone thinking of setting up such a programme:

1 Because women's issues are so often viewed as frivolous, women-only training can easily gain the reputation of the 'girls' day out'. Thus it must receive clearly articulated support from top management if it is to function as a credible in-house educational programme. Similarly top-down support must be given to those attending the women-only training. It often helps if the training is run by authoritative external trainers.
2 Be prepared to face accusations of sex-discrimination when instituting women-only training programmes and be prepared to offer male-facilitated male-only training in order to offer men the opportunity to address sex-role issues in a safe environment as well (Fonda 1986). One might also consider bringing these groups together at some point, and if this format is utilized, it is imperative that male and female facilitators are used and that they are able to serve as positive role models in their interactions with each other (Sean 1986).
3 Ideally the programme should be offered in several modules, separated by weeks or months (Fritchie 1986). Many of the issues that arise in women-only training are highly emotional ones that require time to process, and many of the concepts may remain abstract until applied and internalized in the work-place (Hammond 1986).
4 It is important that women-only training be targeted at a specific group of women (for example, top-level managers or first-line supervisors, not both) or address a specific issue. Otherwise participants may find that they have nothing in common but their gender.
5 In organizations in which this training is being offered in-house a decision must be made as to whether participants should be nominated along set criteria, or self-selected. The former method allows the organizers to create the relative homogeneity they desire, and may serve as an effective organizational reward, but the method may result in a less highly motivated group of participants and may engender resentment among those

who were not selected. When the course is being offered by external agencies, the latter should be involved in deciding on the method of selection.

6 Residential workshops constitute an ideal learning environment. If child-care is a problem, it is important to give serious consideration to its provision in a way that makes the women feel their work is appreciated rather than that they are a problem.

7 The issue of 'Why Women Only?' should be addressed in the opening session of the course (Fritchie 1986), and ideally also in the course of advertising literature.

8 Guard against the wholesale acceptance of the male model of doing things, of teaching women to be more like men. Loden's (1985) popular book, *Feminine Leadership or How to Succeed in Business Without Being One of the Boys* is recommended for anyone embarking upon the facilitation of such training. Loden fills the reader with a strong appreciation of the unique characteristics that women bring to the work-place, a healthy perspective from which to embark upon women-only training.

9 Although it is critical that women's concerns should not be discounted and that participants be allowed to express their negative feelings, it is also important that the training draw to a positive conclusion. This goal requires a skilled facilitator with a positive view of life, one who is experienced in dealing with negative reactions and is not easily drawn into anger herself.

10 Ensure that none of the training materials are sexist in their assumptions or their language. Although it counteracts this non-sexist ideal, the group facilitator must be a woman.

11 Avoid an anti-male stance, if for no better reason than it encourages the workshop to develop a female-victim/male-persecutor tone, a tone that is damaging to the self-concepts of the participants. The examination of male sex-role issues is one effective way to achieve a balanced perspective.

12 It is imperative that women-only training be seen as an adjunct to, rather than a substitute for, more traditional organizational and occupational training. Such training must be treated merely as one specific part of a comprehensive career development programme for female employees.

Of course training programmes specifically designed for women in management do not provide the complete answer to the problems women managers encounter at work. They are most effective when supported by good family, organizational and social arrangements which take into account the issues raised by women having careers. Women's training programmes provide only a starting-point for women but, so far in our experience, it has proved to be a cathartic starting-point.

References

Arey, M. L. (1987) Du Pont backs personal safety with Employee Rape Prevention Program, *Business and Health*, 5, 1: 56.
Arles, E. (1977) Male–female interpersonal styles in all male, all female and mixed groups, in A. G. Sargent (ed.) *Beyond Sex Roles*, St Paul: West.

Bargh, L. (1986) Awareness raising through training, *Journal of European Industrial Training*, 10, 1: 23–7.

Bunker, B. B. and Seashore, E. W. (1977) Power, collusion; intimacy-sexuality; support, in A. G. Sargent (ed.) *Beyond Sex Roles*, St Paul: West.

Collins, E. G. C. (1983) Managers and lovers, *Harvard Business Review*, Sept–Oct; 142–53.

Colwill, N. L. and Erhart, M. (1985) Have women changed the workplace?, *Business Quarterly*, 49, 4: 27–31.

Colwill, N. L. and Josephson, W. L. (1983) Attitudes toward equal opportunity in employment: the case of one government department, *Business Quarterly*, 48, 1: 87–93.

Colwill, N. L. and Pollick, M. (1987) The mentor connection update, *Business Quarterly*, 52, 2, 16–20.

Colwill, N. L. and Roos, N. P. (1978) Debunking a stereotype: the female medical student, *Sex Roles*, 5: 717–22.

Cooper, G. and Davidson, M. (1982) *High Pressure; Working Lives of Women Managers*, Glasgow: Collins/Fontana.

Fonda, N. (1984) Developing personal effectiveness: a course for women, *Women and Training News*, 15: whole issue.

——(1986) Single-sex vs mixed-sex training, *Journal of European Industrial Training*, 10, 7: 28–33.

Frank, R. H. (1978) Why women earn less: the theory and estimation of differential qualification, *American Economic Review*, 68, 360–73.

Fritchie, J. (1986) How to design women's training that gets results, *Journal of European Industrial Training*, 10, 7: 10–14.

Hammond, V. (1986) Management training for women, *Journal of European Industrial Training*, 10, 7: 15–22.

Harlan, A. and Weiss, C. L. (1980) Moving up: women in managerial careers – Third progress report, unpublished manuscript, Wellesley College, Center for Research on Women, Wellesley, Mass.

Licata, B. J. and Popovich, P. M. (1987) Preventing sexual harassment: a proactive approach, *Training and Development Journal*, 41, 5: 34–8.

Lockheed, M. E. and Hall, K. P. (1976) Conceptualizing sex as a status characteristic: applications to leadership training strategies, *Journal of Social Issues*, 32, 3: 11–124.

Loden, M. (1985) *Feminine leadership, or How to Succeed in Business Without Being One of the Boys*, New York: Times Books.

Novarra, V. (1982) Management education: case for women's studies, *Women's Studies International Forum*, 5, 1: 69–74.

Sean, R. (1986) Men and equality in organizations: training strategies, *Journal of European Industrial Training*, 10, 8: 9–12.

Spero, M. (1987) Self-development for women managers in the retail industry, *Industrial and Commercial Training*, 19, 5: 9–12.

Spinner, B. and Colwill, N. L. (1982) Communication, in N. L. Colwill (ed.) *The New Partnership: Women and Men in Organizations*, Palo Alto, Calif: Mayfield Publishing.

Vinnicombe, S. (1987) What exactly are the differences in male and female working styles? *Women in Management Review*, 3, 1: 13–21.

Vinnicombe, S. and Colwill, N. L. (1987) Should women in management have their own training programmes? *Occupational Psychologist*, special issue 'Gender Issues in Occupational Psychology': 19–21.

Zimmerman, D. H. and West, C. (1975) Sex roles, interruptions and silences in conversation, in B. Thorne and N. Henley (eds) *Language and Sex: Difference and Dominance*, Rawley, Mass: Newbury House.

Acknowledgement

The authors wish to express their appreciation to Cranfield School of Management and the Centre for International Business Studies, Department of Marketing, University of Manitoba, for the travel and literature review grants that made this work possible.

Part II
The problems traditionally associated with working women

5 | Sexual harassment at work

Janet E. Stockdale

Issues and context

He would continually ask me how my sex life was, and who I was going out with. Would I like to go off one day for a walk, dinner, whatever? He was always leering and making remarks about my personal appearance and looks.

I discussed it with my colleagues and friends, and told one of his peers about his behaviour, but without naming the person concerned. Nothing happened and I feel responsible to some extent, because I didn't know how to tell him the remarks were unwanted. It's a male-dominated office and there is always sexual banter, and it is very difficult to state all the time that it is not pleasant. I've got to work with these people after all.

I became very angry and depressed. I was less efficient at work (I wouldn't approach him for advice on how to do the job), I didn't want to go to work and I avoided certain people at work. I suffered from stress and physical symptoms including colitis, panic attacks and depression. I wasn't the only person to suffer from this man's attentions but, as the only 'professional' member of the staff affected, the administrative staff used to come and tell me their experiences as well.

(An environmental health officer, female, talking about a male superior, quoted in Phillips, Stockdale and Joeman 1989)

Sexual harassment at work is not a new problem. The behaviours that constitute it have been a source of concern to generations of working women. In the past they were seen as an inevitable part of the working environment, but now there is growing awareness that they transgress the acceptable standards of male–female interpersonal behaviour.

The issue of definition is fundamental to discussions of sexual harassment at work and estimates of its incidence. One all-embracing view sees sexual harassment as the way men exert social control over women; at work it is merely sexism in a specific location. This definition, which restricts sexual harassment to male behaviour towards women, logically excludes men as victims. A less global definition of sexual harassment is implicit in some survey research where respondents are asked about a range of behaviours assumed to constitute harassment. But any externally generated definition ignores how the individuals themselves define the problem. This raises the issue of whether the 'victim' has to consider the behaviour as harassment for it to be so defined.

Available estimates suggest that at least one in ten and possibly as many as one in two working women experience sexual harassment at work. The majority of harassment involves women being harassed by men, and my analysis of the issues will reflect this dominant, and some would argue defining aspect of sexual harassment at work. However, in no way is this focus intended to deny the reality of the experiences of women and of men who suffer other forms of sexual harassment.

In order to understand the nature of sexual harassment at work we need a theoretical framework for examining its origins and effects. The recognition that sexual harassment is a problem in the work-place and has a detrimental effect on individual well-being and organizational efficiency should lead to strategies aimed at minimizing its occurrence but which also provide effective measures for dealing with it.

Incidence, definition and measurement

Awareness of sexual harassment has grown over the last decade (Backhouse and Cohen 1978; Brewer and Berk 1982; Farley 1978; Gutek 1985; Hadji-fotiou 1983; MacKinnon 1979; Meyer et al. 1981; Read 1982; Rubenstein 1988; Sedley and Benn 1982) and there is a substantial body of research aimed at establishing the scale of the problem (cf. Joeman et al. 1989). This cannot be measured by the number of formal complaints because of workers' anxieties about the consequences of voicing their unease, particularly in the absence of an established grievance procedure. In North American studies, incidence levels of sexual harassment towards women at work range from early estimates of between 70 and 90 per cent (cf. Farley 1978), which may have been inflated by the use of self-selected respondents, to later estimates of between 25 and 50 per cent (cf. Canadian Human Rights Commission 1984; Gutek 1985; USMSPB 1981). Equally wide-ranging estimates are provided by survey data from member states of the EEC, which may reflect variations in sampling and measurement criteria rather than differences in the magnitude of the problem (Rubenstein 1988). In Britain a number of studies have reported incidence figures of around 50 per cent for example, among secretarial staff (Alfred Marks Bureau 1982), women managers (Cooper and Davidson 1982) and women in a variety of occupations (Leeds TUCRIC 1983). More recently, a survey of 1,000 workers in Britain (800 women and 200 men) found that 16 per cent of the women in the sample reported experiencing harassment in their current job (Phillips et al. 1989). This figure is in stark contrast to the reported incidence rate of 2 per cent among men.

There is clear evidence that the behaviour that an individual defines as sexual harassment depends on their gender, with women consistently defining more experiences as harassing than men (cf. Collins and Blodgett 1981; Gutek 1985; Powell 1986). In the survey reported by Gutek (1985) sexual touching showed the largest gender gap, with 84 per cent of women, compared with 59 per cent of men, considering it to be sexual harassment. Furthermore, individuals, men and women, differ widely in their personal definitions. So, while complimentary comments and suggestive remarks constitute harassment for some individuals, for others they do not (cf. Gutek 1985; Powell 1983).

Although such data indicate the impossibility of obtaining a unanimously agreed definition, there is some consensus that, put most simply, sexual harassment is unwanted sexual attention (Stockdale 1986). In this study the major category of serious sexual harassment at work involved abuses of authority, such as promise of advancement or threat of reprisal. 'Trivial' examples of sexual harassment included a variety of behaviours, but 20 per cent of respondents, the majority of whom were women, thought that there was no such thing as trivial incidents of sexual harassment at work. For the women respondents sexual harassment at work was distinguished from similar behaviour outside by the difficulties of escaping such attentions and of challenging the right of the harasser to indulge in such behaviour.

In contrast with many analyses of sexual harassment and people's perceptions (cf. Pryor 1985), within the policy arena definitions frequently make no gender assumption about target or perpetrator (cf. Crocker 1983; Somers 1982; TUC 1983). Although in some policy definitions the harasser must have some explicit power or authority over the target, in my view this is not a necessary condition. While mutual attraction is implicitly excluded from many formal definitions, the distinction between attraction and harassment is a difficult one in the context of the power differentials existing both within work organizations and in educational institutions between staff and students (cf. Glaser and Thorpe 1986).

In order to understand the nature of sexual harassment it is important to appreciate not only its defining attributes but also the types of behaviour possessing these attributes, the contexts in which such behaviour occurs and the characteristics of the harasser and those who are targets of harassment. In our recent study (Phillips *et al.* 1989) the picture of sexual harassment that emerged from the analysis of 160 incidents reported by our respondents was a mixture of isolated incidents and continuing behaviour, most frequently occurring in the worker's own work-place, and initiated primarily by men toward women. Two-thirds of the reported incidents were harassment by colleagues, over half of whom held positions senior in status to the person being harassed, while the majority of the remainder involved harassment by clients or customers. There were two major categories of incident: sexual comments, innuendo and verbal advances (43 per cent), in some cases accompanied by threats or offers of reward; and physical contact (44 per cent), sometimes in the context of comments and advances.

Causes of sexual harassment

What do the victims of sexual harassment perceive to be the reasons for such behaviour? Stockdale (1986) found that the primary motives underlying sexual harassment were perceived to be sexual desire and powerplay – gaining, asserting or maintaining power and status. However, whereas men were twice as likely to attribute sexual harassment to sexual desire rather than to power-play, the reverse was true of women. In our recent study (Phillips *et al.* 1989) the harasser was seen as entirely responsible for initiating the behaviour in over three-quarters of the incidents (cf. Gutek 1985). However, in some cases the work-place atmosphere was perceived as encouraging harassment (18 per cent), for example when 'macho' behaviour was the norm and harassment was widely accepted or when its friendly atmosphere led to a confusion of signals; or the person harassed believed they were partly at fault (11 per cent), by their failing to be more assertive, or inadvertently encouraging comments or advances.

On the basis of previous analyses of women's work status (Nieva and Gutek 1981) and more specifically of sexuality at work (Tangri *et al.* 1982), Gutek (1985) considers three classes of model which offer explanations of sexual harassment at work. The natural/biological interpretation is used to argue that what has been called sexual harassment is merely sexual attraction. According to this view such behaviour is neither sexist nor discriminatory and does not have harmful consequences. Most importantly, this approach admits the existence of the behaviour but denies the intent to harass. According to Tangri *et al.* (1982) one version of this model suggests that, because men have a stronger sex drive, they more often make sexual advances in all settings, including the work-place. This perspective is compatible with the individual deficit explanation (identified by Nieva and Gutek 1981) which attributes sexual harassment to women's own deficiency in handling an approach or the deficiency of individual men in controlling their natural drives.

The organizational (or structural institutional) perspective assumes that sexual harassment is a result of opportunity structures created by organizational climate, hierarchy and specific authority relations. People in higher positions can use their power – which is perceived as legitimate within the organizational structure – to coerce lower-status individuals, who are usually women, into engaging in sexual interactions (cf. Nieva and Gutek 1981; Tangri *et al.* 1982). Sociocultural or sex role models focus on the power differentials of men and women, the motivation of men to maintain their dominance over women, and the socialization of women to acquiesce in general or to specific female sex role ideals (cf. Farley 1978; MacKinnon 1979; Nieva and Gutek, 1981; Tangri *et al.* 1982).

In response to the view that none of these models by itself appears to constitute an adequate explanation of sexual harassment, Gutek proposes a model that incorporates elements of all three approaches, emphasizing the effects of sex role expectations in an organizational context. This is known as sex role spillover (Gutek 1985; Gutek and Morasch 1982).

Sex role spill-over refers to the carry-over into the work-place of gender-based roles, that are usually irrelevant or inappropriate to work (cf. Nieva and Gutek 1981). Sex role expectations are carried over into the work-place for a variety of reasons. For example gender identity seems to be a more basic cognitive category than work role (Bem 1981; Kessler and McKenna 1978; Laws 1979); and women may feel more comfortable with stereotypically female roles in some circumstances, especially if they feel men at work have difficulty accepting them in anything other than a traditional female role (Kanter 1977). Gutek's research provides some support for predictions generated by the sex role spill-over model, with women in non-traditional male-dominated jobs, who are seen as 'role-deviates', reporting more sexual harassment than women in traditionally female jobs (cf. Leeds TUCRIC 1983). A major advantage of the sex role spill-over approach is that it focuses attention on the work-place and its environment, which may offer a more tractable arena for change than society in general.

What are the features of both the working environment and the way society is structured that encourage the occurrence of sexual harassment? Occupational segregation and gendered working spheres are seen as playing an important role in many analyses of sexual harassment in the work-place (cf. Gutek 1985; Stanko 1988). As Hakim (1979) points out, segregation has two components. The jobs that women do are different from those done by men (horizontal segregation) and women work at lower levels than men in the occupational hierarchy (vertical segregation). There is ample evidence that both forms of gender segregation are a pervasive feature of the work-force in Britain and scant evidence of change (Alban-Metcalfe and West, Chapter 12 in this volume; Cockburn 1988; EOC 1989; Roberts *et al.* 1988).

Gutek argues that sex segregation of work calls attention to gender – the single most noticeable aspect of people – and therefore facilitates sex role spill-over, the assumption that people in particular jobs and the jobs themselves have the characteristics of only one gender. This view is endorsed by Deaux and Major (1987) who identify sex role spill-over as just one example of the activation of gender beliefs and expectations, both descriptive and prescriptive, which affect male–female interaction. Gutek extends her analysis to a consideration of the effects of the sex ratio at work, which she differentiates into three components: sex ratio of occupation, of job, and of work group, which jointly affect day-to-day work experiences and provide the context in which work roles may be defined. According to Gutek's analysis, when the sex ratio of an occupation is significantly skewed, aspects of the sex role for the dominant gender spill over into the occupational work role, especially if the numerically dominant gender also occupies the high-status positions in the work group. The form and effects of the sex role spill-over depends on whether the person is in the majority or minority sex.

For example, the person in the minority – usually a woman – is seen as a role deviate, because of an incongruence between the sex role of the majority gender, which has spilled over into the occupational work role. The woman perceives the differential treatment she receives to be discriminatory, and to constitute harassment when the content is sexual. In contrast, a woman in an occupation which is female dominated is expected to fulfil those aspects of the female sex role emphasized by the particular job, and there is substantial overlap between the work role and female sex role. In this situation, although women may recognize that their job contains aspects of sexuality, according to Gutek they are less likely to view and report sexual harassment as a problem at work, because 'it is part of the job'. Men in comparable situations do not encounter the same problems as women, because women do not focus on male sexuality in the same way that men choose to focus on female sexuality. Moreover, when men working in a female-dominated work group do encounter social-sexual behaviour, they are less likely to perceive it as discriminatory or to label it as harassment because of the wider context of gender relations in society and the underlying issues of power and control.

Stanko (1988) argues that gendered working spheres provide the context but not the script for coercive sexuality at work. While concurring with Gutek that women's employment spheres, largely composed of care-giving and service jobs, contribute to the sexualization of women in those positions, Stanko sees sexual harassment as another example of male domination in women's everyday lives. In her view women's experiences of sexual harassment are not bound by traditional or non-traditional occupational spheres, but are bound by the wider experience of male dominance, power and economic control (cf. Farley 1978; MacKinnon 1979). From her examination of secretaries' work experiences, Pringle (1989) argues that sexual harassment is only one aspect of sexual power structures, and that sexuality in the workplace is so pervasive as to be invisible. In her view it is necessary to analyse the complex role that gender and sexuality play in the day-to-day negotiation of power at work.

A broader theoretical context is provided by social-psychological models of gender-related behaviour which recognize the fundamental significance of gender in social categorization and interaction, by providing the core of an individual's identity (cf. Goffman 1977; Stockard and Johnson 1979). Williams's (1984) integrative analysis of gender and social identity theory (Tajfel 1978) offers a productive perspective on sexual harassment. According to social identity theory, that part of a person's self-concept which derives from social group membership is constructed by embracing those outcomes of intergroup social comparison processes which make a positive contribution to self-esteem. Williams argues that, while social identity created in this way-referred to as agentic social identity (cf. Bakan 1966) – is an analogue of the type of personal identity encouraged in men, it is possible that a group may also gain meaning communally, thus reflecting processes of affiliation and attachments to others. To the extent that agentic and communal processes of constructing and evaluating social identity have different implications, and are differently encouraged in the sexes, we can expect men and women to be predisposed to behave in different ways.

Sexual harassment may be viewed as a corollary of the agentic style of identity construction whereby men define themselves as different from and better than women. Men's use of agentic definitions of identity based on status, prestige, authority and power can make women targets of unwanted sexual attention in normal social settings. When such behaviour is transferred to the work-place women's vulnerability increases dramatically because of the implicit or explicit threat to their future employment and economic viability. The responses of many women to sexual harassment, such as their reluctance to report such behaviour, protecting the harasser's identity and seeking support from close friends (cf. Phillips *et al.* 1989), can be seen to reflect not only their lack of confidence that any action will be taken, but also the fact that the victim is acting in a communal style.

Sexual harassment serves to reinforce the status quo. The imposition of unwanted sexual attention is a routine means of exercising the unequal power relations which exist between bosses – usually men – and workers – usually women. With its origins in polarized gender relationships and inappropriate sex role expectations, sexual harassment makes it difficult for women to achieve equal working relationships and makes it unlikely than men will recognize the discrimination faced by women. The failure to initiate change and to eradicate sexual harassment reflects the pervasiveness of male power (Ragins and Sundstrom 1989) and men's understandable wish to retain this power by means of protectionist strategies, involving collusion and mutual support. Sexual harassment is a barrier to the full integration of women into the labour market, and its removal demands the degendering, both of work categories and of areas of responsibility and expertise in society as a whole.

Theoretical perspectives link sexual harassment to the broader domain of social-sexual behaviour in the work-place and in society in general. However, they leave us with the practical problem of devising strategies for dealing with sexual harassment and minimizing its costs to the individual and the organization.

Personal and organizational costs of sexual harassment

The severe personal (Loy and Stewart 1984) and organizational costs (USMSPB 1981) associated with sexual harassment are compelling reasons for attempting to eradicate it from the work-place. In addition to obvious costs associated with sexual harassment litigation and the resulting media publicity, there are the hidden but equally real costs arising from emotional stress, which may be manifested in physical symptoms, absenteeism, staff turnover, low productivity, poor morale and reduced job involvement and satisfaction. In their large survey of government employees, the US Merit Systems Protection Board (USMSPB 1981) reported that one-third of the women who had been sexually harassed felt that their emotional or physical condition had deteriorated as a result of their experiences. Gutek (1985) found that the major reactions to experiencing sexual harassment were disgust and anger, and a substantial proportion of women reported that sexual harassment affected how they felt about their jobs and how they related to people at work. The overwhelming response to sexual harassment of women in our recent study was anger, with nearly two-thirds of the incidents provoking this reaction, but the consequences were pervasive affecting women's emotional well-being, behaviour and efficiency (Phillips *et al.* 1989).

A consistent research finding is that very few women report incidents of sexual harassment to their employer or someone in authority (USMSPB 1981; Gutek 1985). This picture is confirmed by the results of our recent study (Phillips *et al.* 1989) in which only 27 per cent of the incidents were formally reported, and in 26 per cent of cases the individual who was harassed did nothing whatsoever. The reasons respondents gave for doing nothing about suffering sexual harassment reflect the widespread difficulties both individuals and organizations experience in dealing with such behaviour. Victims commonly thought that their complaints would not be taken seriously or they were too stunned and embarrassed to do anything. Other reasons for inaction included: harassment being the norm at work; the seniority of the harasser;

individuals wanting to avoid retribution; and feeling that they needed to prove themselves in the company. The finding that in some cases no action was taken because there was no procedure or union representative available, and in others because of the identity of the person to whom they would have to report the incident (e.g. a male manager or head of department with a reputation for sexual harassment himself), highlights the importance of having clear company policies and a sympathetic reporting procedure.

All of these results point to the serious impact of sexual harassment on individual well-being and organizational effectiveness. The stress associated with coping with sexual harassment imposes a high cost which affects both individual and organizational performance. Obviously it is difficult to cost the effects of sexual harassment in the work-place, but there is little doubt that financial penalties are substantial. Based on calculations of the cost of replacing staff, paying medical insurance claims and sick leave, and absorbing costs associated with reduced productivity, the US Merit Systems Protection Board (1981) estimated that sexual harassment cost the Federal Government 189 million dollars over a two-year period. However, evidence suggests that many organizations underestimate the need to take effective action against sexual harassment (Collins and Blodgett 1981; Dolecheck and Dolecheck 1983; Petersen and Massengill 1982). Management might be more willing to take positive steps and introduce sexual harassment policies, procedures and educational programmes if they were made aware of the costs of inaction.

As Backhouse and Cohen point out, 'Sexual harassment is not a personal problem. It is a *personnel* problem' (1978: 174). Although there are individual actions which may minimize the occurrence of sexual harassment and personal coping strategies and actions for dealing with such behaviour, solutions to the problem of sexual harassment demand recognition of the corporate responsibility for ensuring the personal safety and well-being of all employees. Organizations must be made aware of the scale and severity of the problem and its implications both for individuals and their work performance, and the long-term organizational benefits of combating sexual harassment.

Organizational responses to sexual harassment

A variety of definitions of sexual harassment and grievance procedures have been adopted by organizations in the USA and a similar pattern is emerging in this country. However, in making comparisons between the USA and the UK the differing legal context must be borne in mind. In the late 1970s and early 1980s in the USA a series of court rulings decided sexual harassment was a form of sexual discrimination in employment, prohibited by Title VII of the Civil Rights Act 1964. In 1980 the US Equal Employment Opportunity Commission issued guidelines in which sexual harassment was defined as sexual attention which is unwelcome, and which has the effect of unreasonably interfering with an individual's work performance, is a condition of employment, forms the basis for an employment decision, or creates an intimidating, hostile or offensive working environment. In the USA the case law on sexual harassment has continued to develop, raising complex and controversial issues relating to the shape of discrimination law and equal opportunities policies (*Equal Opportunities Review No. 12* 1987a).

In this country and much of Europe the role of litigation has been less prominent. Rubenstein (1988) argues that existing laws within the member states of the European Community (EC) are not suitable for dealing with the problems caused by sexual harassment at work. He recommends specific legislation aimed at protecting workers against the risk of sexual harassment and encouraging employers to establish and maintain working environments free of sexual harassment. In Rubenstein's view sexual harassment should be regarded as discrimination on the grounds of sex contrary to Article 5(1) of the Equal Treatment Directive 1976. Only within the United Kingdom and in Ireland is there judicial recognition that sexual harassment can constitute unlawful sex discrimination. The Sex Discrimination Act 1975 has two clauses under which a claim of sexual harassment can succeed. Section 1(1) (a) states that it is unlawful to treat a person less favourably on grounds of sex, while Section 6(2) (b) of the Act makes detrimental treatment by an employer on grounds of sex unlawful. Furthermore, although under Section 41(1) of the Act the employer is liable for any discriminatory action taken by employees in the course of their employment, employers may escape liability if they can show that 'reasonably practicable steps' have been taken to prevent discrimination (Section 41(3)). This is a potentially powerful argument in encouraging employers to adopt a clear policy against sexual harassment and to institute effective procedures for dealing with complaints.

In addition, many trade unions have initiated campaigns against sexual harassment and the Equal Pay and Opportunity Campaign have issued guidelines for employers and unions dealing with the issue (cf. *Industrial Relations Review and Report (IR-RR) 384* 1987; *Labour Research* 1983; *Labour Research Department Bargaining Report 68* 1987). The Equal Opportunities Commission has also provided legal support and representation in fighting sexual harassment. There are now a range of legal cases in the UK which illustrate ways in which the law can be invoked by victims of sexual harassment (cf. *IDS Brief 282* 1984; *IDS Brief 362* 1987). However, as Rubenstein (1988) points out, even in the UK, where the range of potential remedies available to the individual litigant or to the Equal Opportunities Commission under the Sex Discrimination Act is broader than elsewhere in the EC, experience suggests that the sanctions available for dealing with sexual harassment (other than compensation to the victim) are either flawed or unworkable in practice. Moreover, the evidential principles in such cases are unlikely to encourage victims to take complaints of sexual harassment to law (cf. *Equal Opportunities Review No. 13* 1987b; *Equal Opportunities Review No. 19* 1988). Overall, the weaker legal position and personal perceptions of the relative merits of different remedies for sexual harassment suggest that, in this country, clear policy statements, combined with effective grievance procedures are currently preferred to legal action which is seen as the last resort.

Recommendations

In my view there are a number of key elements in devising an effective strategy for dealing with sexual harassment:

1 A workable definition, which informs employees that certain behaviours, whether intended or not, are recognized by the organization as unacceptable and as damaging to the victim's work and personal well-being.
2 A clear policy and a grievance procedure that is fair to all parties involved. If well-publicized, they signal that an organization is committed to addressing the problem and they can help, not only in resolving individual cases, but also in discouraging potential harassers. Sexual harassment is difficult to challenge when procedures for unbiased mediation are inadequate or non-existent, especially since harassers often receive both overt and covert support from colleagues and workmates.
3 A confidential but effective source of advice, guidance and support for those who experience sexual harassment. The reporting process and source of organizational support in resolving problems of sexual harassment, either through informal means or by lodging a formal complaint, clearly influence the effectiveness of any procedure. Many women prefer to discuss the issues and options with a woman, and are likely to be deterred from making a complaint about a supervisor or manager if the reporting procedure requires the person in question to receive the complaint and initiate the investigation.
4 Information and education. These help men and women at all levels in an organization to see the 'reality' of sexual harassment: men are made aware of the impact of imposed sexual attention and women perceive they have the right to challenge such behaviour.

Future research, policy and action

Understanding sexual harassment demands further analysis of the role of societal, organizational and individual factors in its occurrence. More comparative data are needed concerning the influence on sexual harassment of such factors as: sex role attitudes, beliefs and expectations; the position of women in the work-force, including the potential vulnerability created by the lack of job protection for women in part-time employment; economic conditions; and equal opportunities legislation. We also need to examine systematically how the characteristics of organizations – the organizational climate, the workplace ethos, power differentials and work practices – can act to facilitate or discourage the incidence of sexual harassment. At an individual level more information is needed about men's perceptions of their behaviour and its impact, and what helps to change it. We need to understand how individual interpretations of economic power and social control interact with the perceived need to defend the status of particular work roles. Furthermore, the fact that many women find it difficult to make it clear that sexual harassment is unacceptable indicates the need to understand how women can be empowered to respond to the indignity they feel.

Accurate estimates of the costs of sexual harassment would act as a powerful factor in encouraging the implementation of strategies for dealing with the problem and preventing its occurrence. A number of employers have already recognized that it is not good management practice to maintain a working environment which allows and, in many cases, encourages sexual harassment. However, some organizations may see sexual harassment at work as a problem for the individual, and may regard action as an intrusion into private and personal relationships. Where organizations are reluctant to take action it is imperative that they are made aware of the scale of the problem and its impact, and of their responsibilities toward their work-forces. We also need to examine the response of management to allegations of sexual harassment and to establish the practical effectiveness of policies and procedures for dealing with the problem.

Sexual harassment may be seen as symptomatic of sexual inequality in society in general. Until this inequality is challenged through education, social change and concerted action, the assumption will remain that women are unable to participate fully and equally in the work-place, and the conditions in which sexual harassment flourishes will continue to exist. This long-term aim should not prevent the immediate translation of our awareness of the individual and organizational costs of sexual harassment at work into effective action. Both commitment and resources are needed to ensure that everyone is aware of the damaging effects of sexual harassment at work and to minimize its occurrence. People in their day-to-day working lives have the right to expect that they will be judged on their skills and abilities rather than defined by their gender.

References

Alfred Marks Bureau (1982) *Sex in the Office – An Investigation into the Incidence of Sexual Harassment*, London: Statistical Services Division.

Backhouse, C. and Cohen, L. (1978) *The Secret Oppression: Sexual Harassment of Working Women*, Toronto: Macmillan of Canada.

Bakan, D. (1966) *The Duality of Human Existence*, Chicago, Ill: Rand McNally.

Bem, S. L. (1981) Gender schema theory: a cognitive account of sex typing, *Psychological Review*, 88: 354–64.

Brewer, H. B. and Berk, R. A. (eds) (1982) Beyond nine to five: sexual harassment on the job, *Journal of Social Issues*, 38, 4: whole issue.

CHRC (Canadian Human Rights Commission) (1984) *Unwanted Sexual Attention and Sexual Harassment: Results of a Survey of Canadians*, Ottawa: Research and Special Studies Branch/Ministry of Supplies and Services, March.

Cockburn, C. (1988) The gendering of jobs: workplace relations and the reproduction of sex segregation, in S. Walby (ed.) *Gender Segregation at Work*, Milton Keynes: Open University Press.

Collins, E. G. and Blodgett, T. B. (1981) Sexual harassment: some see it . . . some won't, *Harvard Business Review*, 59, 2: 76–95.

Cooper, C. and Davidson, H. (1982) *High Pressure: Working Lives of Women Managers*, London: Fontana.

Crocker, P. L. (1983) An analysis of university definitions of sexual harassment, *Signs: Journal of Women in Culture and Society*, 8, 4: 696–707.

Deaux, K. and Major, B. (1987) Putting gender into context: an interactive model of gender-related behaviour, *Psychological Review*, 94, 3: 369–89.

Dolecheck, C. C. and Dolecheck, M. M. (1983) Sexual harassment: a problem for small businesses, *American Journal of Small Business*, 7: 45–50.

Equal Opportunities Commission (EOC) (1989) *Women and Men in Britain: A Statistical Profile*, London: HMSO.

Equal Opportunities Review No. 12 (1987a) Sexual harassment law in the United States, March/April: 18–25.

Equal Opportunities Review No. 13 (1987b) Evidence as to sexual attitude admissible in harassment cases, May/June 42–4.

Equal Opportunities Review No. 19 (1988) Evidential principles in sexual harassment cases, May/June: 41–4.

Farley, L. (1978) *Sexual Shakedown: The Sexual Harassment of Women on the Job*, New York: McGraw Hill.

Glaser, R. D. and Thorpe J. S. (1986) Unethical intimacy: a survey of contact and advances between psychology educators and female graduate students, *American Psychologist*, 41, 1: 43–51.

Goffman, E. (1977) The arrangement between the sexes, *Theory and Society*, 4, 301–31.

Gutek, B. A. (1985) *Sex and the Workplace*, San Francisco, Calif: Jossey-Bass.

Gutek, B. A. and Morasch, B. (1982) Sex ratios, sex role spillover and sexual harassment of women at work, *Journal of Social Issues*, 38, 4: 55–74.

Hadjifotiou, N. (1983) *Women and Harassment at Work*, London: Pluto.

Hakim, C. (1979) *Occupational Segregation: A Comparative Study of the Degree and Pattern of the Differentiation between Men and Women's Work in Britain, the United States and Other Countries*, London: Department of Employment, Research Paper No. 9.

IDS Brief 282 (1984) Sexual harassment at work, August: 1–4.

IDS Brief 362 (1987) Sexual harassment, December: 7–10.

Industrial Relations Review and Report (IR-RR) 384 (1987) 20 January, 2–6, Sexual Harassment at Work.

Joeman, L. M., Phillips, C. M. and Stockdale, J. E. (1989) *The Risks in Going to Work: Bibliography*, London: The Suzy Lamplugh Trust.

Kanter, R. M. (1977) *Men and Women of the Corporation*, New York: Basic Books.

Kessler, S. J. and McKenna, W. (1978) *Gender: An Ethnomethodological Approach*, New York: John Wiley.

Labour Research (1983) Sexual harassment, September: 234–5.

Labour Research Department Bargaining Report 68 (1987) Sexual harassment at work, December: 4–11.

Laws, J. L. (1979) *The Second X: Sex Role and Social Role*, New York: Elsevier.

Leeds TUCRIC (Trade Union and Community Resource and Information Centre) (1983) *Sexual Harassment of Women at Work*, Leeds: TUCRIC.

Loy, P. H. and Stewart, L. P. (1984) The extent and effects of the sexual harassment of working women, *Sociological Focus*, 17, 1: 31–43.

MacKinnon, C. (1979) *Sexual Harassment of Working Women: A Case of Sex Discrimination*, New Haven, Conn: Yale University Press.

Meyer, M. C., Berchtold, I. M., Oestreich, J. L. and Collins, F. J. (1981) *Sexual Harassment*, New York/Princeton, NJ: Petrocelli Books.

Nieva, V. F. and Gutek, B. A. (1981) *Women and Work: A Psychological Perspective*, New York: Praeger.

Peterson, D. J. and Massengill, D. (1982) Sexual harassment: a growing problem in the workplace, *Personnel Administrator*, 27: 79–89.

Phillips, C. M., Stockdale, J. E. and Joeman, L. M. (1989) *The Risks in Going to Work: The Nature of People's Work, the Risks they Encounter and the Incidence of Sexual Harassment, Physical Attack and Threatening Behaviour*, London: the Suzy Lamplugh Trust.

Powell, G. N. (1983) Sexual harassment: confronting the problem of definition, *Business Horizons*, 26, 4: 24–8.

—— (1986) Effects of sex role identity and sex on definitions of sexual harassment, *Sex Roles*, 14, 1/2: 9–18.

Pringle, R. (1989) *Secretaries Talk: Sexuality, Power and Work*, London: Verso.

Pryor, J. B. (1985) The lay person's understanding of sexual harassment, *Sex Roles*, 13, 5/6: 273–86.

Ragins, B. R. and Sundstrom, E. (1989) Gender and power in organisations: a longitudinal perspective, *Psychological Bulletin*, 105: 51–88.

Read, S. (1982) *Sexual Harassment at Work*, Feltham: Hamlyn.

Roberts, K., Richardson, D. and Dench, S. (1988) Sex discrimination in youth labour markets and employers' interests, in S. Walby (ed.) *Gender Segregation at Work*, Milton Keynes: Open University Press.

Rubenstein, M. (1988) *The Dignity of Women at Work*, A report on the problem of sexual harassment in the member states of the European Communities: Parts 1–11 (EC469), Brussels/Luxembourg: Commission of the European Communities.

Sedley, A. and Benn, M. (1982) *Sexual Harassment at Work*, London: National Council for Civil Liberties.

Somers, A. (1982) Sexual harassment in academe: legal issues and definitions, *Journal of Social Issues*, 38: 23–32.

Stanko, E. A. (1988) Keeping women in and out of line: sexual harassment and occupational segregation, in S. Walby (ed.) *Gender Segregation at Work*, Milton Keynes: Open University Press.

Stockard, J. and Johnson, M. M. (1979) The social origins of male dominance, *Sex Roles*, 5: 199–218.

Stockdale, J. E. (1986) Sexual harassment in a university setting, Paper presented at the London Conference of the British Psychological Society, December.

Tajfel, H. (ed.) (1978) *Differentiation Between Social Groups: Studies in the Social Psychology of Intergroup Relations*, London: Academic Press.

Tangri, S., Burt, M. R. and Johnson, L. B. (1982) Sexual harassment at work: three explanatory models, *Journal of Social Issues*, 38, 4: 55–74.

TUC (Trades Union Congress) (1983) *Sexual Harassment at Work*, London: TUC.

USMSPB (US Merit Systems Protection Board) (1981) *Sexual Harassment in the Federal Workplace: Is it a Problem?*, Washington, DC: US Government Printing Office.

Williams, J. A. (1984) Gender and intergroup behaviour: toward an integration, *British Journal of Social Psychology*, 23, 4: 311–16.

6 | The female reproductive system and work

Jacqueline Bates Gaston

This chapter reviews current research on women's reproductive processes in the context of work outside the home. As well as menstruation, pregnancy and the menopause, the longer developmental phase of the climacterium has been included, since women from their forties to their mid-sixties are often viewed as menopausal, even though physiologically they may in fact be pre- or post-menopausal.

When we consider women at work, we cannot ignore the fact that they are biologically very different from the male and that the latter is perceived as 'the norm'. Each of the following sections briefly seeks to demonstrate that women's experiences are influenced by more than physiology and changes in hormonal levels. Women's lives are often determined by cultural stereotypes as well as social and environmental structures, and the research shows parallels across the reproductive processes. Stereotypes also condition women's re- actions to their normal developmental phases. Perceptions of women in- fluence how they are valued in the work-place and their careers suffer further because they take time off work to produce and nurture the next generation. Unfortunately, much of the research has focused on the negative rather than the positive aspects of female reproduction.

Menstruation and work

The menstrual cycle is important as it occurs thirteen times per year for half the life-span of most women. Popular mythology claims that women are constant- ly unstable, unreliable, unpredictable, likely to be irritable and moody and generally perform badly around the onset of menstruation. This view is universal throughout the world (Finn and Finn 1981; WHO 1981; Bates Gaston 1987).

Mood and emotionality

Frank (1931) first described the pre-menstrual syndrome (PMS) as a collection of feelings, which coincided regularly with the days preceding menstrual bleeding. Well over 100 possible changes have been attributed to this syndrome, which is reported to affect between 5 and 95 per cent of women (Harrison *et al.* 1985). Despite years of research there is still no agreement over the precise diagnosis. Ussher (1989) states that PMS 'provides scientific legitimacy for the traditional raging hormone theory. As it assumes the status of a known illness, a syndrome, it gives scientific backing to discrimination against women'.

Perceptions of menstruation

Koeske (1980) found that both men and women are likely to attribute negative moods occurring in the pre-menstrual and menstrual phases to underlying biological processes, while negative moods experienced at other times are attributed to environmental factors. In an industrial study, (Bates Gaston 1987) I found that female factory workers and male and female managers all held negative beliefs about mood in relation to the menstrual cycle. In response to an item from the Menstrual Attitude Questionnaire (Brooks-Gunn and Ruble 1980) – 'A woman's moods are not influenced in any major way by the phase of her monthly cycle' – almost 88 per cent of male managers, 94 per cent of female managers and 70 per cent of female employees *disagreed* with the statement (total surveyed 440). Studies have reported no consistent mood fluctuation across the menstrual cycle (Golub and Harrington 1981; Lahmayer *et al.* 1982 and O'Neill *et al.* 1984).

Positive behaviours

Some researchers (Ederlyi 1962; Morris and Udry 1970; May 1976) have reported positive behaviour and mood changes in the pre-menstrual phases of the cycle. Some women report greater creativity and energy around menstruation. Asso and Braier (1982) suggest that there is a strong likelihood that autonomic activation increases during the pre-menstrual phase of the cycle. Although the research findings into mood and menstruation have not all been negative, the stereotype of instability is the one which prevails.

Motor and cognitive performance

Ryan (1975) found that approximately one-third to one-half of women questioned in a survey believed that performance is impaired around menstruation. Various studies reported that while many women expect to show a decline in performance and ability around menses onset, this does not necessarily occur, even amongst women who most expect in (Altenhaus 1978; Munchel 1979; Bates Gaston 1987). In a review of the area, Sommer (1983) stated that 'out of 81 performance tests carried out in 35 independent studies only 14 support a hypothesis of either pre-menstrual or menstrual delibitation'. Others investigated intellectual performance and also found no support for pre-menstrual decrements (Bernstein 1977; Golub 1976; Walsh *et al.* 1981).

Work performance

In a historical analysis of the literature on menstruation and work, Harlow (1986) argued that the long-held assumption that normal menstruation impairs women's performance at work cannot be supported by scientific evidence. Industrial studies are nevertheless surprisingly rare given the importance of women's aspirations for equal treatment in the work-place. Redgrove (1971) studied the output of four laundry workers over twenty-five complete cycles. She found no effect of menstrual phase on job performance and in a subsequent study of nine punch card operators and three typists the same findings were obtained. Smith (1950a; 1950b) demonstrated that no single phase of the menstrual cycle yielded losses in efficiency more frequently than any other phase, with the exception of women performing work of 'high mental' difficulty, although this was balanced out by a higher level of work at menstruation. In a longitudinal, industrial study (Bates Gaston 1987) in which forty-six 'naive' women in a clothing factory were studied for thirty-three weeks, I found no overall menstrual or phase decrement in performance. Some women's performance was statistically significantly superior on menstruating days. There was greater variability across cycles than across phases, which indicated that women's performance was probably more affected by situational or environmental variables than by regular hormonal changes. These findings were similar to those reported by Wilcoxon *et al.* (1976), who examined stressful environmental events, and Rossi and Rossi (1977), who investigated mood state and day of the week, and found that these measures accounted for more of the variance in negative affect than cycle phase.

Absenteeism as a work performance measure has been studied and has usually assumed that women's work and men's work is comparable in terms of pay and satisfaction. Gafafer (1942) estimated women's frequency of absence to be 60 per cent higher than men's, but the proportion attributable to menstruation was responsible for only 0.29 days per person per year and Svennerud (1959) found that dysmenorrhea accounted for 3.7 per cent of absences in factory workers and 2.5 per cent of absences in office workers. However, Jones and Jones (1981) report that a recent gynaecological textbook claims dysmenorrhea to be the most frequent cause of lost work time. So the 'weakness' medical model still persists. In a three-year prospective study of the distribution of illness within the menstrual cycle, Friedman *et al.* (1978) found no discernible relationship of illness or disability across the cycle. They found that reported illnesses, accidents, medical consultations and hospital admissions were randomly distributed throughout the menstrual cycle and that reported menstrual symptoms were infrequent. In an analysis of the data on absenteeism and lost time in the clothing industry (Bates Gaston 1987), I found no statistical differences when overall menstrual and non-menstrual days were compared. I also found that absenteeism and lost time were highest on Mondays and least on Fridays. This agrees with the research of Pocock (1973) and Dansereau *et al.* (1978), who found day-of-week absenteeism effects for male workers. It seems that female workers are not ruled by 'raging hormones', but are merely subject to environmental changes and demands like their male colleagues.

The application of research and theory on social expectations and menstrual cycle behaviour suggests that attitudes and expectations about menstruation may themselves affect women's behaviour and self-evaluations. If a woman believes that menstruation has a negative effect on performance she may become more anxious around menses onset and avoid participation in a variety of activities (Brooks-Gunn *et al.* 1977). Since attitudes influence perceptions of behaviour and assessment of situations and people, it seems important that the area of performance, as well as beliefs, needs exposure in the work context. My survey (Bates Gaston 1987) revealed that 71 per cent of male managers, 62 per cent of female managers and 63 per cent of female factory workers felt that women have to accept that they 'may not perform as well when they are menstruating'. The research evidence is overwhelmingly against 'the incapacitated, unstable and weak' model of menstruating women, but within our society this stereotype remains, often perpetuated by women themselves.

Pregnancy and work

Work and maternal well-being

A woman's career and her childbearing years run in parallel. Various estimates (Norwood and Waldman 1979; Marieskind 1980) suggest that over half of all women are in paid employment. Married women, under 35 years with at least one child at home, are the largest grouping. For many women there is no choice about returning to work after childbirth. Oakley (1984) points out that there has been a large increase in one-parent families with 'four out of five headed by women'; 40 per cent of women work part-time compared with 4 per cent of men, which means they are financially disadvantaged (Chiplin and Sloane, 1982). This affects their autonomy and control in the family unit.

Often a family is taken out of the poverty trap by a mother's earnings, although the debate about maternal employment is still a dilemma for many, including mothers themselves. Strangely, few would question paternal employment in the context of the birth of a child. Ussher (1989) says that mothers find themselves in a double bind. Women who stay at home are likely to be isolated, dependent and liable to suffer from alienation and depression, but if they go out to work, they have to maintain their jobs and take most of the responsibility for child-care and housework. The socially constructed 'ideal mother' remains at home with her child. Despite the fact that women are now working more hours outside the home, husbands and fathers still contribute little time or energy to child care or household maintenance (Goff-Timmer, Eccles and O'Brien 1985). Indeed the wife's working status has very little effect on the husband's time-use patterns either inside or outside the home. There is a tendency for women to move into less favoured sectors of employment like part-time work following childbirth (Daniel 1980; Moss 1980) and women with pre-school children are more likely than others to be doing evening shift-work (Rees and Palmer 1970). This probably reflects a solution to the need to work and the conflict and guilt that many mothers feel in taking on a full-time day job.

Health

It is often assumed that involvement in the two major roles of paid employee and home-maker results in negative health consequences. Otto (1979) and Szalai (1972) found that dual-career women reported insufficient time for rest or recreation. 'Dual-career women may well be an understatement. Most working women do housework, mother-work, wife-work and paid-work. Each of these functions have clearly differentiated behaviour and emotional commitment. If a home-maker goes to work as a temporary break from a repressive and highly confused home situation, and, if the type of job she obtains enhances her level of self-esteem and social contacts then employment could have a positive impact on health and well-being (Baruch *et al.* 1983; Waldron *et al.* 1982).

Benefits of work

There is considerable evidence to suggest that employment is valued by mothers as offering escape from captivity in the home and for involving the mother in social relationships (Lopata 1971; Gavron 1966; Oakley 1979). The positive benefits of employment for mothers and their young children have been highlighted by the research of Brown and Harris (1978). Their study on depression and psychiatric illness found motherhood to be a risk factor, with the risk being higher for working-class women (as opposed to middle-class women) with young children under 6 years. Employment outside the house was identified as a factor protecting against maternal depression, and they suggested that the mediating structure was the effect of employment on a mother's self-esteem. However, it has also been found that positive outcomes depend on supportive relationships and on individual personal and family situations (Parry and Shapiro 1986; Haw 1982).

Looking at the issue from a different perspective, Jimenez and Newton (1982) examined job orientation, adjustment to pregnancy and early motherhood. They found women who adapt well to work also adapt well to child-rearing, and that women who scored high in job commitment had more favourable psychological and emotional experiences in the first pregnancy and postpartum period on some measures, and the degree of job commitment was not related to reported maternal attachment behaviour or attitudes. Women who scored high on job interest tended to wait longer before starting a family, worked longer into pregnancy and planned to return to work earlier.

Pregnancy and occupational hazards

(A more detailed consideration of this field, including methodological issues, can be found in Chapter 7). Chamberlain and Garcia (1983) suggest that, in general, working during pregnancy is not, in itself, a health risk, but that the foetus is highly susceptible to harmful or toxic agents in the work-place especially during the first trimester when a woman is often unaware not only that she is pregnant, but also of the risks that working environments hold. The literature on maternal exposure is far more extensive than that on paternal exposure, and yet an investigation into the chemical and physical exposure of parents found that male workers exposed to anaesthetic gases, chloroprene, hydrocarbons and vinyl chloride were associated with adverse outcomes of the pregnancies of unexposed wives who did not go out to work (Stobrino *et al.* 1978).

There are tremendous problems in identifying environmental and occupational hazards which are injurious to reproduction and inter-uterine development (Abdul-Karim 1984). Exposure to a multitude of potentially harmful agents makes it difficult to single out the causative agent, and, since human experimentation is unethical, and animal research is not always generalizable or dependable, much relies on observation (usually retrospective) of relationships between exposures (with concomitant time delay) and outcome of pregnancy. New chemicals are being introduced daily to keep up with the rapid changes in technology in highly competitive industries but the rate at which these chemicals are produced make efficient and exhaustive testing unattractive to the producers.

The research evidence is often conflicting and contradictory. Hemminki *et al.* (1980a) and Hemminki *et al.* (1980b) examined rates of spontaneous abortion in a variety of maternal occupations. They found that women who worked with industrial chemicals like some plastics and metals in pharmaceutical and electronics industries all had increased risk of miscarriage. However, others studied workers in a pharmaceutical industry and found no elevation in miscarriage rates in pregnant laboratory workers exposed to chemicals (Kolmodin-Hedman *et al.* 1981). The conflicting evidence may well depend on specific chemicals investigated.

Research has found that medical laboratories contributed to spontaneous abortions and possibly birth defects with exposure to solvents being cited as the probable hazard (Strandberg *et al.* 1978; Meirik *et al.* 1979). The medical professions generally have been investigated in relation to exposure to anaesthetic gases, but again the evidence is contradictory. A survey of 5,700 pregnancies of women doctors reported that conceptions which occurred when the mother was in an anaesthetic appointment resulted in smaller babies, higher still-birth rates and more congenital malformations of the cardiovascular system than the pregnancies of other female doctors in the survey. However, they found no significant abortion rate between the two groups (Pharoah *et al.* 1977).

Supporting evidence was supplied by Spence *et al.* (1977) and Tomlin (1979), who also reported that the babies of male anaesthetists had an increased incidence of congenital malformations. An association between exposure to anaesthetic gases and higher incidence of pre-term labour and spontaneous abortion rates as well as low birth-weight infants has been reported (Vessey and Nunn 1980). Contrary evidence is supplied by other studies in the area. One study by Knill-Jones *et al.* (1981) gathered exposure incidents prior to pregnancy outcome. Ericson and Kallen (1979) used recorded incidents of exposure, rather than relying on retrospective self-reports of personnel in the study. These latter two studies did not confirm a relationship between exposure to anaesthetic gas and adverse pregnancy outcome (also Schwartz 1985). Several features make interpretation of the research findings in this area very difficult because specific gases involved in the studies are not usually indicated and sometimes staff would be exposed to more than one gas.

Infections

Nursing staff are exposed to a wide variety of infections which can have negative implications for pregnancy. Diseases such as rubella, hepatitis B virus, herpes simplex, cytomegalo-virus, influenza, toxoplasma gandii, HIV and syphilis have all been associated with neonatal and maternal illnesses, spontaneous abortions and birth defects (Coleman and Dickinson 1984). A study of pregnant nurses found that those who cared for prematurely born babies and infants with congenital defects gave birth themselves to infants with an elevated rate of birth defects. Nurses who reported overt infective illness during pregnancy had twice as many congenital defects in their babies than those who reported no illness (Haldane *et al.* 1969). Protection should be provided for paramedical staff who are in contact with viral infections at work.

Radiation

Other workers at risk in the health care sector are those exposed to ionizing radiation. The amount of radiation received depends on the rate given off, the exposure time, the distance from the source and the type of shielding used (Hunt 1978). Nurses, X-ray technicians, dental assistants and ancillary workers can be at risk from the scattering X-rays from portable machines, from cobalt and radium implants in patients and when organizing patients for treatment. There is growing concern for the long-term effects of low doses of radiation and that ionizing radiation can lead to higher incidences of skin cancer, sterility, genetic damage and leukaemia. Naturally women of childbearing age working near radiation have to be particularly vigilant and informed, because the greatest dangers are to the embryo and foetus.

Industry

Outside the health care sector other industries have been investigated for exposure risk to the pregnant woman. Rachootin and Olsen (1983) in a Danish study reported that working women exposed to high levels of noise, textile dyes, lead, mercury and cadmium had increased infertility rates. A review of the area confirmed the association of lead exposure to sterility in women, embryotoxicity, growth retardation in the foetus, increased perinatal deaths and developmental disabilities (Rom 1976). Lead exposure is common in manufacturing industries, in paint pigments, in craft and artistic work and in the glass and ceramics industries. Peters *et al.* (1984) also found consistently high mortality rates due to anencephaly, spina bifida and congenital heart disease in glass and pottery workers, especially amongst those whose jobs involved contact with dyes and glazes.

Other work associated with risk to pregnant or potentially pregnant women covers a wide range of occupations. Female beauticians may be at risk because aerosol gases and hair dyes have been connected with birth defects (Stovall *et al.* 1983; Peters *et al.* 1984). Raw cotton dust in the clothing and textile industries have been associated with foetal damage (Stellman 1978) and the use of vinyl chloride and benzene in manufacturing employment with reproductive failure. An increase in perinatal mortality rate in leather industries where workers were exposed to silicone sprays, ethyl acetate and latex-based adhesives has been reported (Clarke and Mason 1985; McDonald and McDonald 1986). The exposure risks in industry are wide ranging and dangers are not always obvious.

Work stress

Questions often asked are 'When should I stop working during pregnancy?' and 'Am I harming the baby if I work until full term?' Some researchers concluded that there was no evidence to suggest differences in the long-term development of children of mothers who worked during pregnancy compared with those not employed outside the home, or, those who worked for spells during their pregnancy (Peters *et al.* 1984). Mamelle and Laumon (1984) stated that 'the fact a woman works, in itself, cannot be said to be a risk of prematurity, given that, globally speaking, housewives show a higher rate of premature birth – 7.2% (houseworkers) as against 5.8% for women who also work outside the home'. However, they hypothesized that strenuous work could have a harmful effect on pregnancy. Their study revealed that the work conditions most likely to lead to premature births were those which involved boring, monotonous work, work in the standing position for more than three hours per day and work requiring physical effort. They also found that as the number of working hours per week increased the rate of premature births also rose. They suggested that where conditions are arduous, then work should be redesigned or lightened to avoid harmful effects on pregnancy. A follow-up study by Mamelle *et al.* (1989) found that women who were encouraged to take leave from strenuous work during pregnancy had a lower pre-term birth-rate than those who continued working. However, other research found no differences in rates of prematurity, Apgar score, birth-weight, perinatal death-rate or malformations (Marbury *et al.* 1984). Those women who worked for all nine months had least problems overall, although interpretation of the data may be confounded by women with poor health dropping out of work early in pregnancy.

Research on physical stress suggests that work should be designed to alleviate occupational fatigue for all workers regardless of gender. Pregnancy often highlights poor work practices and most jobs would benefit from ergonomic scrutiny. The pregnant female form is usually seen as 'awkward' in ergonomic terms. Few adjustments are made in the work-place to accommodate the changing shape and needs of the mother to be. Pregnant women need more break-time snacks to avoid sickness, extra rest, bathroom facilities and nutritional food selections in cafeterias and vending machines (Chamberlain and Garcia 1983; Tabor 1983).

There has been very little postnatal research regarding recuperation time needed before returning to work. Chavkin (1984) criticizes the medical model which recognizes the need for physical recuperation after birth, but not the need for nurturing the new baby, or for recovery from lack of sleep experienced by most mothers. Few employers have crèches or nurseries for mothers to breastfeed their babies and few even consider providing facilities for breast-feeding mothers to express their milk and store it while at work. Medical science acknowledges 'breast is best' but society pays lip-service to the idea.

Women have undergone surgical sterilization to keep their jobs in high-risk chemical plants (Scott 1984). Some American companies ban women from certain work locations unless they are sterile because of the threat of employee legal action. Female employees have been threatened with termination of employment or reassigned to different departments. Concern for the foetus and its right to grow in a toxic-free environment are of course essential, but exclusionary policies like these can foster discrimination against women in well-paid jobs. Few employers have seen the need to ban women as nurses or teachers even though such professions present signficant risks to the potential foetus. Scott makes the point that if all non-sterile women were banned from low-wage occupations, not enough men could be found to replace them. If we accept the exclusionary approach we help to establish the principle that a company can deal with health and safety problems by removing vulnerable workers rather than tackling the fundamental issue of safety in the work-place for everyone.

Chavkin (1984) makes the point that as long as women bear the major responsibilities for domestic work and child-rearing then employers will weigh the costs of providing related services against the benefits of female employment. But if men and women shared these tasks equally, the costs of providing services and benefits such as paternity leave would become part of the necessary expense of hiring *all* workers.

Children are a nation's resource and therefore support during pregnancy and for the new-born child should be a matter for public as well as private concern.

The menopause, climacteric and work

The menopause is the final stage in a woman's reproductive cycle. It marks the end of menstruation and reproductive capabilities when oestrogen levels decline and ovulation ceases. This usually occurs around 51 years of age in industrialized societies (McKinlay *et al.* 1972) and has not changed appreciably for over a century, which contrasts with age at menarche, which has steadily decreased (Asso 1983). The climacteric is the period, usually between 40 and 65 years, during which a variety of mid-life changes – both physical and social – are taking place, including the menopause. Kitzinger (1983) states that hormone levels fall from the mid-twenties onwards. Changes around the menopausal time are gradual, like ageing itself, and happen in the context of other life events, for instance, death of parents or spouse, maternal role redefinition and career and life reassessments.

Is there a menopausal syndrome?

The menopause or climacteric tends to be blamed for negative changes which take place in women's lives. The causes are usually placed in a medical/ hormonal framework which categorizes reported symptoms within a disease/ deficiency context. McCrea (1983) stated that since the availability of synthetic hormones in the 1960s, the recommended 'treatments' usually include hormone replacement therapy (HRT) for falling oestrogen levels as though the decline is abnormal. As with menstruation the term 'syndrome' is commonly associated with the menopause indicating a collection of symptoms needing treatment. There is a lack of agreement as to the epidemiological status of menopausal complaints which result in inconsistencies in diagnosis and to debate on whether reported symptoms are due to the menopause or to ongoing developmental and social factors (Hunter *et al.* 1986). Others have argued that there is no support for a specific menopausal syndrome because reported symptoms can be experienced at any time during the life-cycle (Neugarten and Kraines 1965; Brown and Brown 1976). Various studies have found that only small percentages of women report severe menopausal symptoms (MacMahon and Worcester 1966; Prill 1977). However, continual reference to a menopausal syndrome reflects the assumption that this normal phase of life is an illness which causes women to be mentally and physically incapacitated. Perlmutter and Bart (1982) demonstrated that women themselves attribute negative moods to the menopause, whereas positive moods are attributed to personality or environmental factors reflecting the findings by Koeske and Koeske (1975) on menstrual mood attributions.

Cross-cultural studies

Kaufert (1982) reviewed cross-cultural reporting of menopausal symptoms and found that a particular society's perception or stereotype of menopause influences how women react. If a society's stereotype of the menopausal woman is negative then women's self-esteem would be under threat – the opposite being true if the stereotype is positive. She also suggests that women whose self-esteem is already low would suffer most psychological distress at this stage. Severne (1982) demonstrated that symptom reporting varied with social class, and suggested that middle-class women are more likely to have more positive self-images and therefore be less susceptible to negative stereotypes.

A study of Rajput women by Flint (1975) found that women in this society experienced positive social changes at menopause – they were allowed out of Purdah and could associate with men as equals for the first time in their lives and consequently they did not report negative symptoms. Other anthropologists have made similar observations (Stenning 1958; La Fontaine 1960; Middleton 1966; Gamst 1969) and have found that societal views of women's status at the menopause influences the outcome of reported symptomatology for each culture. The hormonal and physiological changes are universal, but the behavioural and cognitive outcomes are varied. Where do these stereotypes and perceptions leave women in the work context in our culture?

Work studies

In western culture women are not rewarded for attaining menopause. Ageing is viewed negatively, middle age can be a time of crises for both men and women and the latter's status often declines. Kahana *et al.* (1981) found that men held more negative stereotypes of the menopause than women, and in 1970 Achte reported that 'the assumption has been put forward that women's ability to work reduces to a quarter of the normal by the menopause'. This suggestion was refuted by my research (Bates Gaston 1987), which found that post-menopausal women's performance was superior to younger women's; I attributed this to work attitudes and values as well as to experience. Unfortunately this is an under-researched area to date.

There is evidence to suggest that, in most cultures, women who were in paid employment reported lower rates of menopausal symptomatology, particularly after their children had left home (Bart 1971). Cooke (1984) found the relationships between reported symptoms and stressful life events were mediated by employment outside the home, making women less vulnerable to life stresses which coincided with the menopause. He stated that paid work might be therapeutic for women during this time. A study by Prill (1977) supported the view that work was beneficial to menopausal women. This research on agricultural and professional workers revealed that both groups reported fewer symptoms of menopause and illness generally than full-time houseworkers.

Severne (1982) also found that having a job outside the home constitutes a favourable influence on reported menopausal symptoms. However, this influence was socially differentiated. For the upper socio-economic group the effect of working outside the home was almost always favourable, but this was not the case for the lower socio-economic group for whom having a job brought additional stress and tension during the peri-menopause. In the pre- and post-menopause, however, having a job was a positive stabilizing factor in both groups. Housewives generally were disadvantaged, with those in the lower socio-economic group reporting greater frequencies of somatic and psychological distress. (See also Dege and Gretzinger 1982; Hunter *et al.* 1986).

Another investigation into health, employment status and menopausal/climacteric women found employed women having fewer health problems and reporting fewer illness behaviours, while the unemployed group reported the most health problems (Jennings *et al.* 1984). Home-makers reported intermediary levels of health compared to the employed and unemployed people in this study. The cause and effect relationship may not be clear as less healthy women may withdraw from employment or choose to stay at home.

However, not all studies have viewed work as the panacea for menopausal or climacteric women. A cross-cultural study by Maoz *et al.* (1978) in Israel, found that the effect of work on the menopause differs across ethnic lines and the authors felt that, although judicial assessment of work efficacy would help some women to cope during this time of change, it may not be beneficial for all. This research found Jews of European, Arab and North African origin suffered less during the peri-menopausal and post-menopausal phases if they were employed. However, the results also indicated that work outside the home for Persian Jews was generally not beneficial. McKinlay and Jeffreys (1974) failed to find a relationship between reported symptoms and employment status, but different methodological approaches may explain the disparities across the research.

Ussher (1989) suggests that instead of examining our internal chemistry we should look to the meaning of menopause in society and the socio-cultural changes which are taking place for women during these years and anthropological studies lend support to this approach. Research on work to date has concentrated mainly on the relationship between employment and the reporting of menopausal symptoms. Managerial perceptions of climacteric/menopausal women's performance in the work-place could be a fruitful area for future research and might help to explain why older women returning to work are disadvantaged in terms of their career development.

Conclusions and recommendations

In reviewing these areas, it is hard not to be pessimistic about equality for women at work. The almost universal acceptance of 'biological determinism', where women's reproductive processes are viewed as abnormal or pathological and needing treatment to maintain stability, contributes towards discrimination against women in the work-place. Such stereotypes are rife in our society. Women need to be aware of the relevant research in order to be able to counter the erroneous assumptions which abound in the work-place.

In twenty years of research in the area I have found that women themselves find it difficult to accept that they are not ruled by their hormones. Women are assessed, mostly negatively, throughout their life-span in hormonal terms, whereas men's physiological changes are considered irrelevant. Women have to be careful not to join the bandwagon in assuming that many of their problems must be hormonally controlled. Instead they should look to society to correct its misperceptions and the resulting inequalities.

Individual

Be informed. Don't be ruled by the myths about 'raging hormones'. Act against biological discrimination in the home, school, social situations, the media and in the work-place. Initiate training programmes for men and women at all levels. Encourage women to view their bodies as the biological miracles they are, not as focal points for illogical taboos.

Organizational

Promote awareness of biological discrimination. Counteract casual remarks which bolster up such discrimination. Support moves towards stronger legislation for equal employment practices. Monitor current progress in recruitment, selection and promotion for women of all ages in your work-place. Campaign for proper facilities for pregnant and nursing women at work and in other public places. Campaign for both paternity and maternity leave. Ensure that the working environment is not harmful to the reproductive processes of either gender.

References

Menstruation and work

Altenhaus, A. L. (1978) The effect of expectancy for change on performance during the menstrual cycle, *Dissertation Abstracts International* 39, 2-B: 968.

Asso, D. and Braier, J. (1982) Changes with the menstrual cycle in psychophysiological and self-report measures of activation, *Biological Psychology* 15: 95–107.

Bates Gaston, J. I. (1987) Menstruation performance and attitudes: an industrial study, unpublished PhD thesis, Queen's University, Belfast.

Bernstein, B. (1977) Effects of menstruation on academic performance among college women, *Archives of Sexual Behaviour*, 6, 4: 289–96.

Brooks-Gunn, J. and Ruble, D. N. (1980) The menstrual attitude questionnaire, *Psychosomatic Medicine*, 42, 5: 503–12.

Brooks-Gunn, J., Ruble, D. and Clarke, A. (1977) College women's attitudes and expectations concerning menstrual related changes, *Psychosomatic Medicine*, 39: 288–98.

Dansereau, F. Alutto, J. and Mackam, S. (1978) An initial investigation into the suitability of absenteeism rates as measures of performance, in D. Bryant and R. Niehaus (eds) *Manpower Planning and Organization Design*, New York: Plenum.

Ederlyi, G. (1962) Gynaecological study of female athletes, *Journal of Sports and Medical Fitness*, 2: 174–9.

Finn, R. and Finn, R. (1981) *Tampax Report 110E*, 59th Street, New York 10022, USA.

Frank, R. T. (1931) The normal causes of premenstrual tension, *Archives of Neurology and Psychiatry*, 26: 1,053–7.

Friedman, E., Katcher, A. H. and Brighton, V. J. (1978) A prospective study of the distribution of illness within the menstrual cycle, *Motivation and Emotion*, 2, 4: 355–68.

Gafafer, W. M. (1942) Disabling morbidity among male and female industrial workers during 1941, and among males during the first quarter of 1942, *Public Health Report*, US Public Health Service, 57, 2: 1,344–7.

Golub, S. (1976) The effect of premenstrual anxiety and depression on cognitive function, *Journal of Personality and Social Psychology*, 34: 99–104.

——and Harrington, D. (1981) Premenstrual and menstrual mood changes in adolescent women, *Journal of Personality and Social Psychology*, 41, 5: 961–5.

Harlow, S. (1986) Function and dysfunction: a historical critique of the literature on menstruation and work, *Health Care Women International* 7, 1–2: 39–50.

Harrison, W., Sharpe, L. and Endicott, J. (1985) Treatment of premenstrual symptoms, *General Hospital Psychiatry*, 17, 1: 54–65.

Jones, H. W. and Jones, G. S. (1981) *Novak's Textbook of Gynaecology*, 10th edn, Baltimore, Williams & Wilkins.

Koeske, R. D. (1980) Theoretical perspectives on menstrual cycle research: the relevance of attributional approaches for the perception and explanation of premenstrual emotionality, in A. J. Dan, E. Graham and C. Beecher (eds) *The Menstrual Cycle* 1, New York: Springer.

Lahmayer, H., Miller, M. and DeLeon-Jones, F. (1982) Anxiety and mood fluctuation during the normal menstrual cycle, *Psychosomatic Medicine*, 44, 2: 119–25.

May, R. (1976) Mood shifts and the menstrual cycle, *Journal of Psychosomatic Research* 20: 125–30.

Morris, N. and Udry, J. (1970) Variations in pedometer activity during the menstrual cycle, *Obstetrics and Gynaecology* 35: 199–201.

Munchel, M. E. (1979) The effects of symptom expectations and response styles on cognitive and perceptual motor performance during the menstrual cycle, *Dissertation Abstracts International*, 39, 7-B: 3,532.

O'Neill, M., Lancee, W. and Freeman, T. (1984) Fluctuations in psychological distress during the menstrual cycle, *Canadian Journal of Psychiatry*, 29, 5; 373–8.

Pocock, S. J. (1973) Daily variations in sickness absence, *Applied Statistics*, 22: 127–37.

Redgrove, J. A. (1971) Menstrual cycles, in W. O. Colquhoun (ed.) *Biological Rhythms and Human Performance*, New York: Academic Press.

Rossi, A. and Rossi, P. (1977) Body time and social time: mood patterns by menstrual cycle phase and day of the week, *Social Science Research* 6: 273–308.

Ryan, A. J. (1975) Gynaecological consideration, *Journal of Health, Physical Education and Recreation*, 46 (January): 40–4.

Smith, A. (1950a) Menstruation and industrial efficiency absenteeism and activity level, *Journal of Applied Psychology*, 34, 1: 1–5.

——(1950b) Menstruation and industrial efficiency: quality and quantity of production, *Journal of Applied Psychology*, 34, 1: 148–52.

Sommer, B. (1973) The effect of menstruation on cognitive and perceptual motor behaviour: a review, *Psychosomatic Medicine*, 35: 515–34.

——(1983) How does menstruation affect cognitive competence and psychophysiological response? *Women Health*, 8, 2–3: 53–90.

Svennerud, S. (1959) Dysmenorrhea and absenteeism: some gynaecological and medico-social aspects, *Acta Obstetrica Gynaecologica Scandinavica*, 38 (supple. 2): 116.

Ussher, J. (1989) *The Psychology of the Female Body*, London: Routledge.

Walsh, R. N., Budtz-Olsen, I., Leader, C. and Cummins, R. A. (1981) The menstrual cycle, personality and academic performance, *Archives of General Psychiatry*, 38: 219–21.

Wilcoxin, L., Schrader, S. and Sherif, C. W. (1976) Daily self-reports on activities, life events, moods and sematic changes during the menstrual cycle, *Psychosomatic Medicine*, 38, 6: 399–417.

WHO (World Health Organisation) (1981) Studies in family planning: a cross cultural study of menstruation. Implications for contraceptive development and use, *WHO Task Force on Psychosocial Research*, 12, 1: 3–16.

Pregnancy and work

Abdul-Karim, R. W. (1984) Women workers at higher risk of reproductive hazards, in G. Chamberlain (ed.) *Pregnant Women at Work*, London: Royal Society of Medicine and Macmillan.

Baruch, G., Barnett, R. and Rivers, C. (1983) *Lifeprints: New Patterns of Love and Work for Today's Women*, New York: McGraw-Hill.

Brown, G. W. and Harris, T. (1978) *Social Origins of Depression*, London: Tavistock.

Chamberlain, G. and Garcia, J. (1983) Pregnant women at work, *Lancet*, i: 228–30.

Chavkin, W. (1984) Walking a tightrope: pregnancy, parenting and work, in W. Chavkin (ed.) *Double Exposure: Women's Health Hazards on the Job and at Home*, New York: Monthly Review Press.

Chiplin, B. and Sloane, P. J. (1982) *Tackling Discrimination in the Workforce*, Cambridge University Press.

Clarke, M. and Mason, E. S. (1985) Leatherwork: a possible hazard to reproduction, *British Medical Journal*, 290: 1,235.

Coleman, L. and Dickinson, C. (1984) The risks of healing: the hazards of the nursing profession, in W. Chavkin (ed.) *Double Exposure Women's Health Hazards on the Job and at Home*, New York: Monthly Review Press.

Daniel, W. W. (1980) *Maternity Rights: The Experience of Women*, London: Policy Studies Institute.

Ericson, A. and Kallen, B. (1979) Survey of infants born in 1973 to 1975 to Swedish women working in operating rooms during their pregnancies, *Anaesthesia and Analgesia*, 58: 302–5.

Gavron, H. (1966) *The Captive Wife*, Harmondsworth: Penguin.

Goff-Timmer, S., Eccles, J. and O'Brien, K. (1985) How children use time, in T. Juster *et al.* (eds) *Time, Goods, and Well-being*, Ann Arbor, Mich.: ISR Press.

Haldane, E. V., Van Rooyen, C. E., Embil, J. A., Tupper, W. C., Gordon, P. C. and Wanklin, J. M. (1969) A search for transmissible birth defects of virologic origin in members of the nursing profession, *American Journal of Obstetrics and Gynecology*, 105, 7: 1,032–40.

Haw, M. A. (1982) Women, work and stress: a review and agenda for the future, *Journal of Health and Social Behaviour*, 23: 132–44.

Hemminki, K., Fransilla, E. and Vainio, H. (1980a) Spontaneous abortions among female chemical workers, *International Archives of Occupational and Environmental Health*, 45: 123–6.

Hemminki, K., Niemi, M. L., Koskinen, K. and Vainio, H. (1980b) Spontaneous abortions among women employed in the metal industry in Finland, *International Archives of Occupational and Environmental Health*, 45: 53–60.

Hunt, V. (1978) Occupational radiation exposure of women workers, *Preventive Medicine*, 7: 294–310.

Jimenez, M. H. and Newton, N. (1982) Job orientation and adjustment to pregnancy and early motherhood, *Birth*, 9: 3.

Knill-Jones, R. P., Spence, A. A. and Lawrie, C. (1981) *Occupation of female doctors and outcome of pregnancy*, Abstract of papers from the ninth meeting of the International Epidemiological Association, Edinburgh, August.

Koeske, R. D. (1982) Toward a biosocial paradigm for menopause research, in A. M. Voda, M. Dinnerstein and S. O'Donnell (eds) *Changing Perspectives on Menopause*, Austin, Tex: University of Texas Press.

Kolmodin-Hedman, B., Hedstrom, L. and Gronquist, B. (1981) Fertility outcome in some Swedish groups occupationally exposed to chemicals, Paper presented at the International Course in Occupational Hazards and Reproduction, Helsinki, Finland, August.

Lopata, H. (1971) *Occupation Housewife*, New York: Oxford University Press.

McDonald, A. D. and McDonald, J. C. (1986) Outcome of pregnancy in leatherworkers, *British Medical Journal*, 292: 979.

Mamelle, N., Bertucat, and Munoz, F. (1989) Pregnant women at work: rest periods to prevent preterm birth?, *Paediatric and Perinatal Epidemiology*, 3: 19–28.

Mamelle, N. and Laumon, B. (1984) Occupational fatigue and preterm birth, in G. Chamberlain (ed.) *Pregnant Women at Work*, London: Royal Society of Medicine and Macmillan.

Marbury, M. C., Linn, S., Monson, R., Wegman, D., Schoenbaum, S. C., Stubblefield, P. G. and Ryan, K. J. (1984) Work and pregnancy, *Journal of Occupational Medicine* 26: 415–21.

Marieskind, H. I. (1980) *Women in the Health System: Patients, Providers and Programs* (esp. pp. 157–88), St Louis, CV: Mosby.

Meirik, O., Kallen, B., Gauffin, U. and Ericson, A. (1979) Major malformations in infants born of women who worked in laboratories while pregnant, *Lancet*, ii: 91.

Moss, P. (1980) Parents at work, in P. Moss and N. Fonda (eds) *Work and the Family*, London: Temple Smith.

Norwood, J. and Waldman, F. (1984) The effect of the mothers work on the infant, in G. Chamberlain (ed.) *Pregnant Women at Work*, London: Royal Society of Medicine and Macmillan.

Oakley, A. (1979) *Becoming a Mother*, Oxford: Martin Robertson.

Otto, R. (1979) Negative and positive life experiences among men and women in selected occupations, symptoms awareness and visits to the doctor, *Social Science and Medicine*, 13A: 151–64.

Parry, G. and Shapiro, D. A. (1980) Social support and life events in working-class women: stress buffering or independent effects? *Archives of General Psychiatry* 43: 315–23.

Peters, T. J., Adelstein, P., Golding, J. and Butler, N. (1984) The effects of work in pregnancy: short and long term associations, in G. Chamberlain (ed.) *Pregnant Women at Work*, London: Royal Society of Medicine and Macmillan.

Pharoah, P. O. D., Alberman, E., Doyle, P., and Chamberlain, G. (1977) Outcome of pregnancy among women in anaesthetic practice, Lancet, i: 34–6.

Rachootin, P. and Olsen, J. (1983) The risk of infertility and delayed conception associated with exposure in the Danish workplace, *Journal of Occupational Medicine*, 5: 392–402.

Rees, A. N. and Palmer, F. H. (1970) Factors related to change in mental test performance, *Developmental Psychology Monograph*, 3, 2, 2: 1–6.

Rom, W. N. (1976) Effects of lead on the female and reproduction: a review, *Mount Sinai Journal of Medicine, New York*, 43: 542.

Schwartz, R. W. (1985) Pregnancy in physicians: characteristics and complications, *Obstetrics and Gynecology*, 66: 672.

Scott, J. A. (1984) Keeping women in their place: exclusionary policies and reproduction, in W. Chavkin (ed.) *Double Exposure: Women's Health Hazards on the Job and at Home*, New York: Monthly Review Press.

Spence, A. A., Cohen, E. N., Brown, B. W., Knill-Jones, R. P. and Himmelberger, D. V. (1977) Occupational hazards for operating based physicians, *Journal of American Medical Association*, 238: 955–9.

Stellman, J. M. (1978) Forum: women's occupational health: medical legal and social implications, *Preventive Medicine*, 7: 281–93.

Stobrino, B. B., Kline, J. and Stein, Z. (1978) Chemical and physical exposures of parents: effects on human reproduction and offspring, *Early Human Development*, 1: 371–99.

Stovall, G. K., Levin, L. and Oler, J. (1983) Occupational dermatitis among hairdressers: a multifactor analysis, *Journal of Occupational Medicine*, 25: 871–7.

Strandberg, M., Sandback, K., Axelson, O. and Sundell, L. (1978) Spontaneous abortions among women in a hospital laboratory, *Lancet*, 18 February: 384–5.

Szalai, A. (1972) *The Use of Time*, The Hague: Mouton.

Tabor, M. (1983) Pregnancy and heavy work, *Occupational Health and Safety* 52: 19–23.

Tomlin, P. J. (1979) Health problems of anaesthetists and their families in the West Midlands, *British Medical Journal*, i: 779–83.

Ussher, J. (1989) *The Psychology of the Female Body*, London: Routledge.

Vessey, M. P. and Nunn, J. F. (1980) Occupational hazards of anaesthesia, *British Medical Journal*, 281: 696.

Waldron, I., Herold, J., Dunn, D. and Straum, R. (1982) Reciprocal effects of health and labour force participation among women: evidence from two longitudinal studies, *Journal of Occupational Medicine*, 24: 126–31.

The menopause, climacteric and work

Asso, D. (1983) *The Real Menstrual Cycle*, Chichester: John Wiley.

Bart, P. (1971) Depression in middle-aged women, in V. Gornick and B. Moran (eds) *Women in Sexist Society*, New York: Basic Books.

Bates Gaston, J. I. (1987) Menstruation performance and attitudes: an industrial study, unpublished PhD thesis, Queen's University, Belfast.

Brown, J. and Brown, M. (1976) Psychiatric disorders associated with the menopause, in R. Beard (ed.) *The Menopause*, Lancaster: MTP Press.

Cooke, D. J. (1984) Psychosocial aspects of the climacteric, in A. Broome and L. Wallace (eds) *Psychology and Gynaecological Problems*, London: Tavistock.

Dege, K. and Gretzinger, J. (1982) Attitudes of families toward menopause, in A. Voda, M. Dinnerstein, and S. O'Donnell (eds) *Changing Perspectives on Menopause*, Austin, Tex: University of Texas Press.

Flint, M. (1975) The menopause: reward or punishment?, *Psychosomatics*, autumn, 16: 161–3.

Gamst, F. (1969) *The Qmant, a Pagan Hebraic Peasantry of Ethiopia*, New York: Holt, Rinehart & Winston.

Hunter, M., Battersby, R. and Whitehead, M. (1986) Relationships between psychological symptoms, somatic complaints and menopausal status, *Maturitas*, 8: 217–28.

Jennings, S., Mazaik, C. and McKinlay, S. (1984) Women and work: an investigation of the association between health and employment status in middle-aged women, *Social Science Medicine*, 19, 4: 423–31.

Kahana, E., Kiyak, A. and Liang, J. (1981) Menopause in the context of other life events, in A. Dan, E. Graham and C. Beecher (eds) *The Menstrual Cycle, Vol. 1: A Synthesis of Interdisciplinary Research*, New York: Springer.

Kaufert, P. A. (1982) Anthropology and the menopause: the development of a theoretical framework, *Maturitas*, 4, 181–93.

Kitzinger, S. (1983) *Women's Experience of Sex*, London: Dorling Kindersley.

Koeske, R. K. and Koeske, G. F. (1975) An attributional approach to moods and the menstrual cycle, *Journal of Personality and Social Psychology*, 31: 473–8.

La Fontaine, J. (1960) Homicide and suicide among the Gisu, in P. Bohannan (ed.) *African Homicide and Suicide*, Princeton, NJ: Princeton University Press.

McCrea, F. B. (1983) The politics of Menopause: the discovery of a deficiency disease, *Social Problems*, 31, 1, October: 111–23.

McKinlay, S. M. and Jefferys, M. (1974) The menopausal syndrome, *British Journal of Preventive and Social Medicine*, 28: 108–15.

McKinlay, S., Jefferys, M. and Thompson, B. (1972) An investigation of the age at menopause, *Journal of Biosocial Science*, 4: 161.

MacMahon, B. and Worcester, J. (1966) *Age at Menopause*, 1960–62 US Vital and Health Statistics, series 11, no 19.

Maoz, B., Antonovsky, A., Apter, A., Datan, N., Hochberg, J. and Salomon, Y. (1978) The effect of outside work on the menopausal woman, *Maturitas*, 1: 43–53.

Middleton, J. (1966) *The Lugbara of Uganda*, New York: Holt, Rinehart & Winston.

Neugarten, B. and Kraines, R. (1965) Menopausal symptoms in women of various ages, *Psychosomatic Medicine* 27: 266.

Perlmutter, E. and Bart, P. (1982) Changing views of 'The Change': a critical review and suggestions for an attributional approach, in A. M. Voda, M. Dinnerstein and S. R. O'Donnell (eds) *Changing Perspectives on Menopause*, Austin, Tex: University of Texas Press.

Prill, H. J. (1977) A study of the socio-medical relationships at the climacteric in 2,232 women, *Current Medical Research and Opinion*, 4, Suppl. 3.

Severne, L. (1982) Psychosocial aspects of the menopause, in A. M. Voda, M. Dinnerstein and S. R. O'Donnell (eds) *Changing Perspectives on Menopause*, Austin, Tex: University of Texas Press.

Stenning, D. J. (1958) Household viability among the pastoral Fulani, in J. Goody (ed.) *The Development Cycle in Domestic Groups*, Cambridge University Press.

Ussher, J. M. (1989) *The Psychology of the Female Body*, London: Routledge.

7 | Reproductive hazards at work

Rosalind S. Bramwell and Marilyn J. Davidson

If possible sterility is the main problem, couldn't workers who were old enough that they no longer wanted to have children accept such positions voluntarily? Or could workers be advised of the situation, and some might volunteer for such posts as an alternative to planned surgery for a vasectomy or total ligation, or as a means of getting around religious bans on birth control when they want no more children.

(*Globe and Mail*, 29 September 1977)

The above extract is from a letter sent to the Occupational Safety and Health Administration (OSHA) in the USA by a member of the National Peach Council, following the discovery that the pesticide DECP was a reproductive hazard. It obviously represents an extreme solution to the problem of reproductive hazard, but reflects the way in which the reality of dealing with reproductive hazards at work may often have more to do with social factors than a scientific assessment of individual risk. The aim of this chapter is to provide a brief review of the ways in which concern may arise over potential reproductive hazards; how such potential hazards may be scientifically evaluated; the types of hazard which exist, and what action can and should be taken to reduce the risks to reproductive health. Emphasis is placed on approaches to evaluating the possible risks of particular exposures because, as will be seen, a comparatively small number of agents have been positively identified as hazardous compared with the hundreds, if not thousands, of suspected sources of reproductive hazard.

It is impossible to do full justice to the large and interesting area of reproductive hazards and their effect on women at work in one chapter; however, it is hoped that this chapter will provide an introduction to the nature of reproductive hazard.

Reproductive hazard

A reproductive hazard may be defined as an exposure which increases the probability of an adverse reproductive outcome. These cover a wide range, from pre-conception (e.g. infertility), through adverse pregnancy outcomes (e.g. miscarriage), to developmental abnormalities in children – both behavioural and physical – which may not manifest themselves for some years (Fletcher 1985). Furthermore, reproductive hazards do not affect only those wishing to have children – other adverse reproductive outcomes include menstrual problems and early menopause; and both male and female occupational exposures are of potential importance for reproductive harm. Mutational damage or interference with sperm production in men can induce sterility or affect the development of their children. Reproductive hazards may be mutagenic or teratogenic. Mutagenesis is damage to the genetic material of reproductive cells: teratogenesis refers to the interference with normal development of the embryo and foetus. These two processes are often difficult to distinguish in their effects, and may interact.

Origins of concern

In a two-year period, 1979 to 1981, seven out of thirteen pregnancies among employees of Air Canada at Dorval Airport ended in miscarriage (City Centre 1985). This unusually high incidence was attributed in press reports to the visual display units (VDUs) the women used in the work, and was one of the earliest reports of 'clusters' of adverse pregnancy outcomes among VDU users. Reports of a localized high incidence of health problems – referred to as 'clusters' – are a common source of anxiety over possible health hazards. The debate over VDUs provides an interesting example of the way in which suspicion may fall on a particular exposure, and an excellent example of the difficulties of establishing whether an exposure does, in fact, constitute an occupational reproductive hazard.

In the USA five clusters of adverse pregnancy outcomes among VDU users were investigated by the US Army Environmental Agency (Tezak 1981), the US Center for Disease Control (Binkin 1981) and the National Institute of Occupational Safety and Health (Lichty 1985a; 1985b; Morawetz 1984). Whilst these investigations found that in some clusters the rate of adverse pregnancy outcomes was significantly higher than that of the general populations using standard statistical tests, they did not find any explanation for these clusters based on environmental exposures or maternal characteristics. Instead, it was suggested that these represent 'expected-unexpected clusters' (e.g. Binkin 1981), an artefact of statistical distribution. Probability theory (binomial distribution) predicts that when an adverse outcome is distributed among a large population (such as VDU users), some groups will, by chance, experience a much higher incidence of adverse outcomes. These will be balanced within the population by other groups experiencing a very low incidence of adverse outcomes, but it is the groups experiencing an abnormally high incidence of miscarriages, birth defects, and so on which are reported in the newspapers. Berquist (1984) has produced a mathematical model for the chance occurrence of adverse pregnancy outcomes in groups of VDU users. He found that the number of groups with high (more than 50 per cent) spontaneous abortion rates predicted from this model is in agreement with or in excess of the number of clusters of adverse outcomes in VDU users reported in the press in the years of 1979 and 1980, when such reports were at their peak.

This explanation is not, of course, satisfactory to those who consider the clusters reported in newspapers represent only 'the tip of the iceberg' (Huws 1987).

It is therefore clear that a high incidence of adverse reproductive outcomes among an occupational group may draw attention to the possibility of a hazard, but can in no way be taken as proof that such a hazard exists. An obvious next step is to conduct an epidemiological study, although the methodological difficulties involved in the study of occupational reproductive hazard can mean that such studies do not necessarily resolve the issue: despite some eleven studies which have been conducted into VDU use and pregnancy outcome over the past twenty years, there is still no consensus as to whether there is any reproductive hazard from work with these machines.

Methodological issues in epidemiological studies

As Mackay (1984) points out, the layperson's expectations as to what studies of this kind can 'prove' may not be justified. No such study can ever prove a negative, that VDU work never has an adverse effect on pregnancy outcome. An effect may exist which is simply too small for detection within the statistical limitations of a study.

What such studies can achieve is to establish whether, having made proper allowance for other relevant factors, an association exists between VDU work and adverse pregnancy outcome. One of the first methodological hurdles to overcome in studies of occupational risks to pregnancy is to achieve a sufficiently large sample size. There are three main reasons why particularly large samples are needed in studies of this kind. Firstly, however large the population chosen for the study of pregnancy outcome, it must contain a sufficient number of pregnancies occurring during the study period. Secondly, adverse pregnancy outcomes are thankfully relatively uncommon. Whilst estimates vary according to method of ascertainment, the usual frequency of miscarriage is approximately 10 to 20 per cent of pregnancies, and congenital defects from 2 to 4 per cent (Fletcher 1985). Thirdly, occupational health risks are generally of a relatively low order (Knill-Jones 1986). For instance, smokers are about twenty times more likely to develop lung cancer than non-smokers; if the risk to pregnancy from VDUs were of this order, it would certainly have been detected beyond reasonable doubt by those studies which have already been done in this area.

The researcher may choose one of three main types of methodology. One approach is to select groups of individuals with different levels of exposure to the suspected hazard (e.g. VDU users and non-users) and compare the incidence of adverse outcomes between groups: these are known as *cohort* studies. Alternatively the difference in exposure may be achieved by comparing pregnancy outcomes over a time period corresponding to the introduction of the suspected hazard in the workplace i.e. by the use of *historical controls*. Both these types of studies may be longitudinal or prospective (i.e. follow subjects through over time), or retrospective (i.e. collect only data about past events). In contrast, in *case-control* (or case-referent) studies, subjects are divided into cases, with adverse pregnancy outcomes, and matched controls or referents with no such adverse outcome to their pregnancy. Analysis is then made to discover any difference in exposure to the suspected hazard between these groups. Such studies are intrinsically retrospective in nature, but have the advantage that they are quick to carry out and may be the only way to study risk factors for rare events (such as birth defects) (Knill-Jones 1986).

Information on exposure and reproductive outcomes may be collected from the subjects themselves by interview or questionnaire and/or from computerized records such as hospital and employment records and census data (these types of data are much more extensive in, for instance, Scandinavian countries than in Britain). One problem with the latter is that incomplete or inaccurate records may lead to *misclassification* of subjects, but there are also potential pitfalls in interview or questionnaire data from retrospective studies.

The main source of disagreement in the interpretation of results from past studies of VDUs and pregnancy concerns the operation of *recall bias* (also referred to as response bias). There are two ways in which this may operate. Firstly, it is suggested that women who have experienced an unhappy pregnancy outcome are more likely to remember potentially hazardous exposures than the control group, who may in contrast not search their memories so carefully for factors which might explain an adverse outcome of which they have had no experience (Knill-Jones 1986). The second, slightly different form, refers to a recall bias about an *outcome* rather than bias about a risk factor which can give rise to a problem. This concerns a possible tendency on the part of a group who are exposed to a factor which is suspected of being harmful – in this case VDUs – to be more scrupulous in their recall of past adverse pregnancy outcomes than a control group of women who are not concerned about any such exposure (Knill-Jones 1986).

In addition, it is suggested that those who consider themselves at risk or have experienced unhappy outcomes may be more likely to reply to questionnaire studies leading to a bias in the results. A low response rate may indicate the operation of *selective non-response* in the study population.

The great advantage of questionnaires or interviews is that it is possible to collect information on other factors known to predict pregnancy outcome such as age, socio-economic status, alcohol and cigarette consumption. If allowance is not made in the statistical analysis of results for these and similar *confounding factors*, then the biases could be serious enough to lead to a completely false interpretation of the effect of the exposure of interest (Knill-Jones 1986).

It is essential, therefore, that a study of occupational reproductive hazard have a good sample size and get a good response rate. The problem of recall bias might best be avoided by conducting a prospective study even though this might involve more time and expense, and proper allowance must be made in the analysis for the operation of confounding factors.

Epidemiological studies will also look for evidence of a dose–response relationship and specificity of effect. The question of dose–response relationships is important in evaluating scientific studies of reproductive hazard. The demonstration that increasing levels of exposure to a risk factor are associated with increasing chances of an adverse outcome is considered to provide strong evidence of a causal association (Knill-Jones 1986). An example of the way in which dose–response relationships have led to the acceptance of an agent as hazardous is provided by the case of dibromochloropropane or DBCP, an agricultural pesticide. At the Occidental Chemical Company plant in Lathrop, California, the lack of pregnancies among the male workers' wives eventually led to an investigation, which showed not only a high proportion of male workers with low sperm counts, but also that this was restricted to workers who had worked there for over three years as opposed to under three months (Whorton *et al.* 1977).

A dose-response relationship is therefore important in establishing evidence of a reproductive hazard, but it is important that 'dose' be properly defined and measured. Several studies of VDU use and pregnancy outcomes have cited the lack of relationship between the amount of VDU work and the incidence of adverse pregnancy outcomes (e.g. Westerholm and Ericson 1986; McDonald *et al.* 1986; Butler and Brix 1986; Ericson and Kallen 1986). As will be seen below, however, one possible source of reproductive hazard from VDUs is the stress involved in many VDU jobs, and this is dependent as much upon quality as quantity of VDU work. Levels of occupational stress may therefore have been a more appropriate measure of dose.

A final issue involved in the interpretation of results is specificity of effect. Again, an example of how a lack of specificity of effect has been taken to counter-indicate the existence of a hazard can be taken from research into VDUs. Most studies of VDU work have looked at the effect on adverse outcomes individually, that is separate analysis has been made of miscarriage, low birth-weight, etc. Several studies have indeed looked for an excess of a specific defect or class of defects (e.g. Westerholm and Ericson 1986; Kurppa *et al.* 1985; McDonald *et al.* 1986). The rationale behind this is that 'experience suggests that if an occupational exposure were to cause abnormal foetal development the defect(s) would be specific' (McDonald *et al.* 1986). Although there have been slight indications of, for example, a slight increase in cardiovascular malformations (Westerholm and Ericson 1986), these studies have produced little evidence of a specific effect. This has been taken as evidence against an effect of VDU work on pregnancy. Nevertheless, it can be argued that, as with the lack of evidence for a dose–response relationship, this may depend on the aspect of VDU work which constitutes a hazard, if hazard there is. Bakketeig *et al.* (1984) suggest that an adverse effect of stress on pregnancy may not consist of a specific effect, but a general increase in the probability of several adverse outcomes. The combination of a range of adverse outcomes in the analysis of results may then be a more appropriate approach to the data.

In conclusion, it can be seen that there are many methodological issues which must be considered in the interpretation of epidemiological studies of occupational reproductive hazards and that straightforward answers to the deceptively simple question 'Is there a risk?' may not easily be supplied.

The situation is further complicated by the different forms which reproductive hazards may take. There are four different basic types of reproductive hazards: physical, chemical, psychosocial and biological (Miller Chenier 1982). Following the suspicion which arose from reports of clusters of adverse pregnancy outcomes among VDU users, the question next arose as to what aspect(s) of VDU work might constitute a reproductive hazard.

Various features of the machine, office and psychosocial environment have been cited as possible causes. These factors provide interesting examples of possible physical, chemical and psychosocial occupational reproductive hazards, but it should be remembered that these are not mutually exclusive. Several of these factors could be operating, either separately or to produce a synergistic effect (Huws 1987).

Physical hazards

Physical hazards are the most widely reported of all occupational dangers but, with the exception of ionizing radiation, research on the reproductive impact of all physical hazards is more limited than for chemical hazards (Miller Chenier 1982). Potential physical hazards to reproductive health which have been suggested in relation to VDUs include radiation, heat and poor posture.

One of the earliest fears expressed about VDUs was that they might emit radiation. Berquist (1986) suggested that possible sources of this anxiety were that some television-type equipment from the 1950s was found to emit measurable quantities of X-radiation, and the claim by a Dr Zaret (1984) that VDUs were causing radiant energy cataracts. Electromagnetic radiation can be divided into ionizing – gamma rays, X-rays and some ultraviolet (UV) – and non-ionizing – microwaves, radio frequency and extra-low and very low frequencies (ELF and VLF). It is well known that ionizing radiation is a dangerous mutagen, teratogen and carcinogen and potential hazards associated with microwaves include burns, cataracts and reproductive effects such as sterility and (possible) congenital malformations and loss of libido and potency. The effects of ionizing and microwaves on reproduction are of very serious concern for workers in many industries including the nuclear energy industry and medicine, but repeated tests in many different countries have shown that VDUs do not emit such radiation (for a review of these tests see e.g. Zuk *et al.* 1983).

Recently, however, an area which has become a source of concern is the effects of the ELF emissions from VDUs on reproduction. All electrical appliances produce weak, low-frequency electric and magnetic fields of mains frequency. The principal source of electric and magnetic fields in the VDU is the 'flyback transformer' (McKinlay 1986). Few measurements have been made of these emissions from VDUs (Berquist 1984), but so far all have shown that, at the operator's position, the ELF emissions are substantially below recommended exposure limits (McKinlay 1986).

Nevertheless, there is widespread concern that pulsed electric and magnetic fields of even very low intensity many interact with biological mechanisms. Concern as to the possible effects of the pulsed magnetic fields emitted by VDUs on pregnancy has centred on laboratory studies using mice and chicks (e.g. Delgado *et al.* 1982; Ubeda *et al.* 1983; Maffeo *et al.* 1984; Juutilainen and Saali 1986; Tribukait *et al.* 1986). It should, however, be emphasized that these experiments have been seriously criticized in terms of both methodology and interpretation of results (e.g. Berquist 1986).

The debate over ELF emissions from VDUs present a good example of one approach to evaluating potential reproductive hazards, that is by the use of laboratory experiments on animals, and the way in which the results of such experiments can arouse controversy even before the difficult task of extending the results of animal studies to humans is attempted.

It has also been suggested that over-heated offices may constitute a reproductive hazard. VDUs produce quite a lot of heat (in the 100–400W range compared with 35–40W for an electric typewriter and 100W from a human body). Depending on the type of VDU, number and density of VDUs in the room, and the capability of the air-handling system, the thermal loading of a VDU work environment may be 30 to 150 per cent greater than without VDUs (Marriott and Stuchly 1986). Other work-places where heat may pose a problem include bakeries, canneries, foundries, garment and textile factories, laundries, mines and smelters (Miller Chenier 1982).

Animal studies have shown that, in females, even slight increases in temperature are sufficient to affect the ovum, often leading to embryo death after fertilization (Monty and Wolff 1974; Ulberg and Burfening 1967). In the male, whose sperm-secreting organs are external to the body to keep them at a lower temperature, increases in temperature may inhibit sperm production, as has been shown in both animal (Howarth 1969) and human studies (Brun and Clavert 1977). However, the effect of ambient temperature on reproductive health of office workers, and especially VDU workers, does not appear to have been the subject of any research.

At the same time, extremes of cold may also endanger reproductive health. For instance, a recent study of poultry slaughterhouse workers in Quebec, where many have to work inside large refrigerated stores, described associations between cold work and menstrual disturbances (Mergler and Venzina 1982).

The physical strains imposed on the body by work during pregnancy can be an important source of harm to pregnancy. For example Mamelle and Lauman (1984), in a French survey of 3,437 pregnant women, found that women involved in physically strenuous work were more prone to premature labour than other working women (e.g. a prematurity rate of 9.2 per cent among shop staff compared with 2.7 per cent among skilled workers). They found five main sources of occupational fatigue: posture, work on machine, physical load, mental load and environment; and that not only did all five sources of fatigue increase the prematurity risk, but also the effects of different sources of fatigue were cumulative.

It has been suggested by Mackay (1984) that if there is a danger to pregnancy from VDU work it may come from having to sit in a constrained posture for long hours. The chance to move around doing other tasks, or at least to take breaks from the machine, is important for all VDU users, but this explanation of reproductive hazard has been questioned. Berquist (1986) argues that only physical activity and standing have so far been associated with miscarriage, so an effect of constrained posture can be only speculated. The office employees' organization City Centre (1985) accepts a possible effect of bad posture on early miscarriage, but considers Mackay's argument to be weak in that women office workers have traditionally occupied low-level sedentary jobs, and one would therefore expect to see the same effect on reproduction in the typing pool. Also, his suggestion could not account for other adverse effects, like congenital defects.

Chemical hazards

One of the earliest studies of reproductive hazards was by Constantin Paul in 1860 into some of the reproductive effects of lead exposure. Mention has already been made of the proven effect of PBCP. Potential chemical hazards are present in practically every environment because chemicals, both elements and compounds, are so much a part of our lives. Just a few examples of the kinds of jobs which involve exposure to potentially harmful chemicals are laboratory (medical scientific, photographic), health-care (anaesthetic gases, medications), factory workers, painters, paper and printing, agricultural (pesticides) and mechanics. Furthermore, housewives and mothers use chemical products for cleaning floors, painting walls, gluing things, fertilizing plants, pest control, and many other activities (Price and Birkin 1989). As the chemical industry continues to expand and to produce new products, the magnitude of the problem increases.

Even modern office workers have expressed fears about chemical hazards. Formaldehyde is known to be released by chipboard furniture. One study suggested that polychlorinate biphenyls (PCBs) – insulating fluids sometimes used in VDUs – were being emitted by VDUs, but later studies suggested that it was the ambient air which was contaminated, and that the PCBs did not come from the VDUs (Benoit *et al.* 1984). There is evidence of reproductive hazard from both these chemicals. With both these possible hazards a major factor is the lack of ventilation or poor air-conditioning systems, which are a problem in many offices.

Psychosocial

Recent years have seen a great increase in the interest shown in psychosocial factors such as stress at work and health issues such as coronary heart disease. Concern has been expressed that the increased levels of stress reported in some studies of VDU users may pose a danger to reproductive health.

There is no evidence of a simple relationship between VDU work *per se* and stress. Some studies have shown high levels of reported psychological distress among VDU workers (e.g. Elias *et al.* 1982; Ghingirelli 1982). Others report no significant difference between users and controls (e.g. Binashi *et al.* 1982). This suggests that the problem is not so much the technology itself but the way it is used (Sauter 1983). Rigby (1987) found that data-input employees experience more pressure in their jobs than technicians, and that speed of work, monotony of job, lack of variety, restricted social contact and pressure from superiors were important sources of stress at work.

The picture which emerges is of high stress at work not, as is commonly presumed, for the 'executive', but for workers in low-grade, boring jobs. Furthermore, these low-grade, boring VDU jobs are largely being done by women (Smith *et al.* 1982; Hunting *et al.* 1981; Evans 1986; Wallin *et al.* 1983), and this distribution of VDU work probably reflects general differences between women's and men's work: women are often employed in this type of low-grade, repetitive job in more traditional industries, such as factory assembly lines. VDU workers in these low-grade, stressful jobs are more likely to experience several different types of work-related health complaints, such as visual problems, headaches and general tiredness (Albury *et al.* 1986; Coe *et al.* 1980; Rigby, 1987). Are they also more at risk of reproductive problems?

The study of the effects of psychosocial factors on reproduction is a relatively new area. Studies have found, for instance, correlations between pregnancy complications and anxiety and life stress (Gorsuch and Key 1974); birth defects and persistent personal tension in pregnancy (Stott 1973); and between low scores of standard clinical tests at birth and lack of self-confidence, uncertainty and anxiety in mothers during pregnancy (Pilowsky 1972); mother's fear during pregnancy for their own health and of something going 'wrong' (Ericson 1976); and other psychological variables. There do not appear to be any research findings on the effects on work-related stress on pregnancy.

Stress may, of course, have an important indirect effect on reproductive outcome if, for instance, it depresses nutrition, causes insomnia or raises smoking and alcohol consumption (Bakketeig *et al.* 1984). As stress may be a much more widespread problem than previously recognized in the kind of low-grade, boring work which is often done by women, the effects of work-related stress on reproductive health, particularly during pregnancy, are obviously an area in which much more research is required.

It has been argued that the debate on reproductive hazards of VDUs, and reports in the popular press, may in itself increase the risk of spontaneous abortion in VDU users. Using this rationale, employers may accede to union demands for a right to transfer away from VDU work for women who are or wish to become pregnant, as contained in several existing 'New Technology' agreements, but still deny the existence of any reproductive hazard *per se* from VDUs and avoid the possibility of damages claims.

Biological hazards

The fourth main type of reproductive hazard is biological hazards. Infections (bacterial, viral or fungal) may cause a variety of problems including sterility in men and birth defects. Those working in health-care and laboratories are most obviously at risk, but also those working with animals, in laundries, and with children (diseases which are relatively non-serious in children may cause more long-term harm in adults: for example mumps can cause sterility in adult men).

Rubella was, in 1941, the first infectious agent to be shown to cause birth defects (Fletcher 1985) and various infections have since been associated, conclusively or speculatively, with birth defects. Surprisingly few studies have been conducted into the reproductive hazards of occupational exposure to infection. Haldane *et al.* (1969) hypothesized that workers caring for infants who had been infected by viral agents in utero could then pass such infections to their own developing foetuses, and indeed they found a higher incidence of congenital defects in the offspring of nurses who had cared for infants with defects or premature defects, and this was particularly high for nurses who had also experienced infectious illness in pregnancy. In contrast, a Swedish study of pregnancy outcome amongst hospital workers yielded equivocal results. Perinatal deaths were significantly raised among medical workers for the first year of the study, but not for the subsequent two years, and there was no significant difference in the number of malformed infants (Baltzar *et al.* 1979).

It will be seen that for all four types of reproductive hazards – physical, chemical, psychosocial and biological – there are many more suspected occupational reproductive hazards than proven ones. This is partly because of the difficulty of proving that a reproductive hazard exists, both by the nature of scientific enquiry itself and because of the practical difficulties involved in conducting and evaluating the results of epidemiological studies. The nature of the suspected hazard will have implications for the research methods adopted, and also for the ways in which the hazard may be avoided or removed from the working environment.

Avoiding reproductive hazards at work

It will be clear that to establish that an occupational exposure does indeed constitute a risk to reproductive health can involve a complicated teasing-out of many different effects, and that a lot more research is needed. The question remains as to what action should be taken when an occupational exposure is shown to be at least a probable risk to reproduction.

One answer seems to be simply to select the workers. A rather extreme example of this point of view may be seen in the extract at the beginning of this chapter. The reality of dealing with reproductive hazards at work may often have more to do with social factors than a scientific assessment of individual risk. It has been known since the last century that exposure to lead by both men and women may result in a variety of adverse pregnancy outcomes, and yet in Britain women are subject to much stricter exposure limits (Fletcher 1985). Fletcher (1985) suggests that while such differences appear to exist in order to protect the unborn child, their effect is in fact to exclude women from a relatively well-paid sector of industry. Surely men have as much right as women to be protected from exposures which may harm them or their unborn children, and women have as much right as men to engage in any form of employment they desire.

An optimistic end-note

In considering the subject of reproductive hazards at work, it is all too easy to view only the bad effects of employment outside the home on women's reproductive health, but this is a false picture. There is evidence that the incidence of some adverse outcomes, e.g. prematurity, is higher among house-wives than working women (Mamelle and Laumon 1984). There is also growing research interest in the positive effects of paid employment during pregnancy. Indeed, employment during pregnancy has many advantages, not only financial, but also in increased social contact, access to facilities such as health-care, and increased self-confidence (Chamberlain 1984).

Conclusion

Clearly this issue is about freedom of choice and employers must ensure that the potential reproductive health hazards in the work environment are eradicated as far as possible. One of the most effective ways of reducing the risk from all possible reproductive hazards, proven or not, is by the education of the work-force in safer working practices within the framework of positive initiatives on health and safety at work. Unfortunately many organizations are sadly deficient in this respect. In the final analysis, there is an urgent need for further well-designed research in order to provide more conclusive and valid answers to the whole area of reproductive hazards at work.

References

Albury, D., Butler, T. and Craig, M. (1986) *Visual Display Units: Health and Safety Survey Prepared for the London Borough of Newham and Newham Nalgo*, London: North East London Polytechnic Company Ltd.

Bakketeig, L. S., Hoffman, H. J. and Titmuss Oakly, A. R. (1984) Perinatal mortality, in M. B. Brachman (ed.) *Perenatal Epidemiology*, New York: Oxford University Press.

Baltzar, B., Ericson, E. and Kallen, B. (1979) Pregnancy outcome among women working in Swedish Hospitals, *New England Journal of Medicine*, 300: 627–8.

Benoit, C. M., LeBel, G. L. and Williams, D. T. (1984) Are video display terminals a source of increased PCB concentration in the working atmosphere? One answer, *International Archive of Occupational and Environmental Health*, 53: 261–7.

Berquist, U. (1984) Video display terminals and health: a technical and medical appraisal of the state of the art, *Scandinavian Journal of Work and Environmental Health*, 10, Suppl. 2.

——(1986) The alleged reproductive hazard of VDU work: an overview, in B. Pearce (ed.) *Allegations of Reproductive Hazards from VDUs*, Loughborough: Humane Technology.

Binashi, S., Albonico, G., Gelli, E. and Morelli Di Popolo, M. R. (1982) Study on objective symptomatology of fatigue in VDU operators, in E. Grandjean and E. Vigliani (eds) *Ergonomic Aspects of Visual Display Terminals*, London: Taylor & Francis.

Binkin, N. J. (1981) *Clusters of Spontaneous Abortions*, Dallas, Texas: Technical Report, Public Health Service Centers for Disease Control.

Bron, B. and Clavert, A. (1977) Modifications morphologiques de l'acrosome chez un homme expose a la chaleur, *Journal de Gynecologie, Obstetrique et Biologie de Reproduction*, (Paris) 6: 907–11.

Butler, W. J. and Brix, K. A. (1986) Video display terminal work and pregnancy outcome in Michigan clerical workers, in B. Pearce (ed.) *Allegations of reproductive Hazards from VDUs*, Loughborough: Humane Technology.

Chamberlain, G. (1984) Women at work in pregnancy, in G. Chamberlain (ed.) *Pregnant Women at Work*, New York: Macmillan.

City Centre (1985) *VDUs and Pregnancy: A Review of the Evidence to Date*, London: City Centre.

Coe, J. B., Cuttle, K., McClellon, W. C., Warden, N. J. and Turner, P. J. (1980) Visual display units, *New Zealand Department of Health*, Wellington (Report W/1/80).

Delgado, J. M. R., Leal, J., Monteagudo, S. L. and Gracia, M. G. (1982) Embryological changes induced by weak, extremely low frequency electromagnetic fields, *Journal of Anatomy*, 134: 533–51.

Elias, R., Cail, F., Tisserand, M. and Christmann, H. (1982) Investigations in operators working with CRT display terminals: relationships between task content and psychophysiological alterations, in E. Grandjean and E. Vigliani (eds) *Ergonomic Aspects of Visual Display Terminals*, London: Taylor & Francis.

Ericson, M. T. (1976) The relationship between psychological and specific complications of pregnancy, labor and delivery, *Journal of Psychosomatic Research*, 20: 207–10.

Ericson, A. and Kallen, B. (1986) An epidemiological study of work with video screens and pregnancy outcome: I–A register study; II–A case-control study, *American Journal of Industrial Medicine*, 9, I: 447–57; II: 459–75.

Evans, J. (1986) Questionnaire survey of British VDU operators, *Proceedings: Work with Visual Display Units*, International Scientific Conference, Stockholm, 12–15 May.

Fletcher, A. C. (1985) *Reproductive Hazards of Work*, Manchester: Equal Opportunities Commission.

Ghingirelli, L. (1982) Collection of subjective opinions on use of VDUs, in E. Grandjean and E. Vigliani (eds) *Ergonomic Aspects of Visual Display Terminals*, London: Taylor & Francis.

Gorsuch, R. L. and Key, M. K. (1974) Abnormalities of pregnancy as a function of anxiety and life stress, *Psychosomatic Medicine*, 36: 352–62.

Haldane, E. V., van Rogen, C. E., Embil, J. A., Tupper, W. C., Gordon, P. C. and Wanklin, J. M. (1969) A search for transmissible birth defects of virologic origin in members of the nursing profession, *American Journal of Obstetrics and Gynecology*, 105: 1,032–40.

Howarth, B. (1969) Fertility in the ram following exposure to elevated ambient temperature and humidity, *Journal of Reproduction and Fertility*, 19: 179–85.

Hunting, W., Laubli, T. and Grandjean, E. (1981) Postural and visual loads at VDT workplaces: I–Constrained postures, *Ergonomics*, 24: 917–31.

Huws, U. (1987) *VDU Hazards Handbook*, London: London Hazards Centre.

Juutilainen, J. and Saali, K. (1986) Effects of low frequency magnetic fields on the development of chick embryos, *Proceedings: Work with Visual Display Units*, International Scientific Conference, Stockholm, 12–15 May.

Knill-Jones, R. P. (1986) Epidemiological approaches to reproductive problems in the workplace, in B. Pearce (ed.) *Allegations of Reproductive Hazards from VDUs*, Loughborough: Humane Technology.

Kurppa, K., Holmberg, P. C., Rantala, K., Nurminen, T. and Saxen, L. (1985) Birth defects and exposure to video display terminals during pregnancy, *Scandinavian Journal of Work and Environmental Health*, 11: 353–6.

Lichty, P. (1985a) *HHE Report 84–297–1609*, Cincinnati, Ohio: NIOSH.

——(1985b) *HHE Report 84–191*, Cincinnati, Ohio: NIOSH.

McDonald, A. D., Cherry, N. M., Delorme, C. and McDonald, J. C. (1986) Visual display units and pregnancy: evidence from the Montreal survey, *Journal of Occupational Medicine*, 28, 12: 1,226–31.

Mackay, C. (1984) Visual display unit operation: possible reproductive effects, Paper presented at the Scientific Conference on Alleged Reproductive Effects from Visual Display Units, London, 29–30 November.

McKinlay, A. F. (1986) The results of measurements of electromagnetic emissions from VDUs and a comparison with exposure standards, in B. Pearce (ed.) *Allegations of Reproductive Hazards from VDUs*, Loughborough: Humane Technology.

Maffeo, S., Miller, M. W. and Carstensen, E. L. (1984) Lack of effects of weak low frequency electromagnetic fields on chick embryogenesis, *Journal of Anatomy*, 139: 613–18.

Mamelle, M. and Lauman, B. (1984) Occupational fatigue and preterm birth, in G. Chamberlain (ed.) *Pregnant Women at Work*, New York: Macmillan.

Marriott, I. A. and Stuchly, M. A. (1986) Health aspects of work with visual display terminals, *Journal of Occupational Medicine*, 28, 9: 833–47.

Mergler, D. and Venzina, N. (1982) Dysmenorrhea among poultry slaughterhouse workers, Paper presented at the Second International Symposium on Epidemiology in Occupational Health, Montreal, 23–25 August.

Miller Chenier, N. (1982) *Reproductive Hazards at Work: Men, Women and the Fertility Gamble*, Ottawa: Canadian Advisory Council on the Status of Women.

Monty, D. E. and Wolff, L. K. (1974) Summer heat stress and reduced fertility in Holstein-Friesian cows in Arizona, *American Journal of Veterinary Research*, 35, 12: 1,495–500.

Morawetz, J. (1984) *HHE Report 83–329–1498*, Cincinnati, Ohio: NIOSH.

Pilowsky, I. (1972) Psychological aspects of complications in childbirth: a prospective study of premiparae and their husbands, in N. Morris (ed.) *Psychosomatic Medicine in Obstetrics and Gynaecology*, Basel : Karger.

Price, B. and Birkin, M. (1989) *C For Chemicals – A New Guide to Household Chemical Hazards*, London: Greenprint.

Rigby, F. L. (1987) A comparison of stress among three types of VDU/computer users, MSc dissertation, UMIST, Manchester.

Sauter, S. L. (1983) Predictors of strain in VDT users and traditional office workers, Paper presented at the International Scientific Conference on Ergonomics and Health Aspects in Modern Offices, Torino, Italy, 7–9 November.

Smith, A. B., Tanaka, S., Halperin, W. and Richards, R. D. (1982) *Report of a Cross-Sectional Survey of Video Display Terminal (VDT) Users at the Baltimore Sun*, National Institute for Occupational Safety and Health, Center for Disease Control, Cincinnati, Ohio.

Stott, D. H. (1973) Follow-up study from birth of the effect of prenatal stresses, *Developmental Medicine and Child Neurology*, 15: 770–87.

Tezak, R. W. (1981) *Occupational Health Special Study: Investigation of Adverse Pregnancy Outcomes, Defence Contract Administrative Services Region, Atlanta*, Technical Report: US Environmental Hygiene Agency.

Tribukait, B., Cekan, E. and Paulsson, L. E. (1986) Effects of pulsed magnetic field on embryonic development in mice, Extended Abstract, International Scientific Conference on Working with VDUs, Stockholm, 12–15 May.

Ubeda, A., Leal, J., Trillo, M. A., Jimenez, M. A. and Delgado, J. M. R. (1983) Pulse shape of magnetic fields influences chick embryogenesis, *Journal of Anatomy*, 137: 513–36.

Ulberg, L. C. and Burfening, P. J. (1967) Embryo death resulting from adverse environment on spermatozoa or ova, *Journal of Animal Science*, 26: 571–7.

Wallin, L., Winkvist, E. and Svenson, G. (1983) *Terminalanvandares Arbetsmiljo – en enkatstudie vid volvo, Goteborg*, Goteborg: AB Volvo.

Westerholm, P. and Ericson, A. (1986) Pregnancy outcome and VDU-work in a cohort of insurance clerks, *Proceedings: Work with Display Units*, International Scientific Conference, Stockholm, 12–15 May.

Whorton, D., Krauss, R. M., Marshall, S. and Milby, R. H. (1977) Infertility in male pesticide workers, *Lancet*, 2: 1,259–61.

Zaret, M. (1984) Cataracts and visual display units, in B. G. Pearce (ed.) *Health Hazards of VDTs?*, Chichester: John Wiley.

Zuk, W. M., Stuchly, M. A., Dvorak, P. and Deslauriers, Y. (1983) *Investigation of Radiation Emissions from Video Display Terminals*, Radiation Protection Bureau, Health and Welfare, Canada, Ottawa.

8 | Problems facing qualified women returners
Daphne F. Jackson

Introduction

This chapter is concerned with the problems of women returners who are well qualified, especially in science and engineering. It might be anticipated that present concerns about demographic trends would mean that such women are being wooed back to work; on the whole this is not the case and a number of reasons for the present position are discussed.

The problem has various aspects, which can be classed broadly as individual or as social. At the individual level, the need for retraining and rebuilding of self-confidence will emerge very strongly. This indicates the necessity of positive action to provide retraining in the form required by these women returners.

At the social level, there is no general recognition of the special skills or needs of qualified women returners. In particular, those responsible for recruiting in many organizations are ill-equipped to deal with this type of non-standard applicant.

Academic research can play its part in clarifying these problems and making them explicit, so that public perception of what is possible and desirable can be changed. This work, however, needs to be based soundly on the actual experiences of women returners. It is these experiences which are discussed here; a substantial number of quotations from reports by women returners are included in this chapter so that the authentic voice of the women themselves may be heard.

The characteristics of women returners

Women returners are not a particularly homogeneous group. What they have in common is that their careers have been interrupted as a result of having children or caring for handicapped or elderly relatives. More women are now thought to be caring for elderly relatives than are caring for young children and this trend will persist with demographic changes.

The impact of family demands on a woman's career is very particular to the individual woman. This is not really understood by well-meaning men who expect an intelligent woman to prepare for her career break and plan her return. It is assumed that the birth-dates of all children can be arranged and that plans made before childbirth can be adhered to. The impact of childbirth is overlooked, as are the needs of older children and adolescents. It is often assumed that career disruption occurs only in association with the arrival of babies, whereas unexpected changes in a partner's employment and the sudden onset of physical or emotional dependency in elderly relatives may prove equally disruptive. Some case histories have been collected (Laverick 1980; Jackson 1984) from members of the Women's Engineering Society. The following extracts illustrate the personal nature of their experiences:

> The actual biological and emotional urge to have children may take even the best by surprise. I have found this side the most difficult to plan as you don't know about or don't believe the emotional commitments until they happen.

> My daughter was born at the beginning of February. . . . I returned to full-time work in mid-April. However I was very miserable, largely because of seeing so little of my daughter. I went effectively part-time until June, when I decided to resign.

> The problems of caring for two children seem to be enormous. I have found a private nursery school for the toddler but there is only one day centre for babies in this city . . . child-minders are okay, but then I have to deliver the children to two different locations unless the toddler goes to the same minder, and that wouldn't be fair.

> My children, although now older, are more emotionally demanding than when young and I get extremely tired.

> My mother was physically okay and was never too bad to be left. The worst thing was the stress – the infuriations and frustrations and coming home to a houseful of gas. . . . When my mother was finally admitted to hospital, a doctor wanted to send her home in the expectation that I would give up my work.

Among women returners in the age group 37–50, the most common pattern seems to be a fairly complete career break from the birth of the first child until the youngest child enters primary school. Younger women appear to be using provisions for maternity leave in order to return to their careers as soon as possible after the birth of each child. The obstacles to a rapid return to full-time work, if so desired, are very great especially if there is more than one child. These women need access to retainer schemes (Engineering Council 1985) so that they can keep in touch with their employers and their profession.

Recognition of skills acquired during a career break

Women do make many and varied efforts to maintain some kind of intellectual activity, for example by helping local primary schools with their computers, tutoring for the Open University or WEA, or working with voluntary groups.

At present, society, employers and women themselves place little value on voluntary work and none at all on the skills acquired in running a home and raising a family. A woman will say that she 'has not done anything in the past few years'. She has, of course, been exercising interpersonal and management skills, motivating the young, controlling finances, and possibly running a transport system.

In collaboration with G. Dearden of the Learning from Experience Trust, I have produced a questionnaire for women returners. This is intended to start women thinking about the skills they have developed from their home-based activities and from part-time or voluntary work. The questionnaire has been sent to about eighty women scientists and engineers. The general comments were favourable but specific comments led to revisions in the initial question-naire. The revised version is given in Appendix 1 (pp. 107–9) so that it may be used more widely.

Interviews have been carried out with a more broadly based and less highly qualified group of women (Howard 1986). This led to a job description for a Home Manager which was contrasted with job descriptions for a number of posts in a high technology company, a local authority, and a service organization.

Women returners should be encouraged to include a statement about their skills in their CVs, and employers must be encouraged to give recognition to these skills. The questionnaire described here is a good means towards achieving this end.

The need for retraining

For women who have taken a long career break retraining is essential. The discussion here of their problems and needs places emphasis on women engineers and scientists who are qualified to the level of BTEC Diploma, HNC, a first degree, or above. For these women retraining must involve up-dating in technical expertise and practical skills. Because of all the other tasks women undertake, it is generally the case that report-writing and team-working skills are retained.

In practice, technical procedures may not have changed very much but almost all areas of science and engineering have become heavily dependent on computers for control as well as calculations, and a new set of 'buzz words' have entered the technical language. New programming languages have been developed, new standard packages exist, and libraries of special routines are available, such as the NAG Library. (This situation will also affect women returning to banking, insurance, accountancy and similar professions.) A biochemist returner commented that

the biggest change I noticed was the increase in use of computers,

but those returners who have used computers with their children or with a local school can rapidly acclimatize to new uses of computers in their profession.

The most important feature of retraining for women is the rebuilding of self-confidence (Roscher 1978). This seems to be just as important for qualified women as for any others. The main problem is the sense of loss of contact with a field of activity which is moving forward very rapidly.

I felt a lack of self-confidence in my engineering knowledge and ability.

In theory, I could keep abreast of technology by reading journals, etc, but I find this difficult, tedious and not very meaningful whilst at home.

After four or five years, I began to lose touch with what developments were being made. Reading papers became a frustration and I was unable to attend seminars to meet people due to family and financial constraints.

Clearly some women find that after a career break their personality and aspirations have changed; they need access to counselling as well as retraining.

I had a dreary job in engineering and the prospect of finishing work was a pleasant one, but I planned to go back into engineering in a more exciting field.

Counselling is needed even for those who want to go back into the same or a strongly related area to their original education and working experience. They have lost touch with their previous employers and with their profession. They find that the local Careers Service is entirely geared to young school-leavers, and although there is now an increasing number of guides for returners (Dobbie 1982; Horne 1983; Wilson 1983; Chapman 1987; Hutchinson and Hutchinson 1986) and directories of available courses (Women Returners' Network 1987), these are not readily obtainable through the local library or the high street bookshop. The more highly qualified the woman is, the more difficult this problem seems:

It is impossible for most would-be returners . . . to find out about available opportunities to begin research again.

The main problem has been discovering where to start in a research field which is almost new to me.

It must be stressed that potential returners do not register as unemployed. In consequence they do not have access to information intended for unemployed or temporarily redundant people. Furthermore, returners not registered as unemployed are ineligible for some retraining opportunities.

The value of part-time retraining

For many potential returners the intermediate step of part-time retraining opportunities and part-time work is valuable or even essential.

Currently I am doing some lectures and supervision on a freelance basis. . . . However, there seems to be a possibility of a genuine part-time job, next year; without this lure I might give up as I feel that I am falling between two stools – work and a genuine home life. Overall then, I feel that part-time work is essential to overcome the problem of a career break.

My return to work has been gradual from the time my youngest daughter started play school and it is only recently, when she is 13, that I have taken a full-time job.

Half-time work has been of considerable help.

There are frustrations, however, because only slow progress can be made and the sense of lack of time can be stressful. Only those with children or elderly dependent relatives can understand the sense of pressure imposed by the need to be home by a specified time and the difficulty of explaining why it is not feasible to stay for the late afternoon seminar or be available during half-term:

> One constant difficulty is the feeling of never having enough time to fit in all the things one wants to do.

> The main difficulty has been coming to terms with being a part-time research worker. Experimental work cannot always be organized on a part-time basis and this has led to some frustrations on my part.

> Family commitments do obtrude; half-term is a problem, as are afternoon seminars.

Another problem is the lack of credibility accorded to part-timers by colleagues and employers. In the academic world it is perfectly respectable to be a part-time secretary or technician or a part-time untenured research worker but part-time tenured posts are rarely available and someone who sought such an arrangement would not be regarded as seriously committed to their career. Some industrial employers will not contemplate part-time posts for professional staff and those that do permit part-time working do not give part-timers the same prospects for promotion as full-timers. A returner to industry has an interesting comment on this matter

> It would be useful if employers would give recognition to part-timers, for example if two years' part-time work equalled one year of full-time work for recognition of service for promotion prospects. . . . It seems to me that taking a career break reduces one's chances of career development above the lower ranks.

Part-time returners can experience difficulties because they are both part-time and mature. Therefore they do not fit neatly into the standard hierarchy and in some cases can feel insecure due to

> a lack of an established place in an existing structure, i.e. young researchers and older established academics.

Age discrimination

Possibly the most serious problem for women is the effect of age discrimination. The use of fixed age-ranges for posts with related salary scales makes it virtually impossible for a woman to return to her career by taking a lower post while refreshing her knowledge and working skills or to keep herself 'ticking over' in a less stressful post while her family demands are high.

The choice of an age-group for each type of post sometimes reflects the view that new intellectual or entrepreneurial progress is made primarily by the young. Current recruiting policies of employers in the field of Information Technology place a low age limit, often less than 30, high in the list of selection criteria, and seem directed toward maintaining the currently low average age in such companies (Information Technology Skills Agency 1988). The working conditions and career development paths are designed to attract young males because of a perceived need to travel at short notice or work unsocial hours, although in practice most IT staff do neither unless they have specific contract commitments (Virgo 1989). That this view is unnecessary is exemplified by the FI Group, which is a highly successful software house employing an exceptionally high proportion of part-time, home-based women.

The view that only the young create new ideas and inventions has led to a particularly discriminatory situation in the universities where appointments to lectureships are often restricted to exactly the age range in which most married professional women will be involved with young children. A woman whose career had been interrupted by very early childbearing would be unlikely to have evidence of the necessary intellectually creative capacity to succeed in competition for these posts while those who have delayed childbearing in order to complete PhDs or obtain Chartered status are likely to be still committed to their children. In 1979, 15 per cent of lectureships in all disciplines were held by women (Rendel 1984). The percentages at the level of reader/senior lecturer and professor were, respectively 5.8 per cent and 2.7 per cent, as shown in Table 8.1, but by 1988 the absolute number of women professors appeared to have fallen (Donoghue 1988). (A more complete analysis of these data over the past ten years has recently been completed (Jackson 1990).) For three years, starting in 1983, appointments to lectureships were made under the so-called New Blood scheme, which imposed an upper age limit of 35. In the first two years of the scheme, women took 8 and 14 per cent respectively of the posts in all disciplines, as shown in Table 8.2 (personal communication from the University Grants Committee). They took no more than 8 per cent of the posts in physical sciences and no more than 4 per cent of the posts in engineering. These low recruitment levels occurred at the same time as the WISE (Women Into Science and Engineering) campaign, which the universities strongly supported in order to recruit more girls into science and engineering courses.

The same situation will arise in the New Academic Appointment Scheme starting in 1989. It must be stressed that the problem is not overt sex discrimination (CUWAG 1988). Heads of Departments often express disappointment that they are unable to short-list a woman candidate. At the same time, little progress has been made in the provision of child-care facilities which would encourage young women to continue their careers. Nor has any progress been made in the provision of part-time tenured posts which would enable older women to apply for posts.

Table 8.1 Women academics

1979	Number	% of total
Professors	105	2.7
Readers/senior lecturers	468	5.8
Lecturers	3,689	15.0
Others	1,216	35.3
All grades	5,487	13.7

Table 8.2   New blood appointments

| | % Women | |
	1983/84	1984/85
Medicine	16	16
Ag/vet	0	0
Biol sci	17	10
Phys sci	8	7
Maths	0	15
Eng/tech	3	4
Arts	31	37
Social st	7	17
Education	—	67
IT	0	16
Total	8	14

Retraining opportunities

Many women have found the courses offered by the Open University of great value, particularly for updating in computing and mathematical methods. Others have acted as OU tutors, thereby keeping both their professional expertise and their teaching skills in use.

The special Open University programme entitled Women in Technology has been extremely beneficial for women wishing to return to work in technology. The scheme was set up in 1981 to provide an opportunity for women qualified in engineering and technology, who had left paid employment for family reasons, to prepare for a return to work (Swarbrick 1984). It involves collaboration between the OU Yorkshire Region and the Centre for Extension Studies at Loughborough University of Technology. A residential weekend at Loughborough provides essential preparation and reorientation; this is followed by the study of technology courses as an Associate Student of the OU. Costs are met by bursaries initially from the Manpower Services Commission and now from the Training Agency and also from the Department of Economic Development in Northern Ireland. Notable features of the scheme are the effort made to contact an isolated group of women separated from their professions, the importance given to advice and counselling right from the enquiry stage, and the very small drop-out rate (Swarbrick 1984).

An increasing number of retraining courses are becoming available (Newton 1987), provided by FE and HE colleges, polytechnics and some universities. Access and Foundation Year courses tend to be intensive courses for those changing direction completely or lacking formal qualifications. Courses under the title of New Opportunities for Women (NOW) tend to be part-time preparatory courses and few emphasise mathematics, science or technology. New higher level courses under development will emphasize management as well as technology (Knott 1989).

Distance learning and college-based courses do have the limitation that the opportunities for high-level practical training are severely limited. Also, they do not offer opportunities for scholarly or creative work which leads to publications in scholarly or professional journals or conference presentations.

The Fellowship Scheme for Women Returners to Science and Engineering

The objective of this scheme is to provide retraining opportunities for qualified women to regain the expertise and self-confidence necessary to conduct advanced research and thereby to regain a position from which they can compete on equal terms for tenured academic posts or senior research posts in universities or industry. The scheme is restricted to physical and biological sciences and to engineering, with emphasis on new technologies such as information technology and biotechnology. These areas are the subject of many university/industry collaborations.

The retraining is achieved by offering flexible part-time fellowships in university departments so that the women returners have access to front-line experimental or computational facilities. The programme for each fellowship contains two integrated components: first, a retraining phase which utilizes the postgraduate lectures, short courses, etc, already offered by the university, and second, a research project conducted under the supervision of a staff member and of interest to the university department and, if appropriate, the sponsor. The fellow may also be given the opportunity to act as a university tutor or demonstrator. There is a simple evaluation procedure consisting of a mid-term report describing the training programme and intended research project and a final report indicating the research standard achieved. These reports are written by the fellows and endorsed by their supervisors. The fellows are asked to state what difficulties they had encountered and how these had been overcome, and also to indicate their future employment plans. An overall report on the progress of the scheme, based on the reports of the individual fellows, has been prepared (Jackson and McCormick 1987).

The Fellowship Scheme was launched in the summer of 1985. The first fellows were appointed from January 1986. Women apply to the Co-ordinator and are asked for a CV, any ideas that they may have about their work, and an indication of the universities to which they can readily travel. The Co-ordinator contacts an appropriate university department where a rigorous interview is carried out. If this is satisfactory, a retraining programme is jointly outlined by the applicant and the university supervisor.

Each fellowship consists of a part-time salary for two or three years and a modest contribution to running costs. The host university provides resources in the form of staff time, space, use of equipment and, in some cases, back-up funding. The Scheme presently depends entirely on the efforts of the Co-ordinator to raise funds. More than 50 per cent of the funding has come from industry and the rest from charitable bodies and institutions. The Co-ordinator also has an important role in counselling some of the applicants and helping them to take their first steps towards re-employment.

Only about 16 per cent of the applications arose as a result of information seen in the national press or professional and technical journals. Details are given in Table 8.3 (Jackson and McCormick 1987), and give a clear illustration of the problems of contacting qualified women who have lost touch with their previous employers and their professions.

Some of the difficulties experienced by the returner fellows have already

Table 8.3   Applications to the Fellowship Scheme

Means of contact	%
Letter in *Woman* magazine	21
Open University	18
Article in *New Scientist*	13
National press and radio	9
Professional and technical journals	8
Personal contact	6
Local press	4
Other	21

been discussed. One of the most positive experiences has been the help received from academic staff and technicians who are, of course, mostly men:

> Team members have, without exception, been friendly and kind and have shown great patience in teaching new techniques.

> Members of the section were generous in giving me programs to look at.

Some of the fellows have become strongly involved in the teaching activities of their departments. One has become a member of a Board of Studies and another is a member of a Staff-Student Liaison Committee.

The fellows are bringing freshness and enthusiasm to their work, irrespective of their ages. Their output of presentations for national and international conferences and of papers (mostly co-authored) is very high. Their enjoyment is evident:

> I haven't enjoyed myself so much for years.

> I am really enjoying the work. I feel it is all worthwhile and that I am making a useful contribution.

> It has been a most marvellous experience for me and has given me confidence to take my place in the academic world again.

Employment prospects following retraining

Despite the growing concern about the demographic trends and skills shortages (Information Technology Skills Agency 1988; Virgo 1989; House of Commons Employment Committee 1987; IT Skills Shortages Committee 1984; 1985a; 1985b; Pearson 1989) and the high investment in the initial education and postgraduate training of potential returners, the returners express anxieties about their prospects. They are particularly concerned about age limits used to define eligibility for posts and conservative employment practices. There seems to be a gulf in attitudes between the leaders of industry and their plant managers. Personnel staff seem unable to adjust recruitment procedures in order to cope with a heterogeneous group with unconventional career backgrounds. A potential returner with a PhD in chemistry and command of five

European languages has failed to receive replies to many applications for posts, which means that she is not even receiving any feedback on why she is not being considered. Even when part-time employment is on offer, advertisements are not placed with the local media or in magazines that are read in waiting-rooms of doctors and dentists.

Professional societies and institutions should be extending their careers guidance and placement services, and making it known that these services can be used by people who have dropped out of their profession but want to return.

After some initial rebuffs and disappointments, all the returners in the Fellowship Scheme who have so far completed their fellowships have obtained further employment, mostly in academic research and industry. Three have obtained university lectureships. It is to be hoped that these successes are the first signs of changes in attitudes to recruitment.

Acknowledgements

I am greatly indebted to all the sponsors of the Fellowship Scheme for their support both to me as Co-ordinator and to the returner fellows. I am very grateful to all the returners who have revealed personal information to me and have thereby developed my understanding of their problems and achievements. Amongst these returners, Dr Elizabeth Johnson has been particularly supportive and has made many perceptive comments.

Appendix 1

PREPARED BY
LEARNING FROM EXPERIENCE TRUST

FOR PROFESSOR DAPHNE JACKSON OF THE UNIVERSITY OF
SURREY

TO BE USED BY

WOMEN POSTGRADUATES IN SCIENCE AND ENGINEERING

SEEKING RE-ENTRY TO EMPLOYMENT
(Revised Version)

This form is designed to help you to identify those talents and skills which you have developed from relevant experience as well as from more traditional and formal educational activities. There is plenty of evidence that employers value mature applicants who can offer the experience of being responsible for others and who have the organizational skills which often develop through the everyday experience of active people.

Full name of applicant . . . .

Address ....

....

(NB SOME OF THESE QUESTIONS MAY NOT BE APPLICABLE IN YOUR CASE,
AND WHERE THIS IS SO, PLEASE PROCEED TO THE NEXT QUESTION)

1. Since you left employment, have you done any of the following?
    (a) Studied for part-time courses, e.g. with the OU, WEA, etc? If so, what did
    the studies cover, and what benefit did you derive from them?

    (b) Private reading, especially of non-fiction?
    If so, what books or periodicals have you read and how did you profit from
    this activity, e.g. in critical thinking, appraisal of problems and possible
    solutions?

    (c) Part-time work?
    If so, specify what was involved, e.g. motivating others, delegating tasks to
    others, identifying the problems of others.

    (d) Work for playgroups, parent–teacher associations, learned societies, sports
    clubs, church or other organizations?
    Did this involve administrative work, budgetary control, committee work,
    chairmanship, report writing, planning and co-ordinating of activities?
    If so, did you develop new skills through these activities?

    (e) Household management for the family?
    Has this involved basic management skills in organizing routines, time and
    budgets for the benefit of husband, children or other relatives and friends?
    Are you conscious of having learned to organize your own time so that
    part-time study or work would be feasible?

    (f) Management of individuals or groups in any of the above activities, e.g. in
    arranging household repairs or employing a home help, which may have
    involved the development of inter-personal skills?
    If so, are you conscious of having acquired or improved these skills since you
    left work, e.g. in negotiation, persuasion, motivation of others, etc.?

(g) Formal communication in speech or writing with individual or groups such as teachers, welfare officers, the local press? If so, are you aware of having improved effective communication with others?

(h) Work using a typewriter, printer or duplicating equipment, home computer, calculator or microprocessor?
If so, can you give specific examples of usage?

(i) Problem-solving in specific situations?
In any of the above situations you may have developed particular techniques for problem-solving or trouble-shooting; on reflection, do you think that these have added significantly to your learning skills?

(j) Attendance at interviews for employment?
If so, have you analysed your performance to identify its strengths and weaknesses and reasons for success or failure?

2. In what respects have you managed to update your academic knowledge or research expertise in the area of your specialism since you left work? (This could involve reading of appropriate books or periodicals, occasional attendance at conferences, watching relevant TV programmes or films, informal contact with relevant industry, etc.)

3. Have you maintained your membership of any professional societies? Have you pressed for a reduced subscription while you are taking a career break?

References

Chapman, J. (1987) *Women Working it Out*, Sheffield: Careers and Occupational Information Centre.

CUWAG (Cambridge University Women's Action Group) (1988) *Forty Years On . . .* , Report on the Numbers and Status of Academic Women, Cambridge: CUWAG Survey Committee.

Dobbie, E. (1982) *Returners*, 2nd edn, London: National Advisory Centre on Careers for Women.

Donoghue, H. (1988) Female professors, *AUT Women*, 13: 2.

Engineering Council (1985) *Career Breaks for Women Chartered and Technician Engineers*, London: Engineering Council.

Horne, J. (1983) New courses and careers for women, *NATFHE Journal*, October: 28–9.

House of Commons Employment Committee (1987) *Skills Shortages*, Second Report for Sessions 1986–87, London.

Howard, K. (1986) *Managerial Skills: Yes, They Can Be Developed in the Home*, Howard Affiliates.

Hutchinson, E. and Hutchinson, E. (1986) *Women Returning to Learning*, Cambridge: National Extension College.

Information Technology Skills Agency (1988) *Changes in IT Skills: The Impact of Technology*, London: ITSA.

IT Skills Shortages Committee (1984) *The Human Factor: The Supply Side Problem*, First Report, London: Department of Trade and Industry.

—— (1985a) *Changing Technology: Changing Skills*, Second Report, London: Department of Trade and Industry.

—— (1985b) *Signposts for the Future*, Final Report, London: Department of Trade and Industry.

Jackson, D. F. (1984) Career development and disruption, in G. Chivers and M. van Ments (eds) *Women in Technology*, Centre for Extension Studies, Loughborough University of Technology.

Jackson, D. F. and McCormick, E. (1987) *Fellowship Scheme for Women Returners to Science and Engineering*, Guildford: University of Surrey.

Jackson, D. F. (1990) Women working in higher education, *Higher Education Quarterly*, to be published.

Knott, M. (1989) Mothers: industry needs you, *The Engineer*, 9 February: 37.

Laverick, E. (1980) Engineering and the future, unpublished talk.

Newton, P. (1987) New educational and training opportunities for women, in *Managing the Career Break*, London: Equal Opportunities Commission.

Pearson, R. (1989) The impact of Europe's 1992, *Nature*, 338: 526.

Rendel, M. (1984) Women academics in the seventies, in S. Acker and D. Warren Piper (eds) *Is Higher Education Fair to Women?*, Windsor: SRHE and NFER-Nelson.

Roscher, N. M. (1978) Updating women chemists for active careers, *Journal of College Science Teaching*, March, VII: 220–2.

Swarbrick, A. (1984) Women in technology scheme, in G. Chivers and M. van Ments (eds) *Women in Technology*, Centre for Extension Studies, Loughborough University of Technology.

Virgo, P. (ed.) (1989) *Towards an Open and Equal IT Careers Initiative*, Report of the Women into Information Technology Campaign Feasibility Study, London: ICL (available from IT Strategy Services, 2 Eastbourne Avenue, London, W3 6JN).

Wilson, V. (1983) Computerised occupational guidance for adults, *Scottish Journal of Adult Education*, 6, 1:18–22.

Women Returners' Network (1987) *Returning to Work: Education and Training for Women*, 1st edn, London: Longman.

Part III
Women's experiences in specific occupations

9 | Women entrepreneurs
Sandra M. Simpson

What is the potential of entrepreneurship for women? Does it offer an escape from the confines of the labour market or does it merely reproduce women's repression in a different form? Does it offer a means whereby women can improve the quality of their lives (particularly in relation to their other commitments) or does it merely increase women's workload? Does society prepare women for entrepreneurship or does it prepare them to subordinate themselves to the caring of others? Is society really ready to encourage women into entrepreneurship?

Although working women have raised their profile in society over recent years, women's entrepreneurship – an increasingly important subsection of the world of work – has received minimal attention. This may be somewhat unexpected in the light of 'The Enterprise Culture' promotion over the last decade, and given the urgent need to inform future policy, this reflects as bad practice. The scale of such 'omission' can be judged by the actual numbers of women entering self-employment: between 1981 and 1987 the figures for women showed an increase of 70 per cent, while for men an increase of only 30 per cent (*Employment Gazette* 1988).[1] Currently in this country women comprise 25 per cent of the self-employed population.

Working women in general have heightened their profile in recent years and this will certainly be maintained in the foreseeable future, not least because of their increasing participation in the labour force (they now form 42.6 per cent of the work-force: EOC 1988). However, the demands of industry are likely to militate against further concern for women in entrepreneurship given problems arising from the projected demographical changes over the next two decades; for example, the 'skills shortage'.

This 'lack of concern' with women's entrepreneurship (which looks as if it may continue) needs to be viewed and understood in a wide context – beyond the bounds of 'The Enterprise Culture' promotion – in terms of women's roles, their particular labour market experiences and labour market demands. Policy-makers have not acknowledged women's varied needs to work beyond positions which do not seriously challenge women's conventionally defined roles. These roles exist as a function of particular relationships which are 'home/family' based – women's first responsibility (as far as traditional ideology is concerned) should be to her partner/family/home. Latitude may be extended at times when wider economic or military needs dictate. Then women are regarded as a reserve army of labour (Bruegel 1979) who can be moved in and out of the labour force on demand. However, the implications of policy are to preserve the family unit, which is seen as man supporting his wife and children. Such a basis for policy is questionable when this particular form of 'unit' comprises such a small percentage of the total 'family' units in the UK. Policy maintains traditional ideology and fails to reflect social reality accurately.

General changes in attitudes themselves have also promoted some latitude for women working, particularly where individual financial imperatives are seen to exist.[2] However, once again, we find unrealistic notions being maintained, for example, the 'pin money' theory. Few women work for just 'pin money' – they work out of economic necessity, either contributing substantially to joint family income, or working to support their family, whether it be as a lone parent or as the only provider of income for the household. Working wives, for example, keep many families above the poverty line (West 1982). In addition, women do not just exist in terms of a set of relationships by which they are defined (and constrained): a large proportion work to support themselves. They also work for a whole range of non-financial reasons concerning individual needs like satisfaction, fulfilment, and so on. The non-family/home-oriented reasons, however, challenge women's assumed primary role. Although they clearly exist they are largely ignored.

When we actually look at entrepreneurship, it is essentially a male phenomenon. The rhetoric indicates 'opportunity for all', although even a superficial analysis reveals messages reflecting a predominantly male image of enterprise. Enterprise promotion has been re-targeted more recently, however, and has been aimed (in theory) specifically at people and areas most affected by unemployment and/or disadvantage (*Employment Gazette* 1988). Although it is well documented that women are disadvantaged, there have been few measures to attract women into self-employment. Neither is due consideration afforded them under the unemployment category as the manner in which the statistics are compiled means that women's real position and needs are underestimated (Martin and Roberts 1984). Demand for various schemes (e.g. Enterprise Allowance Scheme (EAS), Business Enterprise Programme) are also underestimated as women are frequently ineligible due to either lost National Insurance Contributions or not being in receipt of benefit. Of the successful EAS applicants between April and October 1987, 28.7 per cent were women compared to 71.3 per cent men (EOC 1988). Statistics on the number of failed applications (by gender) were not available. All in all, women are largely ignored.

Why then do women choose self-employment?

The context of women's labour market experiences, which is best characterized by the term 'occupational segregation' (Hakim 1979), provides some powerful indicators to this question. Women are concentrated in low-skilled and poorly paid occupations. They have fewer opportunities for training and generally poor prospects. Work engaged in is often unchallenging and unsatisfying (Wainwright 1978; Webb 1982). They need to be better qualified and work harder than their male counterparts in order to progress (Cooper and Davidson 1984). Various 'female' occupational areas of the economy suffer long-term unemployment (Sinfield 1981; West 1982). Women are more likely to suffer redundancy (Coyle 1984) and are poorly represented by unions (Hunt 1982). Some geographic areas just do not provide opportunity for paid employment. Women returning to work after some break for child-rearing frequently suffer downward mobility, or find the demands of formal employment too inflexible to accommodate their domestic roles (Brotherton *et al.* 1987a). Frequently self-employment is turned to out of frustration with inequality in career prospects (Hymounts 1986), or other unrewarding experiences in employment (Brotherton *et al.* 1986; Simpson *et al.* 1986; Goffee and Scase 1985; Scase and Goffee 1982).

Of course, some provision to encourage women into entrepreneurship does exist, though generally it is neither widely available (on a geographic basis) nor accessible (it may not accommodate women's family roles in terms of timing, and crèche facilities). Where 'encouragement' does exist, we are talking about local initiatives – not national policy. This token approach contrasts sharply with the USA where efforts of federal agencies have been co-ordinated to provide specific support for women (for example, Interagency Committee on Women's Business Enterprise 1980). In this country business advisory and support agencies are seen as taking little notice of the needs of women in practice although, of course, their services are 'available to all' in theory (Truman 1989), failing an already substantial and increasing percentage of their potential clientele. The widespread lack of awareness that women frequently face distinct problems in accessing support and advice (Turner 1989), for example, coping with negative attitudes, is not helped by agencies and other commercial sources of advice being almost exclusively staffed with male 'advisers'. Acknowledging the scale of the problem or ascertaining real need is made difficult by statistics being compiled in a gender-blind manner and evaluation of services being carried out in primarily quantitative terms (Truman 1989).

In terms of policy and action women entrepreneurs are, in effect, a 'non-issue'. And yet they continue to make important contributions to the economy in a variety of ways, not least by their increasing contribution to entrepreneurship, where they face the usual problems in starting up and running their business and have additional gender-specific hurdles to overcome (Brotherton *et al.* 1987a; Carter and Cannon 1988; Goffee and Scase 1985; Halpern 1989; Koper 1989; Turner 1989).

How does research on entrepreneurship contribute at the level of policy?

For some considerable time and to a great extent the research community has reflected the prevailing (traditional) ideology, legitimizing entrepreneurship as male. The vast majority of entrepreneurship research has, until more recently, concentrated on all male samples. Such theories as exist are theories of male entrepreneurship and are of limited application. As in most other countries, excepting the USA, there is only a small body of work involving women entrepreneurs in the UK. In general, research has contributed to our understanding of entrepreneurship only in a limited way and for a great variety of reasons that go way beyond the gender-bias of most samples. The restrictive role of financial considerations, for example, in this process should not be underestimated. The picture which emerges from these studies is, however, generally not clear unless we firmly attach the results to the very specific 'conditions' under which they were conducted. And herein lies a particular difficulty – to interpret and apply the research. The following are a selection of the problem areas.

Much early literature debates at length the question of how 'entrepreneur' should be defined. The debate has not yet concluded, which means a variety of 'working' definitions are adopted, the justification of which is rarely made clear. The bases for defining entrepreneurs have ranged across the following: length of time in business; number of others employed (Creigh 1986); level of turnover; innovation (Schumpeter 1954); propensity for risk-taking; success (Hornaday and Aboud 1971); scores on need for achievement (McClelland 1961), and so on. Beyond the gender bias, few studies adequately represent (or even address the issue of) ethnic minorities and/or different socio-economic groups. Often a very wide, or extremely narrow, range of occupational areas are included. Much work has concentrated on samples from a very restricted locality; while others have covered a wide geographic area. Little has yet been done in any systematic way to try and take into account the specificity of particular labour markets or local economic conditions. Approaches have remained at the level of discussion or subjective observation (Brotherton *et al.* 1987b; Bruno and Tyjebee 1982). There are few studies which can make any contribution beyond that offered by a cross-sectional approach. Continuing debate over method has often resulted in the polarization of qualitative and quantitative approaches, rather than a more fruitful integration.

What we are left with, generally, are single variable explanations which prove to be overly simplistic and do not take account of the breadth, depth and existence of complex interactions of numerous variables. Social deprivation theory (Boswell 1973) and notions of entrepreneurs being deviant and nonconformist (Kets de Vries 1977) are merely two examples of how piecemeal the information is to aid understanding of entrepreneurship.

Our understanding of women's entrepreneurship has also struggled to advance. Primarily we have only a small body of work to consider and this is compounded by the different approaches taken: we have studies which have concentrated on women only (e.g. Carter and Cannon 1988; Cromie and Hayes 1988; Goffee and Scase 1985); we have few studies which have decided at the outset to compare women and men (Birley *et al.* 1986; Watkins and Watkins 1986); and we have other studies which, although including women and men in the sample, did not set out to make comparisons at the outset (Brotherton *et al.* 1987b; Johnson and Storey 1989). All off these studies are liable to suffer some or many of the research 'problems' outlined previously, but most critically, they allow us to make only limited contributions to inform policy, for example, in terms of differences which may or may not exist between women and men.

Research findings

What might we currently conclude from research which has, in some way, taken account of women entrepreneurs and how does this relate to male entrepreneurship research generally? There is a range of descriptive information available on samples covering ages, types of businesses, educational background, and so on. Results are, however, often contradictory: women have been found to start 'stereotypical' or traditional women's businesses (Hisrich and Brush 1983; Watkins and Watkins 1983); there is no relationship between gender and industrial sector chosen (Gomolka 1977); women are setting up in male-dominated areas although traditional female areas (that is service industries) predominate (Hisrich 1986). Women are unlikely to be as well qualified as men (Johnson and Storey 1989; Watkins and Watkins 1986); women have higher educational backgrounds than men (Carter and Cannon 1988; Hisrich and O'Cinneide 1986); women and men have that same educational level. Women in business are on average older at start-up than male counterparts (Hisrich 1986; Johnson and Storey 1989); women are younger than male counterparts, (Birley *et al.* 1986; Hisrich and O'Cinneide 1986; Welsch and Young 1982). What we do find, consistently across female and male samples, is that previous employment/work experience predominantly drives the choice of new business formation (Brotherton *et al.* 1987b). This gives us a double-edged sword. On the one hand, setting up in some area where you have knowledge/experience would seem, at the level of common sense, to be of considerable advantage. However, where start-up is in response to redundancy, for example, new businesses may be setting up in a contracting/declining market. The implications for women may be considerably more serious where their previous employment/work experience is likely to have restricted them to female stereotypical areas which may be at greater risk in terms of failure (for example retailing). It is also perhaps more likely that women have had less work experience in areas which might aid them in running businesses (for example financial management).

Beyond descriptive information, most findings from research work can be broadly categorized under the following headings:[3]

1 Motivations to go into business
2 Problems/barriers faced at start-up as well as when running the business
3 Typologies of female entrepreneurship

Motivations

The main motivators for women are the need for independence and challenge (Brotherton *et al.* 1987a; Carter and Cannon 1988; Cromie and Hayes 1988; Schreier 1975; Simpson and Pearson 1989; Schwartz 1979). Similar motivations have been found in studies of male entrepreneurs (e.g.

Simpson *et al.* 1986) although some conclusions seem to have been drawn prematurely:

> Our perception is that the topic [female entrepreneurship] is becoming increasingly a non-issue from a research perspective. While differences exist between male and female entrepreneurs, thus far they are outweighed by the similarities.'
>
> (Ronstadt *et al.* 1986)

Some investigators have concentrated on the reporting of similarities while glossing over the differences, while others do the reverse. At this stage all we can be sure about is that things have not yet been sufficiently well clarified. Differences in women's and men's motivations have been found (for example, accommodating personal/domestic commitments mentioned by women but not men: Simpson *et al.* 1986). However, we must remember that there are dangers in making what may be simple and superficial comparisons between women and men. Consider the notion of independence. For women there may be no single notion of independence, it is likely to be defined differently by women at different stages in their lives, relative to experience, age, commitments. For example, compare women 'returners' with women frustrated by the limitations of the formal labour market (Carter and Cannon 1988). Men may not have similar varied commitments to face over the life-span; however, notions of independence may also vary relative to their experience, age, etc. Clarification is obviously needed.

The difficulties of precisely focusing our picture of women's entrepreneurship are illustrated by the following extract. This might also reasonably be interpreted as indicating 'similarities', particularly in the light of other research:

> in terms of motivations, men are often motivated by the drive to control their own destiny, to make things happen. This drive often stems from disagreements with their boss or a feeling they can run things better. In contrast, women tend to be motivated by independence and achievement arising from job frustration where they have not been allowed to perform to the level they are capable of.
>
> (Hisrich 1986: 69)

This is a crucial issue. Overpreoccupation with either similarities or differences will result in entrepreneurs' being treated inappropriately. This will do nothing to improve the prospects for either women or men, to say nothing of the economy. Considering gender differences all too frequently leads to individuals being slotted into mutually exclusive categories. Motivations can rarely be usefully reduced to single variable explanations.

Problems

The problems women and men face when setting-up and running a new business indicate considerable common ground: general worry about finance, business failure, lack of finance, lack of business skills. However, some of these commonly shared problems would seem to be exacerbated by gender for women. For example lack of finance (Schwartz 1979; Hisrich 1986; Hisrich and Brush 1983); lack of business knowledge, skills, experience or training (Hisrich and Brush, 1983; Schwartz 1979; Watkins and Watkins 1986); discrimination/difficulty in obtaining finance (Brotherton *et al.* 1987a; Epstein 1989; Halpern 1989; Pellegrino and Reece 1982; Schwartz 1979).

In financial terms women are less likely to have access to collateral required by financial institutions (and this situation is worse for Third World women: Epstein 1989). Selection criteria giving access to financial resources often conspire against women; that is they often require more than a modest starting capital, they look for a particular track record in terms of previous experience, they demand particular growth objectives, they look for a certain employment potential and are frequently restricted to the manufacturing sector (Halpern and Szurek 1987). Where financial institutions have a single 'male' model of entrepreneurship, women generally are not taken seriously, and women with particular domestic commitments even less so – they are 'not a good risk'.

> I was asked if my fiancé was going to support me through the initial stages of starting up the business . . . when he went along about business, nobody asked him if *I* was going to support *him*!

> I was asked about . . . oh, I suppose it was very politely put . . . you know, along the lines of 'the patter of tiny feet' . . . and having admitted that it was a consideration *in the future* I was asked, in a very fatherly and kindly way, what I wanted to be bothering my head about all this business nonsense for?
>
> (Former manager of one of the largest branches of a
> well-known national firm)

Divergence between women and men comes in the form of problems that women experience which men do not. Gender poses an additional dimension with which women have to contend. For example not being taken seriously as a woman (Brotherton *et al.* 1987a; Carter and Cannon 1988; Hisrich 1986; Hisrich and O'Brien 1981; Simpson and Pearson 1989; Stevenson 1983); felt intimidation, lack of confidence (Stevenson 1983); role conflict (competing demands of 'family' and business: Simpson and Pearson 1989; Stevenson 1983); lack of support (Simpson and Pearson 1989; Stevenson 1983). In the context of women's experience in education, employment and in terms of role expectations, the additional set of problems seems predictable.

Not being taken seriously may take many forms – from less than positive attitudes of family to downright negative and hostile attitudes from financial institutions (Carter and Cannon 1988). Whatever form it takes, women receive little support. These experiences tend to undermine women's confidence and credibility and it requires extra effort from women to overcome them (Carter and Cannon 1988). Earning credibility is something women seem to have to work hard at (as in the formal labour market) – whether it be with colleagues, customers or employees.

Women enter the labour market handicapped by an education which not only restricts their 'choices' (Byrne 1978; Holland 1980; Stanworth 1988; Weiner 1987; WNC 1983) but also is seen as largely irrelevant in preparation for entrepreneurship (Watkins and Watkins 1986). They remain concentrated in low-skilled occupations and are unlikely to have had the kinds of experiences which might help them prepare for entrepreneurship. The overall effects are in lowered confidence.

Acknowledging the effects of role conflict is not meant to reinforce the notion that women invariably adopt wife/partner/family commitments. For some women, careers/business or family are viewed as distinct alternatives and they make a choice between the two. For others however, there are attempts to combine both, which for many women leads to conflict since the larger part of child-care and housekeeping still falls to women. Women in business generally see themselves as fulfilling a number of different roles in their lives, for example, partner/wife, businesswoman, mother, housekeeper/manager, joint breadwinner, sole breadwinner, and so on. Conflict experienced doesn't seem to depend on whether women are married or not, or whether they have children or not: more conflict is experienced by women with children still living at home, than those without children or those with children who are no longer living at home (Simpson and Pearson 1989).

This study found the amount of support women receive from their partners is limited, in other words, traditional role models are usually maintained. In a nation-wide sample of women in business over half were receiving very little support. They reported that their partners, although trying to be verbally supportive and encouraging about the business, wanted them to fulfil their previous domestic/family responsibilities. The partners in addition hadn't taken on any more responsibility for the domestic area, neither did they help in the business (Simpson and Pearson 1989). The position of women in business contrasts sharply with that of men, whose wives provide a variety of often unpaid, and frequently undervalued services to their husbands' businesses, particularly during the start-up phase, without which the business venture might not get under way (Scase and Goffee 1980a; 1980b; 1982). In addition women often take on full responsibility for the family/domestic situation to allow the husbands to concentrate on their business venture.

The 'support' situation for women may be even worse than some of this research implies. Although nearly half of a particular sample reported their partners' attitudes as being generally verbally supportive (Simpson and Pearson 1989), it is clear from additional questions that women still perform the bulk of household and family chores. One survival strategy employed seems to be either enlisting help from family members or buying in services (paid for by women) for child-care and/or housekeeping. However, accurately quantifying the support may be difficult as evidenced by the piloting of Martin and Roberts's (1984) work, where women reported sharing domestic work equally; in fact, the women were seen to be doing considerably more. While a marriage partner may be viewed as a 'stabilizing' factor in business for men, it is not generally the case for women (Watkins and Watkins 1986).

The hopes that entrepreneurship may be a means of overcoming gender subordination (Goffee and Scase 1985) seems misplaced. Women may certainly escape some of the confines of the formal labour market but these are replaced with a range of problems to face in entrepreneurship which are gender related. The evidence doesn't suggest that conjugal roles are being renegotiated – women are still performing the 'double shift'.

Typologies

Limited research has been carried out which attempts to categorize business-women in particular ways, by proposing specific typologies (Goffee and Scase 1985; Cromie and Hayes 1988).

Goffee and Scase propose four categories into which women might fit based on: their attachment to entrepreneurial ideals (that is belief in economic self-advancement); an adherence to individualism and strong support for the work ethic and profits (seen as just rewards for efforts and sacrifices); and the extent to which they accept conventionally defined female–male relationships (that is subordination to men). The four resulting categories are summarized below:

1 'Conventionals'   highly committed to entrepreneurial ideals and to conventional ideas about gender roles. Any conflict between business and personal situation is likely to be contained by maintaining stable no-growth business situation.
2 'Innovators'   highly committed to entrepreneurial ideals but reject prevailing notions of subordinate female role. Strongly motivated by profit and growth and business is primary life interest, with relationships either secondary, or not figuring at all.
3 'Domestics'   limited commitment to entrepreneurial ideals, the business is constrained by strong attachment to traditional female role which is considered as primary.
4 'Radicals'   low commitment to entrepreneurial ideals and to conventional female roles, and business is geared towards helping to overcome women's subordination.

An attempt to validate the assertions made by Goffee and Scase (1985) was taken up by Cromie and Hayes (1988). Their conclusions do indicate some similarity with Goffee and Scase's categorization. However, while Goffee and Scase's judgements for classification were consistently based on women's marital status, Cromie and Hayes stress the possession of children as an important distinguishing feature. Overlap between the two studies was in the category of 'Innovators', most of whom rejected conventional female roles and were highly committed to personal achievement. No 'Radicals' appeared in their Cromie and Hayes sample. The 'Conventionals' of Goffee and Scase become 'Dualists', who have successful careers which impose strain on their role of child-rearing and where business ownership allows them to fulfil both domestic and career roles. 'Returners' is a category which is likened to Goffee and Scase's 'Domestics', all of whom interrupted their career to have and raise children. However, these women's child-rearing roles were diminishing and it is proposed that this might lead to some change in attitude towards the business.

There is cause for concern in the way Cromie and Hayes consider 'Innovators' as having similar experiences and being motivated by similar incentives as male entrepreneurs; that is they set up business due to a variety of unsatisfactory employment experiences (they make comparisons with men based on work by Scase and Goffee 1980a; Stanworth and Curran 1973). The comparison would seem to be superficial. It is not clear how reality or perception of sex discrimination by women which is included can be considered a 'similar' experience.

Such typologies do not acknowledge changes women may go through in relation to their experience of entrepreneurship as well as other changing commitments over the life-span. This is a critical point for entrepreneurship policy in general. Although the work acknowledges that women entre- preneurs are not a homogeneous group, the experience of subordination, for example, is rather presumed to be homogeneous. Applications of this work are limited. The samples are small; they come from restricted geographical areas and comprise, on the one hand, only 'female' type businesses (for example retail, service sector, craftwork) and, on the other hand, women in the process of start-up or who had been in business for less than six months.

The dangers inherent in applying models derived from such limited data are all too evident. For example,

> It is unlikely that Dualists, who are seeking self employment, should receive high priority in terms of entrepreneurial training or grant aid . . . since their enterprises are likely to remain very small the required level of managerial competence is minimal and since the home is used as the business premises and little equipment is used small amounts of grant aid are all that is required for these businesses.
>
> (Cromie and Hayes 1988)

Given the lack of systematic research it is unclear what the justification is for such an implication. Many new businesses, women's and men's, are started up from home and in a small way. There is no work which indicates such limited preliminary classifications have any predictive value in terms of future sur- vival, growth or success. (Neither is there any systematic research which indicates women entrepreneurs are less successful than men.) Being judged purely in terms of conventional business objectives means only a small proportion of women from these studies (that is the 'Innovators') would have a real chance of gaining access to support services and finance. Some preliminary classification which is used as the basis for ascertaining 'suitability' or access to 'support' services will work against many entrepreneurs, both men and women. A substantial proportion of men facing redundancy or unemployment now set themselves up in business, not to 'create an empire' but purely to recreate the job that they lost (Brotherton *et al.* 1987b). Similar classification would exclude them from gaining access to 'support'.

What we have here are fixed categories which do not allow for movement/ change over time and which have no demonstrable predictive value. They would seem to work against promoting entrepeneurship and economic advancement, and are liable to reinforce stereotyping since the categories themselves are reflections of such stereotyping. The value of this work may come from its acknowledgement that entrepreneurs are not a homogeneous group. Some classification is likely to be extremely useful in evaluating an entrepreneur's position particularly in relation to gaining access to support, advice or training and in ensuring what is offered is in terms that the entrepreneur can benefit from.

There is additional research which supports this concern surrounding categorization and stereotyping and its possible negative outcomes and lends further support to the importance of 'evaluation' in relation to 'promoting'/'supporting' entrepreneurship.

Given that business failures are frequently associated with cash flow difficulties, financial management strategies was one of the many concerns of a two-year study of Nottingham entrepreneurs (Brotherton *et al.* 1987b). Businesses were categorized as either 'Strategic' or 'Operational' (these categories were not considered static and movement from 'Operational' to 'Strategic' was observed over the period of study). Being Strategic involved being forward-looking, predictive, using up-to-date financial information and having an awareness of the impact of decisions in one area of the business on others; for example, accepting orders and cash flow. Being Operational involved having a reactive approach, using historical financial information (for example, certified accounts) if any, and where decisions about a large order, for example, were taken on the basis of 'a big order is good business' without any calculations as to how this might affect the finances of the business. The Strategic approach is argued as being more likely to lead to survival and ultimate success than the Operational approach. In terms of strategies adopted, women were significantly different from men; 69 per cent of women adopted a Strategic approach, compared with about 33 per cent of men. The different approaches cannot be explained in terms of previous employment experience, which, for the men, meant a Strategic approach was likely to be associated with a background of experience of management, or financial management control. The Strategic women were less likely than the Strategic men to have had such a background. Although sampling problems are acknowledged as presenting difficulties, nevertheless these findings are a warning against supporting stereotypes. Explanations can be only speculative, however. Women's domestic roles do provide a range of valuable experiences upon which they may draw. In addition, the problems and barriers they face may mean they have to become more strategic in order to overcome them.

There are clear arguments for precisely this sort of study to be undertaken, concentrating on strategies that may help survival and ultimately success, as well as those which may help women and men overcome the varied range of problems faced in business ownership. Concern with the strategies women use to overcome problems they face has received more recent attention by the construction of case studies of women business owner/managers (Carter and Cannon 1988). The problems varied: they had to work hard to earn credibility with business colleagues, customers and employees; they were often under-capitalized; they frequently experienced hostile and negative attitudes from sources of finance; they often experienced role conflict and had to cope with less than supportive family attitudes.

The strategies used by these women to overcome such problems varied according to their attitudes and experience. Younger women tended to opt for training in business where they lacked management and business experience. Older women sometimes adopted a strategy of depersonalization, where they played down their femininity in order to gain credibility. Some women would exploit their femininity to their own advantage in certain situations.

Confrontation was used, although rarely. The most frequently encountered strategy was networking with other women in business.

Throughout this chapter, concern has been expressed over comparisons made or implied between women and men entrepreneurs, and some of the implications of such comparisons have been considered. A few more issues need to be raised. Comparisons are frequently made in such a way that serves to uphold and legitimize a male norm, and women are viewed as deviating from this norm (and deviation is clearly viewed as inferior). Given the balance of power in society residing in the male, an obvious strategy for women is to adopt the male norm. Clearly many women are doing precisely that and in some cases not only are adopting male behaviour but also are choosing not to have a family. Women remain undervalued, however, because they are women, almost regardless of whether they are seen to be deviating from the male or female norm. However, this situation of women's being undervalued is becoming less comprehensible than in previous decades in the face of the realities of women's increasing participation in the labour force and in self-employment and in the fact that women's breaks from the labour market are becoming increasingly shorter. Arguments concerning women's creating their own problems (for example, the 'lessons they learnt at their mother's knee' – in terms of their being less assertive, confident and so on) fail to acknowledge the responsibility society has in shaping an individual's experience – they conveniently, rather than convincingly, 'blame the victim'.

Comparisons are acceptable where they are used to broaden our understanding of phenomenon, not where they are used to uphold an ideological position which unfairly relegates certain individuals based on unrealistic assumptions stereotypes and conclusions.

As far as understanding entrepreneurship is concerned a number of steps need to be taken, including the many listed at the beginning of the chapter. The existing popular stereotype of the entrepreneur upholds tough, competitive, highly ambitious, motivated and determined behaviour in a male mould, which pursues, to the virtual exclusion of all else, profit, expansion and so on. We need now to accommodate and accept the range of backgrounds and motivations during new business formation (which have been clearly demonstrated to exist) in order to move forward and support entrepreneurship in an efficient and effective manner. The acceptance of 'competing' roles is very much needed to widen opportunities for all entrepreneurs. If we continue to promote entrepreneurship in its present form, which allows only for pursuing conventional entrepreneurial objectives and fails to account for the existence of entrepreneurship beyond a very narrow form, a large percentage of the business population will remain unsupported.

Prospects for the future?

A number of alternative prospects for entrepreneurship were proposed in the opening paragraph of the chapter. What conclusions might now be drawn and how might these be related to future prospects?

Entrepreneurship may allow escape from the confines of the formal labour market; however, women still face a number of gender-related barriers which they need to overcome. The quality of their lives may be somewhat improved in terms of personal achievement and independence, however, running a business is likely to increase women's work-load and they will, unlike men, remain largely unsupported by their husbands or 'partners' at present.

The restrictions of educational and employment experiences have already been documented. How consistent is this pattern of 'limitation' in relation to society's preparation of women for entrepreneurship? Child-rearing practices continue to transmit the dominant ideology (Grabrucker 1989; Hunt 1983). We are still raising little girls to be little girls and little boys to be little boys. Post-school and 'pre-labour market' experiences are consistent too, for example:

> there is not one factor tending to gender-conformity in the Youth Training Scheme but many, and that they are interrelated and unlikely to be corrected by superficial measures . . . the sexual discrimination that occurs is passive rather than active and in many cases it is unconscious. There is however clearly some conscious and active sex-specific selection going on in recruitment.
>
> (Cockburn, 1987)

Many of the chapters in Part III of this book illustrate that the pattern of 'limitation' is consistent: women are still being prepared primarily for the presumed traditional roles they will undertake. The question needs to be asked whether the caring supportive role women generally offer is likely to facilitate running a business? On the one hand it means women come to entre-preneurship with a range of important skills, concerning communication and organization, for example. On the other hand it may leave women predisposed to take, for example, a less than assertive approach in dealing with a variety of individuals like bank managers, customers and employees. In terms of women's typical labour market experiences, they are less likely than men to have had positions and responsibilities in employment which prepare them well to deal with some aspects of their business.

Is society then ready to encourage women into entrepreneurship?

Official views still regard the spheres of work and home as strictly separate: income maintenance, services for children/elderly/handicapped, continue to be based on the assumption that the primary role of women is based in the home and in the care of the family, while the primary role of men is in the field of formal employment (e.g. Land 1978). Projected demographical changes and their likely consequences (that is the increased demands of industry due to the 'skills shortage') are very unlikely to improve the prospects of women being better encouraged, prepared and supported in entrepreneurship; in fact, the consequences might be negative. For example, over the period 1985–95 in the UK there will be a drop of 1.1 million in the age range 15–19 (EOC 1988) and industry is expected to make considerable efforts to attract more women into the work-force. Similarly an expected increase of 50 per cent in the over-65 age group between 1985 and 2035 (from 8.4 million to 12.4 million: EOC 1988) will have a number of implications for women: not only will this increase constraints on women's employment opportunities due to inadequate social service provision (and the assumption that women, not men, look after ageing relatives) but it may increase demand for employees (many of whom are women) within the sectors which provide care for this elderly section of the population. Childcare provision in this country remains grossly inadequate. Attitudes women experience from a variety of sources – partners/husbands, family, financial institutions, support and advisory services – are, in the main, less than supportive. At present, there is little to encourage optimism about potential for change which will improve the situation for women entrepreneurs.

How then might the prospects for women in entrepreneurship be improved?

At the level of the individual action by women entrepreneurs themselves, a number of strategies should prove useful. Better preparation for entrepreneurship is one alternative: by undertaking training and pursuing support and advice. Where little seems to be available or is not particularly accessible, continued enquiry may stimulate improved provision or, at least, awareness of a need. Women may need to adopt particular strategies consciously in order to overcome barriers. Pressure may force choices to adopting male behaviour, using confrontation, sublimating gender, or emphasizing femininity to their advantage. Although no doubt pragmatic in particular circumstances, it seems unlikely that these strategies have much potential for women being perceived more credibly (which would seem to be an important long-term goal). Support groups in a variety of forms would seem to provide a valuable way forward, as well as networking other business women (facilitated by membership of particular women's business organizations). Marketing and public relations, which raise awareness and maintain the profile of women entrepreneurs, are essential in order to effect changes in attitudes to women by both sexes.

At the broader 'collective' level, it is more difficult to envisage from where the moving force for change will come. As the numbers of women in business continue to increase, so will recognition of their social importance. This recognition, even if it is based purely on economic imperatives, should effect change. Those professional services offering support to businesses (banks, accountants and so on) might realize that they are failing to exploit a considerable market opportunity. There is a significant role to be played here in terms of 'training' or awareness courses, which should also improve sensitivity to the needs of entrepreneurs in general. A more aware (and financially motivated) climate is likely to respond better to a range of needs like improved child-care provision and appropriately targeted tax benefits. Eventually change will filter into the educational system, including post-school training.

Entrepreneurship may offer potential for women but it is a potential which is, as yet, largely unrealized. It is time for the driving force of economic imperatives in our society to outweigh the limitations of traditional attitudes towards women in general and women entrepreneurs in particular.

Notes

1 This pattern of increasing numbers of women entering self-employment is not purely a UK phenomenon: it is apparent elsewhere in the world (Halpern and Szurek 1987; USA Small Business Administration 1985).
2 Working women are not a homogeneous group. These comments are, of necessity, generalizing, but at the level of policy account needs to be taken of differences in culture and class.
3 The point has already been made about the difficulties of making comparisons and interpreting research studies. To avoid endless qualification in discussion, the reader is directed to the original source material.

References

Birley, S., Moss, C. and Saunders, P. (1986) The differences between small firms started by male and female entrepreneurs who attended small business courses, in R. Ronstadt, J. A. Hornaday, R. Peterson and K. H. Vesper (eds) *Frontiers of Entrepreneurship Research 1986*, Proceedings of the Sixth Annual Babson College Entrepreneurship Research Conference, Babson College, Wellesley, Mass.

Boswell, J. (1973) *The Rise and Decline of Small Firms*, London: Allen & Unwin.

Brotherton, C., Leather, P. and Simpson, S. M (1986) Social psychological dimensions in job creation, Paper delivered to the Occupational Conference of the British Psychological Society, University of Nottingham, January.

—— (1987a) Job creation: new work for women?, *Work and Stress*, 1, 3: 249–59.

—— (1987b) *Information Technology in the Development of Nottingham's Inner City: An Evaluation of the Advanced Business Centre*, Final Report to the Manpower Services Commission, Dept. of Psychology, University of Nottingham.

Bruegel, I. (1979) Women as a reserve army of labour: a note on recent British experience, *Feminist Review*, 3: 12–23.

Bruno, A. V. and Tyjebee, T. T. (1982) The environment for entrepreneurship, in C. A. Kent, D. L. Sexton and K. H. Vesper (eds) *Encyclopaedia of Entrepreneurship*, Englewood Cliffs, NJ: Prentice-Hall.

Byrne, E. M. (1978) *Women and Education*, London: Tavistock.

Carter, S. and Cannon, T. (1988) *Female Entrepreneurs: A Study of Female Business Owners; their Motivations, Experiences and Strategies for Success*, London: Department of Employment Research Paper, no 65.

Cockburn, C. (1987) *Two-Track Training: Sex Inequalities and the YTS*, Basingstoke: Macmillan Education.

Cooper C. L. and Davidson, M. J. (1984) *Women in Management*, London: Heinemann.

Coyle, A. (1984) *Redundant Women*, London: Women's Press.

Creigh, S. (1986) Self-employment in Britain: results from the Labour Force Surveys 1981–1984, *Employment Gazette*, June: 183–94.

Cromie, S. and Hayes, J. (1988) Towards a typology of female entrepreneurs, *Sociological Review*, 36, 1: 42–6

Employment Gazette (1988) 1987 Labour Force Survey – Preliminary Results, London: Department of Employment, March.

Epstein, T. S. (1989) Female petty-entrepreneurs and their multiple roles, Paper presented to the Women in Enterprise/University of Bradford Women Entrepreneurs Conference, University of Bradford, April.

EOC (Equal Opportunities Commission) (1988) *Women and Men in Britain: A Research Profile*, London: HMSO.

Goffee, R. and Scase, R. (1985) *Women in Charge*, London: Allen & Unwin.

Gomolka, E. (1977) Characteristics of minority international and small business enterprises, *American Journal of Small Business*, July: 178–84.

Grabrucker, M. (1989) *There's a good girl*, London: Women's Press.

Hakim, C. (1979) *Occupational Segregation: A Comparative Study of the Degree and Pattern of the Differentiation between Men's and Women's Work in Britain, the United States and Other Countries*, Research Paper no 9, London: Department of Employment.

Halpern, M. (1989) Business creation by women, and financing, Paper sent for presentation to the Women in Enterprise/University of Bradford Women Entrepreneurs Conference, University of Bradford, April.

Halpern, M. and Szurek, J. (1987) Women Entrepreneurs: motivations, situation and perspectives, Summary of study conducted for the EEC, September.

Hisrich, R. D. (1986) The woman entrepreneur: characteristics, skills, problems, and prescriptions for success, in D. L. Sexton and R. W. Smilor (eds) *The Art and Science of Entrepreneurship*, Cambridge, Mass: Ballinger.

Hisrich, R. D. and Brush, C. (1983) The women entrepreneur: implications of family, educational and occupational experience, *Frontiers of Entrepreneurship Research*, Babson Park, Mass: 255–70.

Hisrich, R. D. and O'Brien, M. (1981) The women entrepreneur from a business and sociological perspective, *Frontiers of Entrepreneurship Research*, Babson Park, Mass: 21–39.

Hisrich, R. D. and O'Cinneide, B. (1986) The Irish entrepreneur: characteristics, problems and future success, in R. Ronstadt, J. A. Hornaday, R. Peterson and K. H. Vesper (eds) *Frontiers of Entrepreneurship Research 1986*, Proceedings of the Sixth Annual Babson College Entrepreneurship Research Conference, Babson College, Wellesley, Mass.

Holland, J. (1980) *Work and Women*, Bedford Way Papers no 6, University of London Institute of Education.

Hornaday, J. A. and Aboud, J. (1971) Characteristics of successful entrepreneurs, *Personnel Psychology*, 24, 2: 42–5.

Hunt, P. (1983) *Gender and Class Consciousness*, London: Macmillan.

Hunt, J. (1982) A woman's place is in her union, in J. West (ed.) *Work, Women and the Labour Market*, London: Routledge & Kegan Paul.

Hymounts, C. (1986) The corporate women – the glass ceiling, *Wall Street Journal*, Dec. 7, 1986: 7.

Interagency Committee on Women's Business Enterprise (1980) *Annual Report to the President*, Washington, DC: US Government Printing Office.

Johnson, S. and Storey, D. (1989) Male and female entrepreneurs and their businesses: a comparative study, Paper presented to the Women in Enterprise/University of Bradford Women Entrepreneurs Conference, University of Bradford, April.

Kets de Vries, M. F. R. (1977) The entrepreneurial personality: a person at the crossroads, *Journal of Management Studies*, 14, 1: 34–57.

Koper, G. (1989) Women entrepreneurs and business credit granting: constraints and possibilities, Paper presented to the Women in Enterprise/University of Bradford Women Entrepreneurs Conference, University of Bradford, April.

Land, H. (1978) Sex-role stereotyping in the social security and income tax systems, in T. Chetwynd O. Hornett (eds) *The Sex Role System*, London: Routledge & Kegan Paul.

McClelland, D. C. (1961) *The Achieving Society*, Princeton, NJ: Van Nostrand.

Martin, J. and Roberts, C. (1984) *Women and Employment: A Lifetime Perspective*, London: Department of Employment and Office of Population Censuses and Surveys, HMSO.

Pellegrino, E. T. and Reece, B. L. (1982) Perceived formative and operational problems encountered by female entrepreneurs in retail and service firms, *Journal of Small Business Management*, April: 15–24.

Ronstadt, R., Hornaday, J. A., Peterson, R. and Vesper, K. H. (eds) (1986) *Frontiers of Entrepreneuring Research 1986*, Proceedings of the Sixth Annual Babson College Entrepreneurship Research Conference, Babson College, Wellesley, Mass.

Scase, R. and Goffee, R. (1980a) *The Real World of the Small Business Owner*, London: Croom Helm.

—— (1980b) Home life in a small business, *New Society*, 30, October: 52–3.

—— (1982) *The Entrepreneurial Middle Class*, London: Croom Helm.

Schreier, J. (1975) The female entrepreneur: a pilot study, Centre for Venture Management, Milwaukee, Wisconsin.

Schumpeter, J. A. (1954) *The Theory of Economic Development*, Cambridge, Mass: Harvard University Press.

Schwartz, E. B. (1979) Entrepreneurship: a new female frontier, *Journal of Contemporary Business*, Winter: 47–76.

Simpson, S. M. and Pearson, E. (1989) Multiple roles and conflict: high hurdles for women entrepreneurs? Paper presented to the Women in Enterprise/ University of Bradford Women Entrepreneurs Conference, University of Bradford, April.

Simpson, S. M., Brotherton, C. J. and Leather, P. J. (1986) The small business boom: social context and social construction, Paper delivered to the British Psychological Society Social Psychology Section Annual Conference, University of Sussex, September.

Sinfield, A. (1981) *What Unemployment Means*, Oxford: Martin Robertson.

Stanworth, M. (1988) *Gender and Schooling*, London: Hutchinson in association with the Explorations in Feminism Collective.

Stanworth, J. and Curran, J. (1973) *Management Motivation in the Smaller Business*, Aldershot, Hants: Gower.

Stevenson, L. (1983) *An Investigation into the Entrepreneurial Experience of Women*, ASAC Proceedings, Vancouver.

Turner, C. (1989) Support for women entrepreneurs across the member-states of the EEC, Paper presented to the Women in Enterprise/University of Bradford Women Entrepreneurs Conference, University of Bradford, April.

Truman, C. (1989) Women and local enterprise agencies, Paper presented to the Women in Enterprise/University of Bradford Women Entrepreneurs Conference, University of Bradford, April.

USA Small Business Administration (1985) *The State of Small Business*, Washington DC: US Government Printing Office.

Wainwright, H. (1978) Women and the division of labour, in P. Abrams (ed.) *Work, Urbanism and Inequality: UK Society Today*, London: Weidenfeld & Nicolson.

Watkins, J. and Watkins, D. (1983) Training needs and the female entrepreneur, Paper presented to the Sixth Annual UK Small Business Conference, Durham, September.

—— (1986) The female entrepreneur: her background and determinants of business choice – some British data, in J. Curran, J. Stanworth and D. Watkins (eds) *The Survival of the Small Firm*, Vol. 1: the Economics of Survival and Entrepreneurship, Aldershot, Hants: Gower.

Webb, M. (1982) The labour market, in I. Reid and E. Wormald (eds) *Sex Differences in Britain*, London: Grant McIntyre.

Weiner, G. (1987) *Just a Bunch of Girls*, Milton Keynes: Open University Press.

West, J. (ed.) (1982) *Work, Women and the Labour Market*, London: Routledge & Kegan Paul.

WNC (Women's National Commission) (1983) *Report on Secondary Education*, London: WNC.

10 | Women doctors
Jenny Firth-Cozens

I recently lost my first baby at 37 weeks. I had just begun my maternity leave and at the end of the three months I was going to take up a consultant's post. My first horrified thought when they told me the baby was dead was, 'Will that mean I have to go back to being a senior registrar?' My consultant rang me the next day to ask if I'd now be able to do a locum, and the hospital personnel officer became irritable and said he'd not had to deal with this before and it was going to be very complicated.

(Female junior hospital doctor)

The one topic that exceeds all others in the literature on women doctors is that of stress – and of suicide in particular. This chapter will review the reports that this group of women are particularly vulnerable and go on to consider what the sources of this stress might be.

Are women doctors more stressed than men?

In order to answer this question with any accuracy we need to consider doctors at various points in their careers and especially to take into account any differences between the sexes during their early training.

Most US studies have reported higher levels of perceived strain in female students when compared with their male counterparts, whether they report use of mental health services (Davidson 1978), or assessments by question-naire (Lloyd and Gartrell 1981; 1984). Since these differences do not appear on intake (Notman et al. 1984) but rather tend to appear and increase during the first six months (Lloyd and Gartrell 1981), it seems they are due, at least in part, to the medical student environment itself.

The differences that occur at various career points were also pointed out by Yogev and Harris (1983). They compared fifteen women resident paediatri-cians, fifteen non-medical academics of similar age and marital status, and fifteen consultant paediatricians. The residents had a significantly lower level of work satisfaction than the others and their self-concept was more negative. Of course, the extreme stress of the junior residency years, and of the first postgraduate year in particular, has featured in a number of studies of both men and women (Reuben 1985; Hsu and Marshall 1987; Firth-Cozens 1987).

Nevertheless, the rates for depression are elevated still higher in women: Hsu and Marshall (1987) found that they were one and a half times more likely than men to be classified as depressed and three times as likely to fall into the severely depressed category. Rates were particularly high in the first post-graduate year. Firth-Cozens (1987) followed a group of 170 fourth-year medical students through to their first postgraduate year. No significant sex differences in stress levels or in job satisfaction and perceptions were found on either occasion, but as junior doctors, the women were significantly more depressed. Hurwitz *et al.* (1987) reported single female doctors as being particularly at risk for impairment (compared to married men and women and single men). In a questionnaire study given at regular intervals throughout the first postgraduate year, women were found to be significantly more depressed and lonely that their male colleagues (Elliot and Girard 1986), though their satisfaction with their career choice, their perceived competence, and their reported levels of fatigue did not differ.

In comparison with other professional groups, women doctors again suffer more stress: Welner *et al.* (1979) interviewed 111 women doctors and 103 women PhDs for the presence of psychiatric illness, and found that 51 per cent of the doctors compared to 32 per cent of the PhDs were diagnosed as having primary affective disorder.

In Britain, however, Salmons (1983) reported no significant differences in psychiatric morbidity between male and female medical students and no female student was reported as committing suicide (although the numbers for both sexes may have been artificially low since, for much of the period covered by the survey, suicide remained an illegal act and so may have been reported as accidental death). This is in sharp constrast to the Pepitone-Arreola-Rockwell *et al.* (1981) study reported earlier, which found that the suicide rate of women medical students was up to four times the rate of age-mates, an identical rate found by Pitts *et al.* (1961) for women physicians. However, there are always problems in comparing the rates of what is a relatively small group (women physicians in the 1970s) with the rates of the millions of women in the general population, especially as the two groups will differ in important ways in addition to size: for example a large proportion of the general population group will not be working and will have lower educational attainment (Carlson and Miller 1981).

A Swedish study (Arnetz *et al.* 1987) has gone some way towards addressing these problems by studying rates over ten years (thus increasing the numbers) and by additionally comparing women doctors to academics who would have a similar educational and socio-economic background. They found that, although male doctors had a similar rate to the general population and an enhanced rate when compared to other academics, female doctors had el-evated rates compared both to the general population and to other academics, though the difference is not quite so great when the comparison is with female academics only, indicating that both groups of women may have suicidal risk factors in common.

Of course, large-scale surveys usually find that women report more psycho-logical symptoms of distress than men do (Banks and Jackson 1982), though if subjects are questioned when at the same stage in life development (that is before marriage and children), these differences do not appear (Jenkins 1985;. Firth 1986). The research reviewed seems to confirm that women begin their medical training with no more psychological symptoms than men do, but their differences occur and increase at least during the student and residency years. Research on more senior doctors is sparse. Despite any limitations in interpretation, it seems clear that women doctors are an occupational group especially at risk for depression and suicide. Various writers have made suggestions as to why women in medicine may suffer especially in this way.

Sources of stress

In 1987 I sent out 92 questionnaires to women doctors in their first postgraduate year, asking them to answer questions concerning symptoms (the depression scale of the SCL-90: Derogatis *et al.* 1973), and concerning the levels and frequencies of perceived stress for a number of items which I had taken from previous literature (this study is reported fully in Firth-Cozens, 1990). There were 70 returns and the mean item depression score was 1.43. This is significantly higher than the overall mean of 1.14 in my earlier study of male and female junior house officers where the women had scored significantly higher at 1.29 (Firth-Cozens 1987). Using the clinically valid cut-off of 1.5, 32 (46 per cent) of these women were showing levels indicative of depression, and 5 (7 per cent) were reporting thoughts of ending their lives. Why such extremely high scores were received for this particular group was not apparent but it is not dissimilar to the depression rate of 51 per cent found by Welner *et al.* (1979).

It was clear that the greatest stressor, both in terms of frequency and level, was the conflict these women had between their careers and their personal life, and the level of perceived stress caused by this was highly related to depression (0.42, $p < 0.001$). The stressor creating the next highest level of stress was sexual harassment at work, though it was the least frequent. While the lack of senior female role models was high in frequency, it did not cause a high level of stress; a similar pattern existed for sexual stereotyping by colleagues ('women can't do X'; 'women makes good Xs', etc.). Although mean scores were low for both frequency and level, where women felt discriminated against they were more depressed ($r = 0.31$, $p < 0.01$). The only other category both high and related to depression is prejudice from patients ($r = 0.39$, $p < 0.01$). These stressors and others will be considered below in more detail.

Conflicts between career and family

As women progress through their medical training it must become quite apparent to them that, despite half their intake being female and large numbers of their sex doing extremely well in assessments, still very few reach consultancy grades in hospital medicine or are unrestricted principals in general practice. For example, Department of Health statistics show that 7.2 per cent of women were consultants in 1970 and 13.5 per cent in 1986. Although the proportions are almost doubled, it is still less than half what would be expected from the 24–31 per cent who graduated between 1970 and 1975 and would have been eligible for consultancy posts. In 1986 the proportion of women in various specialities was as follows: 37 per cent in child psychiatry, 19 per cent in anaesthetics and the same in paediatrics, and 17 per cent in general psychiatry. Only 7 per cent of cardiologists and 0.6 per cent of general surgeons were women. They are, however, over-represented in other branches of medicine; for example in 1985, 60 per cent of community health doctors were women, though only 26 per cent of district medical officers (the top grade) were women (Smyth 1988; Allen 1988). Cartwright (1987), reviewing US trends, concludes that 'women are choosing the same specialities they did in the past, for practically the same reasons'. Bauder-Nishita (1980) reported that, in California at least, women are still mainly found in the lower-status and traditionally nurturant specialties. Very small proportions of women doctors hold positions of power as deans, professors, or within the Royal Colleges or medical societies; for example, by 1985 only 9 per cent had seats on College councils and central policy committees. These data suggest that women are giving up medicine or many branches of it after qualifying, or that there is a bias against women in senior posts in certain medical specialties.

Within ten years of qualification 85 per cent of married female graduates have children (Stephen 1987). Becoming a consultant means working around 85 hours a week for 12 years or more; for doctors (male or female) to have families during those main reproductive years, it seems there must still exist the career assumption that someone else is at home doing at least minimal care-taking. The General Household Survey of 1986 showed that women generally still have less free time than men whether they work full- or part-time; that is they are still doing considerably more of what the survey calls 'essential activities' than men are. In addition women doctors – and women health workers in general – spending the day in a caring role will, if they have a family, need to spend their free time also nurturing others.

With evidence for bias being at best anecdotal, the most compelling explanation for the career inequalities is that women doctors make compromises in their career paths sometimes for marriage and more often for children. Schermerhorn *et al.* (1986) found that the importance of 'compatibility with the spouse's career preference' in choosing a career specialty in medicine increased with their respondants' ages. Berquist *et al.* (1985) found that specialty choice was heavily influenced by patient contact, the family, and working fewer hours. The compromises may be seen as due to·the woman doctor herself, to her partner (if she is in a relationship), to her children, or to a career path and training unsuitable for those who want children and desire a less than minimal parenting role; whatever their cause, they come after a training that is longer and that leaves less time for self-development than other professions. It is not surprising that such large personal compromises might cause resentment and unhappiness as aspirations fade.

One woman client of mine who presented with severe depression and suicidal ideation had planned throughout her training to go into Accident and Emergency. Her husband was an engineer and travelled often, so when she had her first child, she found herself unable to cope with the long on-call duties, and began to train as a general practitioner. Her second daughter was born when she had been accepted in a practice for a year, and at the same time her husband left her. Despite huge efforts to maintain her work-load and her family, her principal refused to make allowances, and she had finally decided to move to family planning as a relatively easy (despite numerous evening clinics) option. Since women are more likely to blame themselves when things go wrong, she attributed her present position (which she despised) as due entirely to herself and her lack of abilities, and the low self-confidence which resulted from this caused her considerable problems in her present job. Learning to be angry at the system and becoming politicized, rather than blaming herself, helped her confidence; her career, although still a compromise, flourished.

These conflicts between career and family have been reported by a number of writers (e.g. Notman and Nadelson 1973; Cartwright 1987; Allen 1988) and it was clearly the most important stressor for the women in my study (Firth-Cozens 1990). The following additional remarks about the causes of stress were made:

> Children – having them and looking after them, and the way they ruin your career.

> Being married – running a household with so little time at home.

> I feel the greatest stress arises from the problems related to personal life. The possibility of pursuing a hospital career and having a family is almost zero.

> The immediate disruption of my career . . . by unplanned pregnancy – no compromises/arrangements made, etc.

> Stress of having to plan a family – i.e. having to decide between a family and career at some point. Difficult to decide when, etc.

What seems most important about these comments is that each one primarily attributes stress to people or circumstances outside of the career structure. Only the last few words hint that change within the structure might be possible. The comments confirm for me the feelings I have had from workshops with and talks to doctors in Britain that the training and career path is carved in tablets of stone. The fact that, since the Sex Discrimination Act 1975, half the annual entrants to medical training are now women, might be thought to necessitate changes – not 'compromises' – towards a more flexible career path, but this seems to occur to doctors, both male and female, remarkably rarely. Isobel Allen's provocative interview study (Allen 1988) should have been the foundation for less rigidity, but a one-day meeting between doctors, researchers and the Department of Health was summed up by the latter as indicating a need for career counselling rather than any change in structure. The anger that was visible throughout the day was ignored, but might indicate that views are beginning to change.

Cartwright (1979) found that women deal with the conflict between career and family in three different ways. First, some become 'superwomen', often tackling a particularly difficult specialty, working full-time, and usually having children and a spouse. One would predict clinically that such a woman was pushed towards perfectionism (perhaps by the feeling that she was loved as a child only for what she could achieve) with the inevitable guilt if 'failure' is apparent to her, either in her job or in her family. Cartwright found such women to be the most vulnerable to stress. The second group were those who chose a 'career of limited ambition' where the career was given a lower priority than the family and usually involves breaks, part-time and salaried work. Although this is less stressful in terms of time-pressures and worries about child-care, such compromises can lead to depression over the loss of cherished hopes. The third group is what Cartwright calls 'medicine is my lust'. These women may choose not to marry or not to have children. She found their career satisfaction high, and stress low, despite some loneliness. In the USA they represent between 20 and 30 per cent of women doctors. Where this is a compromise (and I am not presuming that it is) it is one that men do not have to make. Without a family, women do at least have more time to nurture themselves rather than the common family situation where the woman provides caring for both partner and children, whether she works or not.

Prejudice and sexism

Despite the large numbers of women graduates, there is still a presumption in language, if nothing else, that doctors are male and that they have wives. Increasingly, it is true, junior doctors are given either sex, but consultants are consistently talked of as male. This is the position with the general public, the patients, the nursing staff and the doctors themselves. In workshops I have noticed that women are usually referred to as 'girls', a term whose usage most other professions have managed to at least reduce. What is worse to me is that, when I have pointed this out as a possible source of stress, both the men and the women on the whole do not see the point I am making. It is as if the medical profession, perhaps by the intensity and isolation of their training, has been untouched by the social changes that affect the rest of us – and its patients.

The prejudice against women doctors that used to exist (Engleman 1974) has been reduced, at least in some specialties such as obstetrics/gynaecology (Waller 1988). My research (Firth-Cozens 1990) showed them to be more empathic than male doctors and Waller (1988) found that women patients viewed women doctors as having a range of good qualities – assertiveness and initiative on the one hand, and tenderness and nurturance on the other. Nevertheless, prejudice from colleagues is still seen to exist. For example Franco *et al.* (1983), surveying the stress and attitudes to working with a pregnant colleague, found that one-third of respondents reported women of childbearing age to be a hiring risk. Men's attitudes were less accepting than women's. Prejudice was reported by 50 per cent of the women studied by Welner *et al.* (1979), though there were no significant differences on this between doctors and PhDs, and other chapters in this book make it clear that the problem is by no means simply a medical one.

An article by Poirier (1986) looks at this prejudice by studying the autobiographies of women doctors. She comes up with fascinating quotes which we hope might be largely of historical interest, for example 'Don't waste my time, silly girl. You're going to be married, my dear, and you will never make a doctor. How absurd can you be?', and a physician who 'liked to pinch [women students] and embarrass them', and a woman who reported sleeping fully clothed in the on-call room because her 'sleeping here bothered the men more than it bothered her'.

In my own study, (Firth-Cozens 1990), sexual harassment at work was low in frequency but high in terms of the stress it caused. Prejudice from patients was relatively high in frequency and the third highest stressor. Additional comments concerning more general prejudice were as follows:

Patients find it hard to understand you are a doctor (and not a nurse), [and you are] more questioned re ability than male doctors by nurses.

Female doctors also have to make a greater effort to nursing staff, as doctors are 'expected' to be male.

Various departments, e.g. ECG, X-ray, tend not to be so respectful to female doctors and . . . more frequently rude and uncooperative.

Can't get away with being so bad-tempered to nursing staff, especially when they haven't carried out instructions.

Conflict with female nursing staff.

Being treated as a nurse by nurses, therefore expected to be both doctor and nurse. Difficulty getting help doing some procedures as a female. Patients treating me like a nurse. Male colleagues expecting females to be married and looking after a husband.

It is clear from these comments that many doctors do consider they experience prejudice from various groups within the work-place. On the positive side, one doctor felt 'many female patients prefer a female doctor so it can be a great help'.

A slightly different point was raised by one respondent:

Relationships with nurses [are another stressor]. With senior nurses it seems to be easy enough but particularly with students and younger staff nurses I find some difficulty. There is such strong identification with other young women, yet the difference in our roles and disparity in power I find confusing. I think men probably find this easier to deal with.

Certainly most of the comments made above concern female nurses, but only this one points to the possible dynamic of the interaction – that the female junior doctor may be equally confused by her position in the hierarchy. The power relationships within the medical world (doctor/nurse/patient) very much reflect those in the family (father/mother/child) with the authority carried by the doctor/father and the nurturing by the nurse/mother. This might explain why women doctors, themselves socialized towards mothering, should elicit prejudice from those in the work environment when they show authority, and should feel less than comfortable in the role itself so long as it is interpreted and valued as one of authority alone. As women doctors become more senior, it is likely that they learn to choose between the nurturing/authority roles; for example, an interview study of twenty women doctors at times of organizational change reported stereotyping to be common. This complaint came because they were often called upon to be 'motherly' as well as medical (Brown and Klein 1988).

A lack of social support

Elliot and Girard (1986), having found women to be significantly more lonely, suggest that in a male-dominated profession they may be excluded from cliques of male colleagues, that there are few women faculty members and senior doctors in medicine, and that the need to delay or decide against childbearing may create 'a loss of synchronicity with women peers in general' (1986: 56). The lack of social support suggested by these factors and the resultant loneliness are certainly likely to be involved in higher rates of depression in women doctors, as they are in other groups (Brown and Harris 1978). One of my respondents wrote:

> Mess social life is based heavily around beer drinking, pool playing, dating nurses, etc. This makes me feel at times as if I am not a valuable person in social terms as I am not interested and miss out the mess.

Marriage, or any other stable partnership, has usually been found to be a support and possible buffer to stress (Cassel 1976; Cobb 1976). It may, however, cause extra stress if partners meet only infrequently, as they must during residency, especially as a recent study on the medical marriage found that satisfaction was related to the amount of time the couple spent talking to each other (Gabbard *et al.* 1987). Reports suggest that medical marriages (generally regarded as a male doctor and his wife) are relatively enduring compared to other professions, but are often unsatisfying (Vaillant *et al.* 1972; Garvey and Tuason 1979). Landau *et al.* (1986) found that over 40 per cent of the residents and fellows in their study reported serious marital problems, and 72 per cent of these believed them to be due to their work, while 61 per cent reported their partner agreed with this attribution.

In a study by Kelner and Rosenthal (1986) women doctors and their husbands were interviewed and most expressed negative feelings about the impact of their training on their relationship. The women expressed considerable anxiety about conflicting role obligations and again, most were planning to work in a field which reduced this impact. They reported that having children was an extra source of strain for women juniors; nevertheless, they considered that the

> benefits of marriage at this stage more than outweigh the disadvantages imposed by additional role obligations [though] the supportive function appears to be stronger . . . for males than for females.
>
> (Kelner and Rosenthal 1986: 23)

This was an interview study of only ten couples but a similar suggestion came from Hurwitz *et al.*'s (1987) empirical study of junior doctors, which showed single females were at a high risk for psychological impairment. These findings are contrary to those such as Gove's (1979), which showed that, within the general population, married women were more at risk than the unmarried, whereas it is unmarried men compared to married who are more at risk. All these potential stressors may be exacerbated within a medical marriage since dual-career marriages present special problems in themselves, especially in Britain, and a career in hospital medicine requires a number of geographical moves. Equally it may be possible that partners are more understanding within such a marriage. Fuller empirical testing is needed to see if married doctors are less stressed than unmarried, and whether this is particularly so for men, rather than for women, and whether having a spouse who is a doctor too is a benefit or a risk in terms of the experience of stress.

The implications for change

The overwhelming requirement to reduce stress for women doctors is to alter the career structure in ways which allow interruptions to the career path and periods of part-time working without an inevitable cost to the final career. New educational methods permit a number of ways that studying can be maintained at home where necessary; in addition, the medical curriculum has often been criticized as being indigestible (Albert and Coles 1988) and overloaded with facts (Reidbord 1983) and the very substance of what makes a good doctor lends itself to challenge.

It seems important, however, that any campaign for a less rigid career structure needs to be carried out by women and men working together. Although women have more pressing needs, male doctors have also argued that a fuller self-development demands access to experiences outside medicine. In a 'Personal View' column in the *British Medical Journal*, Charles Essex (1986) described his own career break when he taught English in Peru. He concludes:

> Different experiences are not guaranteed to broaden the mind. But to be denied the opportunity because of the singlemindedness required to ascend the career ladder will lead to a poverty of character. I think that it is to the detriment of all that it is becoming increasingly difficult for doctors to be vagrant in their careers.
>
> (Essex 1986: 693)

In the USA they are estimating an enormous surplus of doctors within the next few years (Tarlov 1981). Of course, this may result in unemployment, but it could equally be the impetus for extended and slowed down training with optional years off for both men and women.

In order to achieve such changes, it is vital that women gain positions of power on College committees and other decision-making bodies. This is best done not as a solitary woman, but in twos and threes to give support to each other. Wendy Savage (in a paper given to the Annual Conference of Women in Medicine) argued that the system of appointing consultants needs to be changed:

> At present the statutory committee is dominated by the consultant in post . . . and lay representation is from token people such as the Chairman of the Health Authority. We need more lay members who are from the community which the hospital serves and have experience of the services; that is, patient groups, the Community Health Council, as well as others with whom doctors work such as nurses, social workers and general practitioners.
>
> (Savage 1987)

The ambivalence of women towards power and competition, and the difficulties that female junior doctors experience with nurses, could be confronted in medical school through women's groups, and assertiveness training, and by courses such as the Tavistock Institute's Leicester Conference where participants are encouraged to find their authority and power within institutions. An increased presence of women at higher grades and on decision-making groups may help to encourage the position that medical practitioners can be authoritative, empathic and nurturing, given a supportive environment. This would be an advantage not only to women doctors and to patients, but also to many male doctors who feel they need to repress their more caring sides (Firth-Cozens 1987).

Considerably more research needs to be carried out concerning the reactions of the public towards women doctors, and their organizations could do much more to promote positive attitudes and to challenge sexism within the media.

Social support could be increased for hospital doctors by the creation of separate messes for women. I realize that this might be seen as a retrograde step by some, but the experiences of the women's movement has been that separate meeting-places and groups lead to greater confidence within the work-place. The loneliness that is likely to be experienced by those at the top of their profession can be reduced by systems of networking both within and outside of medicine, such as those which have been introduced by women managers.

The career of medicine is interesting and fulfilling to men and women alike. The problems that exist are almost all structural ones that can be changed. But first there needs to be an acknowledgement with a view to change by those in power that women are a necessary and important part of the work-force at all levels, and by women that they have as much to offer as men and an equal right to reach the top of the career for which they were trained.

References

Albert, J. S. and Coles, R. (1988) The indigestible curriculum, *Archives Internal Medicine*, 148; 277–8.

Allen, I. (1988) *Doctors and their Careers*, London: Policy Studies Institute.

Arnetz, B. B., Horte, L., Hedberg, A., Theorell, T., Allander, E. and Malker, H. (1987) *Acta Psychiatrica Scandinavia*, 75: 139–43.

Banks, M. H., Clegg, C. W., Jackson, P. R., Kemp, N. J., Stafford, E. M. and Wall, T. D. (1980) The use of the General Health Questionnaire as an indicator of mental health in occupational studies, *Journal of Occupational Psychology*, 53: 187–94.

——and Jackson, P. R. (1982) Unemployment and risk of minor psychiatric disorder in young people, *Psychological Medicine*, 12: 789–98.

Bauder-Nishita, J. (1980) Gender specific differentials of medical practice in California, *Women and Health*, 5: 5–15.

Berquist, S. R., Duchac, B. W., Schalin, V. A., Zastrow, J. F., Barr, V. L. and Borowiecki, T. (1985) Perceptions of freshman medical students of gender differences in medical specialty choice, *Journal of Medical Education*, 60: 379–83.

Brown, G. and Harris, T. (1978) *Social Origins of Depression: A Study of Psychiatric Disorder in Women*, London: Free Press.

Brown, S. and Klein, R. (1986) Women physicians: casualties of organizational stress, *Journal of the American Medical Women's Association*, 41: 79–81.

Carlson, G. A. and Miller, D. (1981) Suicide, affective disorder and women physicians, *American Journal of Psychiatry*, 138: 1,330–5.

Cartwright, L. (1979) The integrative challenges of the young woman doctor: step beyond the barriers, in *Proceedings of 18th Annual Conference on Research in Medical Education*, Association of American Medical Colleges, Washington, DC.

——(1987) Occupational stress in women physicians, in R. L. Payne and J. Firth-Cozens (eds) *Stress in Health Professionals*, Chichester: John Wiley.

Cassel, J. C. (1976) The contribution of the social environment to host resistance, *American Journal of Epidemiology*, 104: 107–23.

Cobb, S. (1976) Social support as a moderator of life stress, *Psychosomatic Medicine*, 38: 300–14.

Davidson, V. M. (1978) Coping styles of women medical students, *Journal of Medical Education*, 53: 902–7.

Derogatis, L. R., Lipman, R. S. and Covi, M. D. (1973) SCL-90: an outpatient psychiatric rating scale – preliminary report, *Psychopharmacological Bulletin*, 9: 13–20.

Elliot, D. L. and Girard, D. E. (1986) Gender and the emotional impact of internship, *Journal of the American Medical Women's Association*, 4: 54–6.

Engleman, E. G. (1974) Attitudes toward women physicians: a study of 500 clinic patients, *Western Journal of Medicine*, 120: 95–100.

Essex, C. (1986) Personal view, *British Medical Journal*, 293: 693.

Firth, J. (1986) Levels and sources of stress in medical students, *British Medical Journal*, 292: 1,177–80.

Firth-Cozens, J. (1987) Emotional distress in junior house officers, *British Medical Journal*, 293: 533–6.

——(1990) Sources of Stress in women junior house officers, *British Medical Journal*, 301: 89–91.

Franco, K., Evans, C. L., Best, A. P., Zrull, J. P. and Pizza, G. A. (1983) Conflicts associated with physicians' pregnancies, *American Journal of Psychiatry*, 140: 902–4.

Gabbard, G. O., Menninger, R. W. and Coyne, L. (1987) Sources of conflict in the medical marriage, *American Journal of Psychiatry*, 144: 567–72.

Garvey M. and Tuason, V. B. (1979) Physician marriages, *Journal of Clinical Psychiatry*, 40: 129–31.

Gove, W. R. (1979) Sex, marital status, and psychiatric treatment: a research note, *Social Forces*, 58: 89–93.

Hsu, K. and Marshall, V. (1987) Prevalence of depression and distress in a large sample of Canadian residents, interns and Fellows, *American Journal of Psychiatry*, 144: 1,561–6.

Hurwitz, T. A., Beiser, M., Nichol, H., Patrick, L. and Kozak, J. (1987) Impaired interns and residents, *Canadian Journal of Psychiatry*, 32: 165–9.

Jenkins, R. (1985) Sex differences in minor psychiatric morbidity, *Psychological Medicine*: supplement 5.

Kelner, M. and Rosenthal, C. (1986) Postgraduate medical training, stress and marriage, *Canadian Journal of Psychiatry*, 31: 22–4.

Landau, C., Hall, S., Wartman, S. and Macko, M. (1986) Stress in social and family relationships during the medical residency, *Journal of Medical Education*, 61: 654–60.

Lloyd, C. and Gartrell, N. K. (1981) Sex differences in student mental health, *American Journal of Psychiatry*, 138: 1,346–51.

—— (1984) Psychiatric symptoms in medical students, *Comprehensive Psychiatry*, 25: 552–65.

Notman, M. T. and Nadelson, C. G. (1973) Medicine: a career conflict for women, *American Journal of Psychiatry*, 130: 1,123–7.

Notman, M. T., Salt, P. and Nadelson, C. G. (1984) Stress and adaptation in medical students: who is most vulnerable?, *Comprehensive Psychiatry*, 25: 355–66.

Pepitone-Arreola-Rockwell, F., Rockwell, D. and Core, N. (1981) Fifty-two medical student suicides, *American Journal of Psychiatry*, 138: 198–201.

Pitts, F. N., Winokur, G. and Stewart, M. A. (1961) Psychiatric syndromes, anxiety symptoms, and response to stress in medical students, *American Journal of Psychiatry*, 118: 333–40.

Poirier, S. (1986) Role stress in medical education: a literary perspective, *Journal of the American Medical Women's Association*, 41: 82–6.

Reidbord, S. P. (1983) Psychological perspectives on iatrogenic physician impairment, *The Pharos*, 2–8.

Reuben, D. B. (1985) Depressive symptoms in medical house officers: effects of level of training and work rotation, *Archives Internal Medicine*, 145: 286–8.

Salmons, P. H. (1983) Psychiatric problems of medical students, *British Journal of Psychiatry*, 143: 505–8.

Savage, W. (1987) What a consultant should be in the 1990s, *Papers of 7th Annual Conference of Women in Medicine*.

Schermerhorn, G. R., Colliver, J., Verhulst, S. and Schmidt, E. (1986) Factors that influence career patterns of women physicians, *Journal of the American Medical Women's Association*, 41: 74–8.

Smyth, E. (1988) Falling off the ladder, *BMA News Review*, 14: 17.

Stephen, P. J. (1987) Career patterns of women medical graduates, 1974–1984, *Medical Education*, 21: 255–9.

Tarlov, A. (1981) *NA Summary Report of the Graduate Medical Education National Advisory Committee, Vol. 1*, DHHS Publication no. 81–651, US Government Printing Office, Washington, DC.

Vaillant, G., Sobowale, N. C. and McArthur, C. (1972) Some psychological vulnerabilities of physicians, *New England Journal of Medicine*, 287: 372–5.

Waller, K. (1988) Women doctors for women patients?, *British Journal of Medical Psychology*, 61: 124–36.

Welner, A., Marten, S., Wochnick, E., Davis, M., Fishman, R. and Clayton, P. (1979) Psychiatric disorders among professional women, *Archives of General Psychiatry*, 36: 169–73.

Yogev, S. and Harris S. (1983) Woman physicians during residency years: workload, work satisfaction and self concept, *Social Science and Medicine*, 17: 837–41.

11 | Computing: an ideal occupation for women?

Peggy Newton

Introduction

Computing appears to be an ideal occupation for women. It's clean and modern and, unlike engineering, it evokes no images of dirty workshops or heavy lifting. It requires a careful approach and attention to detail – skills in which women excel (Linn 1985). The work is often flexible and increasingly allows the possibility of working from home. Yet in recent years the proportion of women entering computing has dropped rapidly. Anecdotal evidence suggests that in the late 1950s and early 1960s almost half the programmers and system analysts were women, whereas by the mid-1980s the figure had dropped to about one-fifth (Lockheed 1985; Newton and Haslam 1988). The trend is even more precipitous in the number of young women studying computer science at universities. In 1977 women accounted for almost a quarter of university entrants in computer science in the UK, whereas ten years later women represented a bare 10 per cent of first-year students (Universities Statistical Record 1988). A stark example of this phenomenon was reported by Southampton University, which had 33 per cent women students on its computing courses in 1978–79 and no female students on their computing courses by 1985–86 (Lovegrove and Hall 1987).

How can this trend be explained? One possibility is that the nature of computing has changed and that girls and women no longer have the intellectual abilities required for computing. However, this seems an unlikely explanation. It does not fit with the body of evidence suggesting a large overlap in the cognitive abilities between females and males (Maccoby and Jacklin 1975). It also contradicts findings from a large survey of US schoolchildren suggesting that girls are superior to boys in several specific areas of programming (Anderson 1987) and studies of children's cognitive abilities showing no gender differences in procedural thinking, which appears to be an important aspect of computer programming (Kiesler *et al.* 1985).

Another possible explanation is that women are turning away from scientific and technological subjects. However, university admission statistics do not support this interpretation. Between 1977 and 1987 there were increases in the proportion of women entering courses in physics, chemistry and engineering. Only the figure for mathematics remained constant at approximately 30 per cent over the ten-year period (Universities Statistical Record 1988).

A third possibility is that girls have been systematically discouraged from applying for courses in computing by their previous experience of computers and their perceptions of computing as a career. This strikes me as the most likely explanation and is the one which will be explored in this chapter. My focus is on the UK, since both the rate of decline and the low proportion of women in the industry are not paralleled in the USA, France and the Far East (*Business Week* 1989; Virgo 1989). I shall argue that several trends have converged to make computing appear an unsuitable occupation for women in the UK. Although these trends are in a large sense societal, they have had a particularly potent effect on adolescent girls when they are faced with important career choices in secondary school.

Changes in computing and its image

The computing industry has changed rapidly in size, in organization and in its public image. Twenty years ago computing was an unknown field to most members of the public. Computers were the province of large organizations, and relatively few people had extensive experience of computers before entering the field. The popular view of computing was neutral and bureaucratic, tied up with large machines, punched cards and the notion that 'you're just a number'. This remote image contrasts sharply with today, where small personal computers are featured in magazines, advertised on television and sold in high street shops. As I shall argue below, the image of computing has become predominantly a male image – tied up with notions of 'boys' toys', of male power and of fascination with technology.

The growth of imagery associated with computers can be seen both in popular culture and in the development of a specialized computer culture. In the everyday world computers have acquired a wealth of cultural meanings, ranging from usage of terms like 'user friendly' to notions of the antisocial world of the hacker and destructive computer games. The development of a specialized computer culture is seen clearly in the barrier of mysterious jargon: RAM, ROM, bit, byte, bus, ASCII, filestore, modem, and so on. Kiesler *et al.* (1985) argue that computing is far more than a set of skills. They suggest that it is a culture 'embedded in a social system, consisting of shared values and norms, a special vocabulary and humour, status and prestige, ordering and differentiation of members from nonmembers' (1985: 453). They contend that initial socialization to this culture is very important and that to become effective in using computers requires both social knowledge of the computer culture and technical knowledge of computers as machines.

Professionalization of computing

With the growth of the computer industry, the knowledge associated with computing has become formalized. In the early days entrants required few, if any, formal qualifications. Many employers trained their own staff and relied on tests of programming aptitude to select their trainees.[1] Although some of these arrangements still pertain, there are now a large number of potential qualifications in computing, including GCSEs, A levels, ONDs, HNDs, City and Guilds, and degrees in computer science. As the field has expanded it has become increasingly professionalized, with the British Computer Society's being empowered to inspect educational institutions and set up formal standards. It may be argued that these changes have enhanced the status of the profession and are characteristic of most professional fields (Perkin 1989; Johnson 1972); however, they have served to limit the number of women and other non-traditional applicants by making entry to the field appear to be lengthy and circumscribed.

Although it is still possible for graduates to enter computing with any degree, recent data suggest that women entering the industry usually have qualifications in computing or an allied field, suggesting an early commitment to computing as a career. In contrast male applicants for computing jobs come from a much wider range of the disciplines, and the majority are from non-scientific backgrounds (Virgo 1989). This pattern provides evidence that women regard computing as a 'man's' world'. To enter this increasingly male-dominated field they feel the need for the record of achievement and feelings of confidence provided by formal qualifications, whereas men are likely to assume that they are naturally 'good at computers'.

How have computers become so clearly a male preserve? Some of the forces which contributed to the gendering of computing clearly reflect the wider cultural influences already discussed; however, I shall argue that one of the most important events influencing young women during that time was the introduction of computers in secondary schools. To understand the basis for this statement it is necessary to look at how and why computers were introduced in schools in the UK.

Computers in secondary schools

Most schools acquired computers under the Micros in Schools Scheme, which began in secondary schools in 1980. Sponsored by the Department of Trade and Industry, the scheme was extended to primary schools in 1982 with the goal of a 'micro in every school' (EOC 1983). This goal was largely achieved in secondary schools by 1984 when 98 per cent of schools reported having at least one microcomputer (BBC 1985). Although the programme was publicized as an educational reform and was accompanied by the DES-sponsored Microelectronics Education Project (MEP), the programme had clear commercial and industrial aims. It can be argued that the scheme was more concerned with supporting the ailing British computer industry and in providing favourable publicity for the sponsoring department than in producing meaningful educational change. Certainly the scheme has been repeatedly criticized for being too rapid and for having neglected many of the educational implications of introducing computers. In their evaluation of the scheme, the Centre for Applied Research in Education noted, 'It was widely welcomed as an enabling measure, but widely criticized as rushed, ill thought out and coercive' (CARE 1988).

Perhaps the most serious problem with the introduction of computers, particularly in mixed schools, was one of access.[2] In 1986 the average number of computers per secondary school was nine and there was wide variability between schools (CARE 1988; Carter 1987). In a survey of 43 schools in Greater Manchester conducted in 1985, Carter (1987) found that the child: computer ratio ranged from 1:85 to 1:124. One survey found that the average time each pupil was expected to spend using a computer was 5.3 hours per term and that many pupils had no contact at all (Carter 1987). An examination of policies for allocating the use of computers in mixed secondary schools suggests that girls were far more likely than boys to miss out on experience with computers. This can be attributed both to the physical and the social location of computers within schools.

Location of computers

The decision to introduce computers in secondary schools first rather than primary schools had the effect of producing clear associations with particular subject areas. Computers were most likely to be located in departments of mathematics or computer studies, thus linking their usage with mathematics and science. This subject link was particularly unfortunate for girls, since they are less likely than boys to have positive attitudes towards science and mathematics (Kelly 1981; APU 1981, cited by Culley 1986: 22). The emphasis on science and mathematics was also reflected clearly in the pattern of teachers receiving training courses in computing and in the educational software currently available for micros. Under the Microelectronics Education Project teachers of mathematics were the most likely to be trained, followed by science teachers, computer studies teachers and geography teachers (BBC 1985). Not surprisingly male teachers were more likely than female teachers to be in charge of computing, thus serving to reinforce the masculine image of computing and to provide both formal and informal barriers to girls' studying computing. The problem was (and continues to be) exacerbated by the shortage of computers and by the attitudes of teachers responsible for them.

Teachers' attitudes

Carter (1987) found that female and male teachers differed sharply in their attitudes towards how computers should be used in schools, how computers should be allocated and on how female teachers might serve as role models for female pupils. In a survey of 54 women and 78 men in charge of computing, he found that female teachers tended to have egalitarian views, believing that computers could be used to teach any subject and that they should be available to all pupils. They also felt that their personal involvement in computing would have a positive effect on girls' attitudes towards mathematics, science and technology. Male teachers saw this effect as much more limited and as being confined primarily to attitudes towards computing. In addition, male teachers had more elitist views, holding that priority for computers should be given to pupils of high ability, particularly boys with an interest in mathematics and science. They also felt that computers were best used in the teaching of mathematics and science. These findings substantiate other research on teachers' attitudes, suggesting that female teachers are more likely to hold egalitarian attitudes towards gender roles, are more likely to be aware of the needs of female pupils, and are more likely to favour 'positive action' measures which will encourage girls to participate in non-traditional areas (Pratt 1985; Kelly *et al.* 1985). Some of the effects of the differences in the attitudes of female and male teachers can be seen clearly in how schools have dealt with the phenomenon of the computer club and access to computers outside of lessons.

Computer clubs

Approximately 80 per cent of schools have computer clubs (BBC 1985; Culley 1986). Computer clubs appear to be equally likely in single-sex schools as mixed schools, but there is wide variation between schools. In some schools only pupils taking Computer Studies options can use the computers outside of lesson time. Other schools give priority to particular year groups or operate a rota system. Another common practice is to give priority to enthusiasts, who are more likely to be boys, or to operate a competitive 'first at the door' policy, which is also likely to favour boys. Some schools have become concerned about girls' lack of participation in computer clubs and have reserved one day for girls only: this often works quite well. However, if the school maintains an open policy on the other days of the week, it frequently results in there being one day for girls-only and four days which are effectively for boys-only (Culley 1986).

Culley found wide variations between schools in the extent to which girls were represented in computer clubs. Girls were most likely to be equally represented in computer clubs when schools operated a quota system and membership was formally allocated to girls and boys on an equal basis. However, girls represented 19 per cent of the pupils using computer clubs, and in 18 of the 190 mixed schools in the survey reported that there were no female members in their computer clubs. Observational data suggest that in many computer clubs boys establish a strongly male culture which is derogatory towards girls and that the girls who participate often find this environment extremely uncomfortable. This pattern of priority being given to males is also seen in the use of home computers.

Home computers

In a survey conducted in 1983, Culley (1986) found that in a sample of fourth and fifth-form pupils ($N = 483$ girls and 491 boys) only 22 per cent of girls, but 56 per cent of boys were likely to have a computer in their home. In a subsample of pupils who were studying for an examination in computing, she found that there was a dramatic difference between female and male students with 28 per cent of the girls and 65 per cent of the boys having a computer at home. Female students without a computer at home may be very seriously disadvantaged because they may find it very difficult to gain access to computers outside the time for formal lessons to complete homework and project work.

It is also worth observing the continuity of attitudes towards gender and computing between home and school. In Culley's survey only 14 per cent of girls but 85 per cent of boys said that the computer had been bought for them; only 9 per cent of girls with a home computer described themselves as the main computer user. Thus at both home and school, males appear more likely to have access to equipment and are more likely to dominate it. Given these experiences, it is not surprising that many girls see computing as a field which is predominantly male. These perceptions are seen clearly in my own data on how young women view computing as a carreer.

Perceptions of computing as a career

My research is based on a sample of 143 female fifth-formers who attended an open day on computing as a career at the University of Manchester in the summer of 1988. These girls represented 48 schools, 11 of which were single sex and 37 were mixed. All were intending to enter a degree course at a university or polytechnic. The sample cannot be seen as representative of schoolgirls and is likely to include a relatively high proportion of computer enthusiasts and girls studying science. However, it provides a useful sample of girls with the academic background necessary to apply for polytechnic and university courses in computing.

As part of my survey, I asked the girls what factors they saw as most important in making a career choice and which ones they expected to find in computing as a career.[3] Their responses suggested that they were most concerned about a job which made full use of their abilities and which also offered opportunities for promotion and paid well. They also valued highly the opportunity to make their own decisions. When these characteristics are compared with the ones that they expected computing to offer, there are some striking discrepancies. While 'makes full use of my abilities' ranked first in the list of 'most important' career characteristics, it ranked as 13th on the factors expected in computing. Another large discrepancy was in 'close involvement with new developments in technology'. Not surprisingly this item was ranked as most characteristic of computing, but it was 12th on the list of important factors in making a career choice. A further area of mismatch was in the opportunity to make one's own decisions. This was highly rated (no. 4) in terms of career characteristics but was seen as quite uncharacteristic of computing (no. 11). Teamwork was also an area where important career characteristics were discrepant with those in computing. 'Working in a team' was seen as highly characteristic of computing, ranking third, and yet it was considered relatively unimportant by these respondents (ranked 12: see Table 11.1).

These findings suggest that these schoolgirls were generally pleased with the material rewards offered by computing but that they were seriously concerned about its intrinsic satisfactions. They clearly did not see it as making full use of their abilities, and they were not motivated by its emphasis on new advance-

Table 11.1 Comparison between rankings: most important factors in career choice and factors expected in computing*

Factor	Most important in career (Rank)	Expected in computing (Rank)
Makes full use of my abilities	1	13
Opportunity for promotion	2	2
Good pay	3	4
Able to make my own decisions	4	11
A career which will last all my life	5	9
Contributes to society	5	6
Working with people	7	7
Opportunity to travel	8	14
Security	9	10
A career which fits in with family commitments	10	5
High status	11	11
Working in a team	12	3
Close involvement with new developments in technology	12	1
Working on my own	14	8

Note: *Based on responses of 76 fifth-forms girls attending an open day in computing.

ments in technology. They also felt some disquiet about patterns of working. They wanted to be in a position to exercise leadership and to make their own decisions, but they perceived it as an industry based on teamwork. As shown below, the comments of girls from mixed schools suggest that they would be unlikely to be comfortable in a predominantly male team.

Why girls don't go into computing

On my questionnaire, I asked why they felt that far fewer girls and women had been going into computing. I found that their most frequent response concerned the male domination of computing. They saw computing as a 'man's world' where girls and women were not welcome:

> It's a man's world – more the kind of thing for boys.

> A lot of boys go into computing.

> [A] computer is boy's equipment.

A salient feature of this part of a 'man's world' was that boys took over; they pushed girls out of the way and they bragged about their knowledge.

> Domineering boys who seem to take over and show off.

> Boys who think they know a lot more about computers.

> [We get] shoved around by boys at school so rarely get access.

> Boys think they know everything; [they] push girls to the side.

Another aspect of boys' claiming superior knowledge was their using it (or assuming it) to put girls down and belittle their knowledge. This clearly made some girls feel as if they didn't want to work in an environment where this would happen routinely:

> [I would] not like working in an environment where men dominate and [I do] not like being put down.

> If girls make mistakes, boys make fun of them.

> Fear of being showed up in front of them.

They were also uncertain about how clever a person needed to be to go into computing. For example, some girls believed that anyone going into computing needed to be a near genius; others thought the job was boring and menial and equated computing with word-processing. There seemed to be little room for anyone between the two extremes:

> It's difficult and complicated . . . you feel you need to be a genius.

> The idea of technology puts many off because it can sound so daunting and hard.

> It's boring and tedious, especially word-processing.

Many girls were put off by what they saw as a separate and almost alien world. One girl described it as 'the mysterious aura surrounding the world of computers'; others complained of the language and terminology:

> Bewildered by all the equipment, disc drives, modems, etc.

> Fancy code names and logos put girls off.

> Strange language.

Girls were also very critical of the way computing was presented at school and of the shortage of machines. Several complained that they were not encouraged to do computing as they were to do other subjects. One girl described how more effort went into encouraging girls to participate in the Harvest Festival than in encouraging girls to learn about computers:

> Girls are not encouraged.

> Girls don't have as much contact as boys.

> [They] don't know much about.

> Very little information.

What can be done?

Schoolgirls are quite clearly rejecting computing as a career and this trend is likely to persist unless there is 'positive action' in schools, in higher education and in industry. Such positive action will involve serious changes in the image of computing, in access to computers and in attitudes towards women in computing. Although each of these issues is considered separately they are clearly interrelated.

Beyond the glossy brochure

Some of the failure to attract women is clearly a failure in marketing and in not presenting an image of the field which is attractive to women. As in attempts to attract women to engineering, material needs to be targeted at women. Currently much of the literature about computing emphasizes advances in new technology, images of being at the 'leading edge', at the 'forefront of technology'. Women are rarely shown and most often appear as decorative sexual objects or as silly brainless creatures, incapable of understanding anything about computers. Changing these images will be difficult because many of the present images are deeply embedded in computer culture. However, a first step must involve finding women already in computing who can serve as role models. They should illustrate the variety of applications of computers, and some of them should clearly represent the human side of computing. These women should be carefully chosen for their communication skills and the image they present to young women.

Access to computers

One of the biggest barriers to women's participation in computing is simply one of access to computers. In mixed schools girls need to be guaranteed access to computers and this probably has to be done formally through 'girls only' sessions for pupils studying computing and 'girls only' sessions for computer clubs. Such measures appear relatively uncommon. Unlike several schools described by Culley (1986) which guranteed access for girls, none of the schools in my sample had girls-only sessions. Research on teachers' attitudes towards equal opportunities suggests such measures are likely to be strongly resisted by many teachers and pupils (Pratt 1985; Kelly *et al.* 1985). However, until computers are much more widely available in schools, there need to be formal arrangements which provide girls with entitlement to computers.

Computer studies and information techonology are frequently seen as unnecessary for the further study of computing. However, my research suggests that these subjects are far more important for girls than for boys.[4] It is here that girls gain confidence in using computers and discover that they have the ability and the interest to proceed. This confidence factor is crucial if they are to enter higher education on an equal footing with their male counterparts.

Attitudes towards women

It may be argued that the highly gendered enviroment of the mixed secondary school is a microcosm of the wider world of industry where women are often not welcome. The computing industry often defends its sexism by arguing that it is a young industry and traditional gender attitudes are not entrenched and so will change. However, information on the position of women in the industry provides little cause for complacency. A survey by *Computer Economics* in 1986 found that women represented 2 per cent of data processing managers, 12 per cent of programmers and 95 per cent of data preparation staff (cited by Cowie 1988). At higher management levels women are even more poorly represented. One study of data-processing management found 2.4 per cent of

board directors were women and only 4.6 per cent of women classify themselves as department managers (cited by Lawrence 1989). Although women
are becoming better represented at senior management levels in business and
finance, particularly in the USA, the high technology world of computing is
widely acknowledged to be a very difficult industry for women who want
advancement. Furthermore, several studies have shown that although women
and men enter the industry at comparable levels, women earn 25 per cent less
than men with 'similar experience' ten years after university (*Business Week*
1989).

Commitment and positive action are needed to provide real career paths for
women. To be effective they are likely to involve changes in company cultures,
in styles of management and patterns of working. American experience
suggests that women are more likely to gain top positions in small companies
where their abilities are recognized and they have a role in creating and
maintaining the cultural ethos (*Business Week* 1989).

Towards the future

Both the academic world and industry need to look very seriously at their
current practice. As the field has grown and acquired status and prestige it has
become more exclusively male. The bold, hard 'high tech' image persists, but
much of computing is about communication, about the interface of people and
computers, about organizing information, and devising new ways to work. If
these images are projected, more women may consider computing as a career.
But for any real change to occur, there is a need for computing to take women
more seriously and to demonstrate a real commitment to providing lifelong
careers for women. It must be more flexible in how it selects people for jobs and
courses, and it should review and validate its selection criteria, especially its
strict age barriers. As part of this exercise it needs to consider a variety of styles
of working, as well as the much-vaunted team approach. The women it wishes
to attract want far more than surface glamour; they want pay, they want
promotion and they want challenge – a career which will make full use of their
abilities.

Notes

1 Computer aptitude tests have been poorly validated and have been criticized for
   their male bias. Most employers continue to use them as an additional selection
   device even when applicants have relevant qualifications in computing, thus
   providing an additional barrier for female candidates.
2 I have focused on mixed schools in this discussion, since they are the more
   common form of secondary schooling in the UK and represent a potent environment for gender stereotyping.
3 Because not all respondents answered all parts of the questionnaire, this analysis
   is based on the replies of 76 subjects. The comparisons reported are based on the
   analysis of respondents' choice of the three most important factors in their career
   choice and the factors which they expected to find in computing.
4 In my sample I found that studying computer studies or information technology
   at GCSE was strongly related to the intention to study computer science at
   university ($\chi^2 = 60.0$, 1df, $p < 0.0001$).

References

Anderson, R. E. (1987) Females surpass males in computer problem solving; findings from the Minnesota Computer Literacy assessment, *Journal of Educational Computing Research*, 31, 1: 39–51.

APU (Assessment of Performance Unit) (1981) *Mathematical Development*, Primary Survey Report no 2, London: HMSO.

BBC Educational Broadcasting Services Research Unit (1985) *Microcomputers in Secondary Schools*, Unpublished report summarized in DES Press Notice 14/85, January.

Business Week (1989) The women who are scaling high tech's new heights, 28 August: 86–9.

CARE (Centre for Applied Research in Education) (1988) *DTI Micros in Schools Support 1981–1984: An Independent Evaluation – Executive Summary and Recommendations*, CARE, University of East Anglia.

Carter, K. (1987) unpublished data, Huddersfield Polytechnic.

Cowie, A. (1988) Screen prejudice, *Guardian*, 25 February.

Culley, L. (1986) *Gender Differences and Computing*, Department of Education, University of Loughborough.

DES (1975) *Curricular Differences for Boys and Girls: Education Survey 21*, London: HMSO.

EOC/London Borough of Croydon (1983) *Information Technology in Schools: Guidelines for Good Practice for Teachers of IT*, Equal Opportunities Commission.

Johnson, T. J. (1972) *Professions and Power*, London: Macmillan.

Kelly, A. (1981) *The Missing Half: Girls and Science Education*, Manchester University Press.

Kelly, A., Baldry, A., Bolton, E., Edwards, S., Emery, J., Levin, C., Smith, S. and Willis, M. (1985) Traditionalists and trendies: teachers' attitudes to educational issues, *British Educational Research Journal*, 11, 2: 91–104.

Kiesler, S., Sproull, L. and Eccles, J. S. (1985) Pool halls, chips and war games: women in the culture of computing, *Psychology of Women Quarterly*, 9, 4: 451–62.

Lawrence, J. (1989) Missing the underused Ms, *Guardian*, 31 August.

Linn, M. C. (1985) Gender equity in computer learning environments, *Computers and the Social Sciences*, 1, 1: 19–27.

Lockheed, M. (ed.) (1985) Introduction: women, girls and computers, special issue *Sex Roles*, 13, 3/4: whole issue.

Lovegrove, G. and Hall, W. (1987) Where have all the girls gone?, *University Computing*, 9: 207–10.

Maccoby, E. and Jacklin, C. (1975) *The Psychology of Sex Roles*, Stanford, Calif.: Stanford University Press.

Newton, P. and Haslam, S. (1988) Girls and computers in secondary school: a system failure?, Paper presented at the British Psychological Society Annual Conference, University of Leeds, April.

Perkin, H. (1989) *The Rise of Professional Society: England since 1880*, London: Routledge.

Pratt, J. (1985) The attitudes of teachers, in J. Whyte, R. Deem, L. Kant and M. Cruickshank (eds) *Girl Friendly Schooling*, London: Methuen.

Universities Statistical Record (1988) Personal communication.

Virgo, P. (ed.) (1989) *Towards an Open and Equal IT Careers Initiative*, Report of the Women into Information Technology Campaign Feasibility Study, London: ICL (available from IT Strategy Services, 2 Eastbourne Avenue, London, W3 6JN).

12 | Women managers
Beverly Alban-Metcalfe and Michael A. West

Most of the literature on management, whether in the form of textbooks or research papers, is based on male perspectives of theories developed predominantly by men, typically on research studies in which females are in the minority, if at all present. The title of an article on the business page of a popular Sunday newspaper printed in the final month of 1989 suggests that little has changed with respect to the exclusion of women in discussions of management issues. It reads 'Why the best man doesn't always win: A firm's most effective man can often be passed over' (*Sunday Times*, 3 December 1989).

The issue is a serious one, not only for women, but also for society, and at the very least for economic growth in current circumstances. The Henley Centre for Forecasting recently predicted that half of Britain's work-force by the year 2000 will be female, that three-quarters of the new jobs created in the 1990s will be filled by women, and that the current figure of 5 per cent of the population of professional and senior management being female will increase significantly. Any increase on a 5 per cent base reading will sound highly significant, but the fact remains that the proportion is appallingly low. There will need to be dramatic changes in the attitudes, values and practices that pervade organizational life simply to kick-start the process. But how can we expect such a commitment when those in the most influential positions are men and little evidence exists of a change in attitudes at the top?

Models of organizational career tracks still reflect the notion of the unbroken vertical path and this is supported from the most recent evidence of the experience of women returning from a 'career-break' to significantly lower positions in the organization (Brannen and Moss 1988). Only 10 per cent of 2,000 employers surveyed by a large personnel organization offered career-break schemes or extended leave period, and presumably only a few of these, if any, were available to men. Even the recent preponderance of articles extolling organizations to encouraging women-returners or to consider women as possible alternatives to men in management and professions reflects the note of desperation in such a plea.

Those of us who are totally convinced of the untapped potential of women in managerial positions are also wary of the danger that this might merely be a replay of what happened during the 1940s when women filled in for their menfolk who had left the firms and factories to protect the nation, but who were 'relegated' to the home on their return.

There is now a substantial body of research on the male-ness of managerial models and academic research in the area of organizational behaviour. We will know that things have changed when we no longer need to write about bias of women in management. However, despite the constant refutation that discrimination no longer exists with respect to women's managerial development there is no real evidence to suggest that this is the reality. So long as the term 'career-break' is used to describe an individual who decides to spend time in activities surrounding child development rather than organizational development, and it is presumed that females are the individuals most likely to undertake such activity, the subject of women in management will need to be addressed. But this is not the only important issue, since there are many other factors that suggest forms of discrimination against women.

In this chapter we shall suggest that traditional discrimination has simply been augmented by new forms of discrimination. However, rather than just illustrating what may be obvious points, we shall go on to address other questions about women managers and their lives. Who are the women managers? What is their experience of managerial work and how are their non-work lives affected? How do they see themselves and what is important to them in their work lives? Finally, we briefly consider by what means might organizational change be brought about.

Our answers are largely drawn from a study which sampled more women managers than any previously in the UK (fuller details of which can be found in Alban-Metcalfe 1984; 1985; 1987; Alban-Metcalfe and Nicholson 1984; Nicholson and West 1988), and which examined job change among 2,304 male and female British managers (1,498 men and 806 women). The study involved mailing questionnaires to a random sample of the roughly 66,000 members of the British Institute of Management (BIM) of whom only about 900 are women. Because of this small proportion the questionnaire was mailed to all female members of the BIM. In addition several professional women's networks were approached to augment the number of women respondents.

Biographical details

The women managers in this study were significantly younger than the men (average 37 years old compared with 48 years amongst the men). The women in general possessed higher educational qualifications with 61 per cent working in the private sector holding first degrees, compared with only 44 per cent of men. In the public sector the percentages were 73 and 65 respectively. The results indicated that women need better qualifications than men in order to achieve similar status positions. Men were more likely to have had a technical education; the women were much more likely to be in 'functional specialist' rather than 'general management' roles than men. Women were scarcely represented among the top echelons of the Fellow of the BIM. Despite the fact that women were vastly over-represented proportionately in our sample (i.e. over 50 per cent of women BIM members were represented compared with only 2 per cent of men) only 8 per cent of the BIM Fellows responding were women.

How do women managers see themselves?

Managers' perceptions of themselves in general and of themselves in work were measured by asking them to indicate how they saw themselves on fifteen semantic differential scales (see Figure 12.1). The scales were as follows:

1 Creative–uncreative
2 Forceful–timid
3 Show feelings readily–keep feelings to myself
4 Trusting–suspicious
5 Relaxed–tense
6 Sociable–reserved
7 Fulfilled–frustrated
8 Happy–sad
9 Intellectual–non-intellectual
10 Confident–unsure
11 Ambitious–unambitious
12 Optimistic–pessimistic
13 Controlling–casual
14 Contented with myself–discontented with myself
15 Like uncertainty–dislike uncertainty.

In general, women perceived themselves as more likely to show their feelings, more sociable, and more intellectual than did men. They were less relaxed and less confident, but felt more fulfilled than the men. However, there were more similarities than differences among the men and women: they perceived themselves in general as equally ambitious, controlling, forceful, creative, trusting, optimistic, happy, content with themselves, and had the same degree of dislike of uncertainty.

There was a remarkable similarity in the way female and male managers perceived themselves at work (controlling for age effects). The only differences were that women felt more tense and perceived themselves as more intellectual than did men; women were also less likely to keep their feelings to themselves.

A comparison was made between the way women perceived themselves at work and how they perceived themselves in general. In order of magnitude of the differences, women saw themselves at work as:

1 More likely to keep their feelings to themselves
2 Less trusting
3 Less fulfilled
4 Less sociable
5 Less relaxed
6 More controlling
7 Less contented with themselves

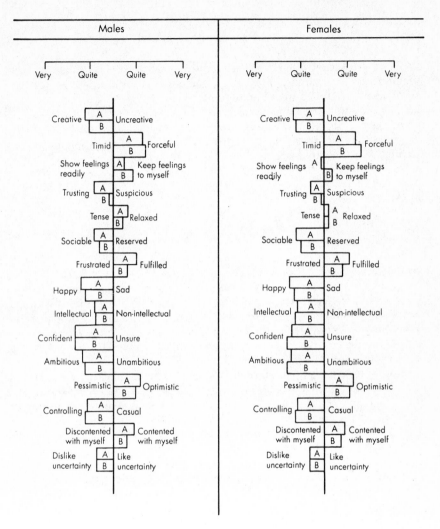

Figure 12.1   Perceptions of self (A) in general and (B) at work for males and females

8 More forceful
9 Less optimistic
10 Less happy
11 More confident
12 Less creative.

At work, men and women perceived themselves to be equally ambitious, controlling and forceful. These results might appear to contradict some previous studies on the characteristics of males and females with respect to managerial traits (e.g. Schein 1975). It is worth noting, however, that the data described in this study arose from individuals' perceptions of themselves, rather than from asking subjects to describe how they perceive the traits of male and female managers in general.

Of the significant differences between women and men's perceptions of themselves at work, it is perhaps not surprising that the women, being better academically qualified than the men, perceived themselves as more intellectual. Neither is it surprising given the differences in socialization which gives permission to women to express emotion but raises injunctions against men doing so, that the women perceive themselves as more likely to express their feelings. There is a tendency to discount and repress the expression of feelings at work, based on the pervasive model that work is more about achieving organizational objectives at the expense of, or ignoring the developments of individuals' needs.

Work and home life

A far greater proportion of women were single or divorced (29 and 10 per cent respectively, versus 3 and 3 per cent respectively for the men). Of those managers who were or who had been married, nearly half of the female sample were without children, compared with just over a tenth of the corresponding male sample. Family size of the female sample was significantly smaller than that of the males. These data are similar to those reported in US studies (e.g. Valdez and Gutek 1987).

Support for domestic commitments from a home-based partner was far less likely for the married women, of whom 90 per cent had partners in paid full-time employment, compared with the corresponding figure of around 25 per cent of the men. The experiences of women and men in dual-career relationships are also totally different. Women refer to the demands of both, work and home, whereas men refer solely to work. Qualitative data (Alban-Metcalfe 1984) bore out Langrish's findings (1981a; 1981b) that men perceived home as a place of refuge, a place to relax and recharge the batteries, whereas women experienced home life as a source of strain and stress presenting women with additional demands and a loss of private time to oneself.

When managers referred to partners' support these were exclusively comments from women. None related to shared domestic duties but solely to psychological support. As many were positive as negative. Teenage children were cited as resenting mother's careers at times, and several comments by women referred to resentment by partners if their careers were judged more successful.

It may well be presumed that the situation with respect to a more equitable distribution of domestic duties had improved but this appears not to be the case in Britain. A recent report of activities of mothers who were in paid employment concluded that of those with partners, even where both partners work full-time, 72 per cent of domestic tasks were done mainly by women.

Research in the USA investigating the relationship between work and family roles for women and men describes work and home demands as being simultaneous for women, rather than typically sequential, as (and when) experienced by men. As to the priorities of family and work demands, the patterns for women and men are typically mirror images. Demands of family responsibilities are allowed and expected to intrude on the work roles of women, and in situations of conflicting demands the family is expected to take priority, whereas the converse is custom and practice for men (Pleck 1977). This has frequently been confirmed by studies investigating discrimination in selection and promotion practices in organizations (see Chapters 2 and 3 in this volume). More starkly stated, marriage and a family are seen as assets for men's careers but liabilities for women's (Bryson *et al.* 1978; Bronstein *et al.* 1987).

Women, it would appear, have to make important life choices not faced by the majority of professional males, and have to carry far greater domestic and career pressures to succeed at both. This directly contradicts the widely held myths such as those identified by Rosen and Jerdee (1974) that male managers believe their female employers are not willing to take risks or make sacrifices for the sake of career development. Let us now turn to look at what motivates women at work, given that so many are prepared to make such sacrifices.

Work preferences

One of the major reasons why women are offered fewer opportunities for management responsibility is that occupational sex-role stereotyping has led to the notion that characteristics commonly associated with a successful manager are more congruent with the traits attributed to men than women (Bernadin 1982; Broverman *et al.* 1975; O'Leary 1974; Basil 1972) and Schein's studies (1973; 1975) showed that these beliefs were held equally strongly by female and male managers. Kaufman and Fetters maintain that:

> the professional literature is replete with theoretical examples explaining women's 'lesser work commitment'. Women are assumed to be less assertive, less ambitious, and less career-oriented than men.
>
> (Kaufman and Fetters 1980: 251)

Anyone who may have hoped that attitudes towards women have become enlightened with time may well become depressed by studies such as Siegfield *et al.* (1981) in which male and female US university students were asked to rate the importance of ten job characteristics for both themselves and members of the opposite sex. The ten characteristics reflect Herzberg's classification of five 'hygiene factors', i.e. those that are extrinsic to the job (for example pay, policy, etc.) and five motivators, i.e. those that are intrinsic to the job (for example achievement, recognition, the nature of the work, etc.). Both sexes rated the motivators as important. However, men tended to underestimate the importance of motivators for women. Motivators included desire for responsibility, advancement, challenging work, a voice in decision-making, and making a contribution to society. Such students are the managers of the future and may be expected to perpetuate these attitudes through the organizational practices in which they become involved.

Irrespective of the gender of the job-holder it is important for organizations to be aware of what motivates their managers in order to support their development and attempt to meet individual needs. And since motivation is a crucial determinant of job performance, greater understanding of what managers want from their jobs and an attempt to assess how they rate their jobs on the aspects they perceive as important can surely help match individual needs to the attainment of organizational goals.

We turn now to examine which aspects of work are important to women managers in the UK and how they compare with the profiles for men. Because far more women proportionately than men were employed in the public sector than the private sector we have conducted separate analyses for the two sectors.

Comparing the differences in work preferences of the female and male managers in the private sector, there were significant differences in fourteen out of seventeen items. Those items which the women rated significantly more highly than the men were:

1   A challenging job
2   An opportunity for development
3   Opportunity for feedback
4   Working with friendly people
5   An opportunity to make a contribution to society
6   Work where accomplishment is appreciated
7   A job which fits in well with life outside work
8   Location
9   Working for an organization that is highly regarded
10 Opportunity to be creative in doing things my own way.

The four items that the men rated significantly more important than did the women were:

1   Fringe benefits
2   High earnings
3   Job security
4   An opportunity to influence organizational policies.

Much has been written about women's lack of commitment to career development and beliefs abound that women are less interested in advancement and in playing an active role in organizational affairs, despite the findings of previous studies such as those of Miner (1974) on 'motivation to manage' scores of women managers, and Terborg's (1977) review of the literature. However, these studies have been based on US samples. The data presented here on managers in Britain also dispute the assumptions of women's lesser career commitment and ambition. Women in this sample were as concerned as the men with opportunity for advancement and were in fact more concerned with challenge, development, and feedback than the men, whereas the men were more concerned with extrinsic factors to the job such as high earnings, fringe benefits, and job security.

Gender segregation in management

It is apparent from the study that women generally occupy male-dominated environments since their bosses, colleagues and subordinates are all more likely to be men than women. In particular women are highly likely to have a male boss and highly unlikely to have a female boss, showing how much the woman manager remains under the control of men at work. Where there are women managers working in an organization there is evidence that there does tend to be gender segregation. Women are more likely to be working alongside women than are men and are more likely to have female subordinates than are men. This suggests that employers may be reluctant to hire women to supervise men and may prefer to hire a woman to manage other women in traditionally female role areas. Other explanations are that women are more likely to hire other women to work for them and that men are reluctant to apply for a job in which a woman is the boss.

When the data on gender segregation are examined in more detail (see Nicholson and West 1988), a revealing picture emerges. In the work areas where women managers are most concentrated (e.g. government and service industries) women are much more likely to be working in gender-segregated areas, that is with or under other women. In the areas where women managers are least concentrated there is very little gender typing, even taking into account the proportionate differences in women's representation. The pessimistic interpretation is that women managers tend to be either the victims of tokenism and/or of gender segregation. Either they are a token group employed to counter the accusation of prejudice and/or they are concentrated in jobs which become gender-stereotyped and subsequently devalued.

The careers of women in management

When the careers of women managers were compared with those of men some clear differences emerged (see Nicholson and West 1988). Men have more upward status moves generally but women are more likely to change employers and to make radical moves outwards and upwards. Furthermore, while men have a high rate of employer-changing predominantly only when they are young, women keep up a high rate of employer-changing throughout their careers. Moreover this high rate of employer-changing is more typical of women with children than those without. It may be that women are having to change employers as spouses move onwards and upwards in their organizations. It may also be that women feel that they have to move organizations to overcome prejudice in their strivings to achieve. A third of women managers said that prejudice had a moderate or greater influence on their careers whereas only 8 per cent of men gave similar responses.

How do women managers describe their experiences?

The predominantly negative comments of women managers and professionals on work and their careers reflect an almost totally different perspective from those of men (Alban-Metcalfe 1984). There is much greater variety in their reasons for work dissatisfaction and these are predominantly gender-related. However, there are views in which women concur strongly with men. These are dissatisfactions with the effectiveness, adaptability and planning vision of top management. Also there is considerable resentment about the lack of training in management skills which seemed to be a relatively common feature in senior management. This perceived deficiency, coupled with the fact that top management appear exempt from any form of performance evaluation, was a source of considerable ill-feeling.

Comments from the women managers fall into three groups: job changes; the benefits and problems of fulfilling major life roles of domestic female, and working spouse/mother; and problems associated with being female in a male-dominated organization or occupation.

Job changes

Comments made by women managers under this heading were in the main quite different in character to those of men. Although company reorganization was mentioned on several occasions, far more frequent reference was made to the job changes which were imposed on managers because their male partners were moving location for career reasons. Several women felt this was reasonable since their male partner received a substantially higher wage and it was therefore considered sensible to allow his career to take precedence. However, others were becoming increasingly resentful of the assumptions that a woman should move regularly for her husband's career advancement, but not vice versa, and the implication that women's careers were of secondary importance. One woman expressed her distress at the consequences of multiple location and job moves:

> While I have managed to make job changes into positive and generally career-enhancing experiences, they were generally made through outside events – i.e. moves to accompany husband, self-employment by necessity. Result: profound sense of insecurity manifested as over-confidence – yet somehow I've retained my basic optimism. My 'career' has been largely disorganized and out of my control.

Some women stated that they had tried to acquire experience in a variety of organizations and functions so as to increase their marketability and enhance later stages of career development. As one put it:

> I have changed direction a number of times deliberately, to give myself the chance to broaden my experience and widen the scope for career development – especially important for a 'working mother'.

But not all job changes were carefully planned. Several women's comments suggested that job changes were often based on luck, fortuitous timing and accident.

An interesting perception of job change emerged from one woman manager's comments:

> I feel that some of the tensions in my job are due to the fact that I have tried to change the objectives in what was seen by staff as a traditionally 'female' job. I

have the full support of my supervisor in this, but found antagonism in some subordinates (male as well as female) as I changed it to a more professional, managerial type of work, and wanted more involvement in a wider area of decision-making.

Many comments reflect women's perceptions of their career situation as grossly disadvantageous despite the enactment of equal opportunity legislation. There were many examples of discrimination in career development opportunities in a wide range of industries and occupations, including computing, medicine, law, accountancy, academic, retailing, production, sales, journalism, banking and local and central government. A good example of this relates to the question posed to a female academic applying for the job of head of department where the majority of lecturers and students were women: 'How would you deal with the antagonism of the (few) male colleagues who would resent working for a female?'

A small minority of women who attempted to 'hide' the fact that they were female by omitting marital status, title and their first name, did this because they believed that being a woman would jeopardize their chances of being considered for a profession which is traditionally 'male'. Examples included civil engineering and computing. They reported that the reaction of employers on greeting them at the interview ranged from annoyance to hostility.

There were recurring comments citing sex discrimination in pay and promotion, when women were better qualified than the men. One clear case concerned a job-sharing scheme in which the female incumbent worked three out of five fays, and the male worked the remaining two days. Despite the fact that they were performing the identical job, the man was paid at a higher level and given the more senior title. Several women mentioned that although they received pay equal to male colleagues doing the same job, they were not given the same title. Moreover, this often occurred when the men were less qualified and experienced than the women. One woman manager described how she sought equal pay and, on refusing a suggested demotion, was made redundant. Another stated that although she was promoted to a higher level than her male colleagues, her title was not changed to reflect this difference.

A perhaps more subtle, and therefore insidious, form of discrimination emerged from the comment of one respondent who saw her role as the token female senior manager:

A very interesting survey! Clarifies my suspicion that I am a woman in a senior management job because it is regarded as woman's work.

Another respondent seemed grateful to the company which employed her while acknowledging its clearly discriminatory treatment of women:

I was lucky enough to find a company that thought women were often better and more conscientious workers than men and they gave me the opportunity of employment, although not equal pay/perks as the men. I am the only female working in a production department with five men of which only one is as highly educated as myself and only two are older.

Gratitude seemed to be a relatively common reaction among women employed in organizations which obviously were discriminatory. The following extract reflect this phenomenon:

> I have never felt discriminated against because I am female, although it is undoubtedly true in this organization that women have to prove themselves beyond reasonable doubt more than men.

Women frequently cited examples of male colleagues, again less well-qualified and experienced, who were promoted considerably more frequently than themselves. Even having a female boss did not always appear to change the experience for women managers. A nurse who commented that her female boss preferred to seek advice and assistance from less qualified men, stated that male nurses appear to have a distinct advantage in promotional opportunities compared with similarly qualified women.

Another form of discrimination perceived by some of the women with young children, related to their having been asked whether their domestic commitments would conflict with work. A further type of discrimination which acts against women's career development prospects is the job place-ment. Thus, for example, several lawyers mentioned the fact that they were prevented from pursuing a career in their particular field of interest, such as criminal law, but were offered employment only in typical 'female-type' specialization such as divorce and family law, while men could choose whichever specialism they preferred. Several women mentioned that they had considered taking their companies to industrial tribunals for sexual discrimi-nation, but feared that it would be too difficult to obtain employment else-where and would feel reluctant to stay in the organization while pursuing a legal case against it.

Domestic and work-related roles

Many females stressed the personal importance of holding a challenging and responsible job, but at the same time were very aware of the very high level of stress and fatigue that they had to accept, since a notable proportion stated that they were still expected to fulfil the traditional domestic role of wife and mother. As one woman stated:

> A man can concentrate on the job knowing that he has a wife at home organizing domestic arrangements, preparing meals, washing, cleaning, etc.

Another commonly expressed opinion was:

> Women have to be superb organizers of both major demands in their lives and moreover we must appear to working colleagues as if we have no problems at all and have to work harder for the same rewards.

There was a substantial number of woman who expressed deep gratitude to their spouses for the support they offered to them in their careers, and without which they felt they could not maintain their jobs. However, there were also comments, though less frequent, from women who had not received support and encouragement from members of their family. Several stated their family thought they should regard their jobs as a mere hobby rather than a career and should be satisfied with the status quo. Of these a few stated they felt that they needed a career so strongly for their sense of self-esteem and well-being; that almost out of a sense of desperation to maintain sanity, they had been determined to pursue this goal despite such difficult circumstances. A good example of this is represented in the following extract:

> I realized that I had to move location in order to obtain the necessary promotion that I knew I needed. I therefore started applying further afield knowing that this mattered to me as much as my marriage. I obtained a post in X-town which I accepted despite my husband's opposition, and bought a small house in which I live from Monday to Friday commuting to Y-town (60 miles away) at weekends. I am very happy and fulfilled, and manage to make life as easy as possible for husband and teenage sons by doing housework, shopping, cooking, washing and ironing at the weekends. My children fully understand the situation and have been most enthusiastic and supportive. It is not an easy life, but I still believe I have been lucky to manage career and family, and, as a woman to be in such a senior management post.

Several women stated that they began working after marriage purely out of financial need but came to realize gradually how important the job was for their psychological well-being. The following is a typical example of this pattern emerging (again the comments have been edited to ensure anonymity):

> In completing this questionnaire, I feel that (1) I may not be the type of person to whom you are trying to reach, i.e. I am not young and I am not a career animal and the reason for that is that I brought up two children, and was quite content to apply my energies to doing a job in the first instance for 'pin' money. Trying to do a job well takes energy and also being a good wife and mother takes even more energy. I have tried very hard to do all very well indeed. However (2) I became frustrated at a dead end job as I saw it in 1970 and wanted a much more fulfilling job and landing my present job has been very rewarding indeed. It has its glamour and meeting top management is very satisfying indeed. But there are periods when the pressure is on and all eyes look to you and your staff to complete satisfactorily some very important issues.

The overwhelming picture that has emerged from comments in this present study is consistent with that of other studies dealing with women combining domestic and work roles; namely as one manager states:

> I'm accepting the fact that if you work in a male-orientated society you must solve domestic problems first.

But another option also emerges with regularity, which is that

> The interest of combining a family life with a professional life is complex, disturbing, satisfying and fulfilling – and one which needs more research.

Having referred to some of the satisfying elements of combining these aspects of life, there are equally frequent references to the frustrating and depressing aspects of attempting to cope with both. Some referred to the frustration in having to accept that there was little or no opportunity for career development because the female manager could not accept a posting to another location. Others with children repeatedly mentioned the lack of opportunity for part-time work in jobs commensurate with their experience, abilities and desire for responsibility. Several mentioned that despite the fact that the nature of their job meant that it could easily be run on flexi-time, and/or from home for most of the time, organizations were totally resistant to any suggestions for changing the organization of work (see Chapter 10 on women doctors). The inevitable price was frustration, even depression, and considerable resentment among managers who had often given several years of satisfactory performance in their jobs. As one woman manager said:

It's hard to reconcile home commitments and personal ambition.

One way in which several women managers dealt with the frustrations of having to abandon a highly responsible and interesting job was to use the 'maternity break' to obtain additional qualifications. Another tactic, referred to by a few, was to change their career ambitions, though it was clear that for many this entailed resigning themselves to accepting a situation they felt to be extremely frustrating.

Being female in male-dominated organizations

The vast majority of comments from women described difficulties arising from being female in a male-dominated organization or occupation. An experience commonly reported is the constant frustration of 'not being taken seriously', and on many occasions women managers of at least equal rank with male colleagues found themselves excluded from formal and informal decision-making meetings. A few referred to the fact that male colleagues, including those senior to them, appeared keen to 'keep women managers in the dark'. One manager stated that on two occasions her job had changed dramatically, and yet in neither instance was she consulted. This may of course be true for men too, but if so it was not commented on by them.

Ironically perhaps, another experience which was commonly expressed was strong resentment received from male colleagues who believed that female managers were receiving preferential treatment from senior management. A further frequent source of irritation to respondents was the suggestion, spoken or implicit, that if a woman is regarded as attractive it may sometimes be presumed that she obtained her position by devious sexual means, and/or that she should not be respected for her professional qualities. An example illustrates this:

When I was appointed as the first female marketing director (one of nine) there was some unpleasant political activity – including the local press – suggesting my appointment was made because I was 'a friend of the MD'. This was quite untrue.

Apart from the need to acclimatize oneself to the regular comments with sexual innuendo referred to by some respondents, a 'masculine' environment appeared to generate other stresses and strains for women. A substantial number felt alienated from environments where there was an overriding emphasis on competition and aggression, and that they felt they had to behave in an entirely 'unnatural' way. A typical comment was

> [Through completing the questionnaire] I noticed that my 'work personality' is far less attractive. It certainly reflects my dislike or feeling it necessary to change my personality at work to reflect what my male management want to see.

Another very strong theme that ran through many comments from women was the feeling of isolation at work, of seeming to operate according to principles quite different from male colleagues, and the constant sense of being under close scrutiny and being tested by a suspicious audience who never appeared to accept you as one of them. Senior managers in particular appeared suspicious, even threatened, and were often unwilling to entrust responsibilities to women managers, even those who were obviously more efficient and experienced than males. As one respondent stated:

> Women have to be twice as good as men to get half the recognition!

Not surprisingly, several women expressed their frustration and depression at the lack of encouragement and support they received from the men around them who did not believe in their capabilities. A few felt very strongly the lack of a female role model. Several stressed the importance of the support given from female colleagues, but two respondents reported experiencing great difficulty working with a female boss, who appeared as discriminatory as past male bosses and felt threatened by other women.

It is clear that although not all comments of the female respondents expressed negative experiences of working in male-dominated organizations, over half referred to problems of discrimination, and these appeared to permeate many aspects of organizational life.

One often experienced constraint for female professionals emerged when they attempted to develop skills and knowledge outside the organization on management development courses. A substantial number of respondents stated that their requests were usually met with subtle, or less-than-subtle resistance (also referred to by a few men). The following extract is a characteristic example:

> I personally experience great difficulty in being allowed to go on any kind of training courses. My requests are either ignored altogether or brushed aside with stupid uninformed comments. . . . Invariably I feel strongly about wanting to join a particular one and end up taking a holiday and paying the fees myself. The men in my company however have no difficulty in going on the courses they wish to follow. I wonder how other women cope with this problem.

People's desire for career counselling advice and help was apparent in many comments, often from women who reported being so disturbed by the problems they experienced at work that they had decided to change jobs, or even more dramatically, to change career. An example of this is

> I would have liked more space in the questionnaire devoted to reasons for job change – or in my case, career change. My own reasons were extremely

complex, and partly connected with the difficulties of a professional career in a very male profession (civil engineering). A second important factor was the realization that my personal motivation did not 'fit in' with the motivation required to be successful and fulfilled in my first choice of career. For a considerable period of time I felt guilty about my 'inadequate' personality before I realized this. I would also like to have commented on the process of analysis and decision-making that I undertook and the pressures I was under from family etc. before I made a radical change in career direction. I would also add that there is little counselling help available to people contemplating career change.

A lack of confidence in one's ability to do a job 'as well as the men' was a persistent theme in many comments. It seemed to be particularly strong when women were entering a new organization or work group, as the following extracts suggest:

Stepping up in the career ladder, and entering a new company to do so, was a time and energy consuming event. I found it very difficult to sell myself and negotiate to a level found easy by men. When I did get the job I was after, I worried a great deal about whether I was living up to the expectations and doing the job well enough.

I was very lacking in confidence in my ability in a managerial career, particularly in the early stages. The change came with my realization of my potential relative to others, particularly male colleagues.

Organizational change

How can changes in organizational policies and practices be accomplished? There is clearly no easy answer. The ability of individuals to overcome organizationally based prejudice and discrimination is limited. However much one seeks to empower the individual to confront these injustices it is likely that she will need support and help if she is not to become frustrated and defeated. One powerful way in which women managers can bring about changes in organizations is to form 'innovation groups' with the explicit intention of bringing about changes in current discriminatory practices towards women (West 1989a; 1989b).

Moscovici *et al.* (1985) have shown that a minority which consistently presents coherent arguments can bring about change within a wider social setting. Moscovici has developed these ideas to explain how minority power groups within society (e.g. women's movements) have brought about change historically, through conflict and conversion processes. By creating strong, cohesive groups it is likely that women managers will develop just such a coherent and consistent approach to bringing about change. Ecological groups, for example, have, through their persistence in presenting a clear, consistent message, had a major influence upon attitudes and practices within society and around the world.

When considering an organizational change it is important for the group to hold to some clear vision because it provides an anchor during the storms and conflict of the change process. As a result the enormous difficulties and inevitable unpopularity of the process are less likely to be overwhelming. It provides guidelines for preparation and a framework for managing resistance, setbacks and potential changes in goals.

It is the attractive, appealing and well-justified content of a vision statement which can by repetition, bring about the conversion of those who are initially neutral or opposed to the change. Social psychological research clearly indicates that a minority viewpoint is more likely to be accepted by the majority if it is argued coherently and consistently. Therefore, the group can prepare by carefully developing, thoroughly understanding and repeatedly rehearsing the content of the vision for the outcome of the change and the plan for achieving it. The greater their degree of unanimity and commitment to the change, the more likely it is to be effected. That means being committed to driving the change through. This requires stamina to maintain the change process in the face of frequent setbacks and stiff opposition. Finally, flexibility is important in listening carefully to the views of those affected and shaping (though not fundamentally changing) the vision in response to overwhelming or convincing evidence.

In order to manage resistance to change the group needs to consider thoroughly all possible objections to the change and build into their arguments ways of responding positively and convincingly. This may mean modifying plans accordingly beforehand. Their counter-arguments should thus be convincing and well-rehearsed. At the same time it is clearly important to listen actively and be seen to listen to the concerns of all those affected. Information dissemination is also important in the change process since much resistance is engendered by misunderstanding. The change agents can try to ensure that coherent and convincing arguments are presented to all those affected by the proposals. In summary they must prepare, rehearse, present, present and present.

In conclusion, this chapter has intended, at a time of apparent growth of opportunities for women, to draw attention to some of the possible hidden obstacles to the realization of their potential. While it focuses largely on the potential injustices to women, careful review by organizations of their culture and procedures are urgently needed in order to create people-friendly environments which enhance self-actualizing opportunities for both women and men. At the same time we have argued that women must be among the agents for change in their organizations – though possibly at the price of popularity – by forming cohesive and active influence groups in order to change existing pervasive and prejudicial practices, attitudes and structures.

References

Alban-Metcalfe, B. M. (1984) Current concerns of female and male managers and professions: an analysis of free-response comments to a national survey, *Equal Opportunities International*, 3, 1: 11–18.
—— (1985) The effects of socialisation on women's management careers, *Management Bibliographies and Reviews*, 11, 3.

—— (1987) Male and female managers: an analysis of biographical and self-concept data, *Work and Stress*, 1, 3: 207–19.

Alban-Metcalfe, B. M. and Nicholson, N. (1984) *The Career Development of British Managers*, London: British Institute of Management Foundation.

Basil, D. C. (1972) *Women in Management*, New York: Dunellen.

Bernadin, H. J. (ed.) (1982) *Women in the Work Force*, New York: Praeger.

Brannen, J, and Moss, P. (1988) *New Mothers at Work: employment and childcare*, London: Unwin.

Broverman, I. K., Vogel, R., Broverman, D. M., Clarkson, F. E. and Rosenkrantz P. S. (1975) Sex-role stereotypes: a current appraisal, in M. T. S. Mednick, S. S. Tangri and L. W. Hoffman (eds) *Women and Achievement: Social and Matrimonial Analyses*, New York: Hemisphere Publishing.

Bryson, R., Bryson, J. B. and Johnson, M. F. (1978) Family size, satisfaction and productivity in dual-career couples, *Psychology of Women Quarterly*, **3**: 67–77.

Bronstein, P., Black, L., Pfennig, J. L. and White, A. (1987) Stepping onto the academic career ladder: how are women doing?, in B. A. Gutek and L. Larwood (eds) *Women's Career Development*, London: Sage.

Kaufman, D. and Fetters, M. (1980) Work motivation and job values among professional men and women: a new accounting, *Journal of Vocational Behaviour*, 17: 251–62.

Langrish, S. (1981a) Women in management: comparative studies using rep grids, PhD thesis, UMIST, Manchester.

—— (1981b) Why don't women progress to management jobs? *Business Graduate*, 11, 1: 12–13.

Miner, J. (1974) Motivation to manage among women: studies of business managers and educational administrators, *Journal of Vocational Behaviour*, 5: 197–208.

Moscovici, S., Mugny, G. and Avermaet, E. U. (1985) *Perspectives in Minority Influence*, Cambridge: Cambridge University Press.

Nicholson, N. and West. M. A. (1988) *Managerial Job Change: Men and Women in Transition*, Cambridge: Cambridge University Press.

Nieva, V. F. and Gutek, B. A. (1981) *Women and Work: A Psychological Perspective*, New York: Praeger.

O'Leary, V. E. (1974) Some attitudinal barriers to occupational aspirations in women, *Psychological Bulletin*, 81: 809–26.

Pleck, J. (1977) The work–family role system, *Social Problems*, 24: 417–27.

Rosen, B. and Jerdee, T. H. (1974) Sex stereotyping in the executive suite, *Harvard Business Review*, 52: 45–58.

Schein, V. E. (1973) One relationship between sex-role stereotypes and requisite management characteristics, *Journal of Applied Psychology*, 57, 2: 95–100.

—— (1975) Relationships between sex-role stereotypes and requisite management characteristics among female managers, *Journal of Applied Psychology*, 60: 340–4.

Siegfried, W. D., McFarlane, I., Graham, D. B., Moore, N. A. and Young, P. L. (1981) A re-examination of sex differences in job preferences, *Journal of Vocational Behaviour*, 18: 30–42.

Terborg, J. R. (1977) Women in management: a research review, *Journal of Applied Psychology*, 62: 647–64.

Valdez, R. L. and Gutek, B. A. (1987) Family roles: a help or a hindrance for working women?' in B. A. Gutek and L. Larwood (eds) *Women's Career Development*, London: Sage.

West, M. A. (1989a). Innovation in groups at work, MRC/ESRC Social and Applied Psychology Unit, University of Sheffield, Memo no 1060.

—— (1989b) Visions and team innovations, *Changes*, 7: 136–40.

13 | A woman's place is at the word processor: technology and change in the office
Catherine Cassell

Introduction

In the UK 40 per cent of all employed women are office workers yet, with notable exceptions (McNally 1979; West 1982), little research has been conducted examining their experience of work (Crompton *et al.* 1982). This is surprising for a number of reasons. First, it is difficult to understand why occupational psychologists have ignored such a large group of the work-force, since as McNally (1979) points out, nearly half of all white-collar workers are women. Second, when one considers that office work is currently in a state of change, as a result of the developments in Information Technology (IT), the situation of women office workers seems ripe for investigation. Although a number of studies have considered the impact that IT will have on the jobs of women office workers (e.g. Softley 1985; Morgall 1983; Barker and Downing 1980), these studies have been conducted mainly from a feminist perspective, rather than emerging from 'mainstream' occupational psychology.

The aim of this chapter is to examine why office work is perceived as 'women's work' and what attracts women workers to clerical jobs. In describing women's attitudes to office work, I shall focus particularly on the concerns and expectations women have about the use of new technology, drawing on findings of a study of female office workers conducted in Sheffield in 1985. From this study conclusions will be drawn about the nature of women's office work, and the role of occupational psychologists in investigating women's work experience. The perspective from which I start is that gender is a crucial organizing factor within work. Gender stereotypes influence the jobs that people do, the pay and conditions associated with those jobs, and the opportunities available to the incumbents of those jobs. Additionally work is crucial to the social construction of gender (Game and Pringle 1984), in that particular jobs have come to be defined as 'suitable' work for women or men. Therefore a consideration of women's office work needs to be seen in the more general context of gender and social relations.

Women: the 'natural office workers'

Office work has changed considerably during the twentieth century and two characteristics are particularly worthy of note. The first is the massive growth of the clerical labour force. In 1850 white-collar workers were 1 per cent of the working population. By 1950 this figure had increased to 10 per cent and by 1970 40 per cent of the working population were white-collar workers (Huws 1982). This increase in clerical labour was matched by the entry of women into office work: the 'feminization' of the clerical labour force (Davies 1974). During the nineteenth century clerical work had been seen as a component of the male managerial role; however, the large number of new jobs that were created were flooded by women. Softley (1985) suggests that there were two major reasons for this. First, women provided cheap labour: they were prepared to work long hours in ill-ventilated rooms for less pay than their male counterparts, and second, the introduction of the typewriter in the 1870s led to a whole new area of work, thus providing the opportunity for women to enter a new occupation that was not yet sex-typed. Additionally women were encouraged to use typewriters because of their 'natural' manual dexterity. Davy (1986) suggests that office work had many advantages for working-class women seeking employment in the first decade of the twentieth century. Apart from being clean and respectable, it provided a viable alternative to domestic service, dress-making and factory work.

Despite the fears expressed by male journalists about the dangers of women working in offices (Softley 1985), the employment of women as secretaries and typists began to grow. As clerical work became predominantly a female occupation its status declined. Morgall (1983) suggests that women were relegated to the low-paying routine tasks, while a new, exclusively male managerial level developed and continued to grow.

In examining how women entered office work, an important element is the ideology that backed up this trend. As women became more accepted as office workers, ideology shifted so that women, as a result of their 'feminine' qualities, became viewed as the 'natural office workers'. As Davies (1974) suggests:

> Women, so the argument went, are by nature adaptable, courteous, and sympathetic – in a word, passive. This natural passivity makes them ideally suited to the job of carrying out an endless number of routine tasks without a complaint. Furthermore, their docility makes it unlikely that they will aspire to rise very far above their station. Thus their male boss is spared the unpleasant possibility that his secretary will one day be competing with him for his job.
>
> (Davies 1974: 258)

This division of labour reflects the general positions that men and women hold in other spheres of life. Patriarchal relations, where men hold positions of control and women are there to service their needs, extended into the office and still, to a certain extent, characterize office life today. Softley (1985) describes how, in addition to clerical work and typing, secretaries are expected to plan their bosses' diaries, make his appointments, make tea, water the office plants and so on. Such expectations lead to many secretaries taking on the role of the 'office wife'. These social aspects of the job are viewed as enhancing the nature of secretarial work, and are often not available to women with the less prestigious office jobs, such as typing. It is important to point out here that 'office work' covers a diverse number of jobs and skills depending on the size, structure and function of the organization. The term 'office work', however, is frequently used as a unitary term (Griffin 1985). This creates problems in understanding women's roles within the office which can be quite diverse. For example a secretary who is a personal assistant will have more discretion and autonomy over her work than a typist who works in a typing pool. There are therefore considerable differences in the roles and statuses of various office workers.

Within the limited research literature on women office workers, stereotypical attributions are often made about their motivation to work. As Lockwood says in *The Blackcoated Worker*:

> A large proportion are young, unmarried women and for many of them clerical work is 'just a job like any other' take up in the interval between leaving school and getting married. It is known that girls are especially attracted to clerical work because of its social status, and also, it may be surmised, because of the opportunity it affords for meeting desirable marriage partners in the blackcoated class.
>
> (Lockwood 1958: 126)

McNally (1979), in reviewing such attitudes suggest that whereas the single woman is viewed as using work instrumentally, the married woman is perceived as working for 'pin money'. This is a particularly inappropriate view in the 1980s and 1990s when more and more women are becoming the primary breadwinner. Work is, more often than not, an economic necessity for both single and married women. As Coyle (1988) points out, only 18 per cent of households in the UK are now supported by a sole male wage-earner.

Cockburn (1987) asks the question of why young women aspire to take on subservient roles in office jobs. Her research involved interviewing young women on government-sponsored Youth Training Schemes for clerical work, about their expectations and aspirations. She concludes that there are a number of reasons why young working-class women view office work as attractive. One reason is the 'glamour' that is associated with certain kinds of office work (Sherrat 1983). Cockburn suggests that advertisements from temporary employment agencies such as Kelly Girl and Brook Street Employment Bureau reinforce the view of the young independent woman with a role to play:

> For young women, struggling in their mid-teens to achieve a workable gender identity, a job that is unambiguously feminine, safe from competition from men, and bestows a little extra femininity on you, is a secure place to be.
>
> (Cockburn 1987: 118)

Secretarial skills and typing make good sense in a world where unemployment is a continual threat for young people. Additionally they provide an entry back into the labour market after bringing up children. The image of the office as a sociable place makes it more attractive to young women than the factory floor. There is the added bonus that women do not have to compete with men for these jobs.

Other studies have considered the aspirations and expectations of women who have worked in clerical posts for a period of time. Crompton *et al.* (1982) conducted interviews with 86 clerical workers in local government, 53 of whom were women. They found that 54 per cent of the women interviewed wanted some form of promotion out of their job, yet only 36 per cent expected it. This is compared with 87 per cent of the male sample who expressed an interest in promotion. The ambivalence that women had about promotion was often related to their domestic commitments. Running a home, for example, conflicted with the demands of extra responsibility at work. This ambivalence also reflects a relatistic appraisal of the opportunities for promotion that are available to clerical workers. Downing (1980) argued that few women ever reach the highest levels of the office hierarchy. Additionally Griffin (1985) suggests that although working in a bank is seen to be one of the most prestigious and secure jobs for a young working-class woman, the young women that she interviewed realized that their prospects were limited.

In view of the stereotypes of office work, it is not surprising that it is attractive to young working-class women. Evidence suggests that young women entering offices know what awaits them and, as Cockburn suggests, 'they are doing the best they can with the opportunities they have inherited' (1987: 120).

IT in the office: the debate

The 'Information Revolution' that has occurred since the mid-1970s has radically altered the nature of information capture, processing, storage and retrieval. The implications of this revolution are crucial for women workers as Pullman and Szymanski suggest:

> The jobs most affected by office technology are clerical jobs. Nineteen million clerical workers, 80% of whom are women, comprise the largest occupational category in the United States labour market. That means that nearly one out of every three working women is in a job that is susceptible to technological change.
>
> (Pullman and Szymanski 1988: 1)

The authors continue by suggesting that the direction in automation is to eliminate the types of jobs at the bottom of the office hierarchy, those typically occupied by working-class white or ethnic minority women. Taking word-processing as an example, Softley (1985) describes how the technology is being advertised as a way of increasing the productivity of typists while reducing labour costs. Research suggests that clerical job losses often accompany the introduction of word-processors (Bird 1980).

Within the modern office there are also likely to be radical changes in the way that work is organized. Some authors believe that these changes will be extremely beneficial in improving the nature of jobs within office work, while increasing office productivity (e.g. Cecil 1980). Other authors view the situation differently however, emphasizing that IT will lead to the de-skilling of workers, increased fragmentation and standardization of work, and the loss of jobs. This debate raises interesting issues for women workers.

In considering the impact that IT will have on women's work, a number of authors have concentrated on the potential of word-processors (Softley 1985; Barker and Downing 1980; Morgall 1983). What distinguishes these authors from others who have considered the potential impact of word-processors (e.g. Cecil 1980) is that they write from a Marxist-feminist perspective, where gender is seen as a crucial process in work organization. Their analysis is therefore set in the context of social relations:

> The impact of word-processing on the office will be to radically re-structure its social relations. It will also, significantly, divest secretarial workers of the control they have over their own labour process. By becoming paced by the machine, they will in effect be rendered machine minders.
>
> (Downing 1980: 276)

An alternative and more optimistic view is that the introduction of word-processing into offices will free women from the more routine aspects of office life allowing them to spend time on other more interesting forms of work. Webster (1988) describes the view of the office of the future that is put across by word-processor manufacturers:

> Elegant young secretaries sit in air-conditioned splendour amongst pot plants, smiling into visual display units. The working environment is portrayed as being cleaner, lighter and more comfortable, the work itself as being more skilled and satisfying for the office worker.
>
> (Webster 1988: 1)

Researchers who have investigated the actual impact of word-processors have found varying instances of work organization around the new technology (Buchannan and Boddy 1982; Webster 1988; Butterriss and Clark 1977). In some cases the jobs of typists have been improved as a result of the introduction of word-processors (e.g. Butterriss and Clark 1977). As more research emerges, the debate continues.

Within the debate the concerns of women office workers about the introduction of office technology have rarely been investigated or expressed. In considering the reactions of women workers to the introduction of IT in the work-place, I would argue that such reactions need to be viewed in the context of the relationship between gender and technology. Traditionally the masculinity of technology (Griffiths 1985) has excluded women both actively, and passively, from its development and use. However, the office of the future will require women to interact regularly with up-to-date technology. The research described here considers some of these issues by focusing on the concerns of female office workers about the introduction of IT into their jobs.

Reactions to the introduction of word-processors in the work-place

Research methodology

This research was conducted with twenty-eight female office workers from four organizations in Sheffield. I purposely chose to interview only women, rather than seeking to compare their experience to those of male workers. When comparisons between the sexes are made, there is a danger that the opinions of women are viewed from the perspective of how they differ from the male 'norm', an approach that is clearly insufficient in describing, categorizing and analysing women's experience of work.

Eight of the women had just begun to use word-processors, while the other twenty had been instructed by their management that they would be using them in the near future. The technique used was that of in-depth semi-structured interviews. I felt that interviewing was the most appropriate methodology. As the issues I was raising could be perceived as sensitive, the interview process would provide the respondents with the chance to develop the issues that they felt were important to them.

Oakley (1982) suggests that the traditional scientific paradigm of 'good' interviewing practice creates problems for feminist interviewers interviewing women. As the primary aim of much feminist research is to detail and validate women's subjective experiences, it is contradictory to feminist principles to use a method that reinforces the status divisions between the interviewer and interviewee. When rapport has been developed it seems inappropriate not to answer an interviewee's questions for example, or to pretend that the interviewer herself has no opinion. As Oakley suggests:

> Where both [interviewer and interviewee] share the same gender, socialization and critical life-experiences, social distance can be minimal. Where both interviewer and interviewee share membership of the same minority group, the basis for equality may impress itself even more urgently on the interviewer's consciousness.
>
> (Oakley 1982: 55)

Therefore these interviews reflected the fact that I was keen to detail the everyday experiences of women while ensuring that the interview situation was a two-way process. If the interviewees asked me questions about my research or about word-processors, I would always answer them directly, rather than handing the question back to them.

The questions within the interview schedule covered various areas including attitudes to present job; views about the introduction of word-processors; attitudes towards training; and the impact of word-processors on secretarial work as a whole. The interviews were tape-recorded and later transcribed in full. The transcripts were then content analysed using a method where response statements from interviewees are divided into a number of themes and subthemes. The interview transcripts are then in a convenient form to describe and categorize the interviewees' responses.

The organizations

Space permits a fuller description of the four organizations where the interviewees worked. Two of them were educational institutions and the other two local authority departments, therefore they were all in the public sector. In the two local authority departments all the interviewees were members of a national trade union (NALGO). Within the other two organizations however, none of the women mentioned any trade union membership or activity. None of the women I spoke to had had any say in the system that was chosen for use within their office. Although in practice they would have been the experts, so to speak, in the day-to-day running of the office, their opinions were not sought. Although in one of the organizations secretaries were asked whether they wanted the technology, they had no say in the system that was then chosen.

I asked all of the secretaries why they thought their employers were purchasing word-processors. The general idea was that employers purchased word-processors because they were the 'in-thing'. Remarks like 'they had to spend their money on something', 'the boss thinks it's a nice piece of furniture', and 'He [the boss] is all into this new technology bit' suggest that from their point of view there had been little consideration about the reasons for purchasing the technology, let alone any coherent implementation strategy. Some of the women pointed out that they could have had a useful input into the decision-making process and should have had some say:

> I would have preferred it if the people whose idea it was would have got us together as a group, or an office, and decided what we needed together, instead of just going out and buying something and saying 'this is what we've got – get trained on it'.

Although the interviewees had a variety of jobs, their tasks could be classified under the general heading of 'administrative-clerical work'. Five were responsible for the work of one particular person, and therefore had higher status jobs. Although most of the interviewees were responsible for the work of a number of people, none of them conducted typing duties alone. For the purpose of this discussion I shall refer to them collectively as 'secretaries'. Generally the secretaries talked about their jobs in favourable terms, their work was varied and they all had control over the pace of work. Demands upon the secretaries varied from organization to organization, and in the case of the educational institutions fluctuated during the year.

Thoughts on word-processors

At least half of the secretaries were pleased about the introduction of word-processors, a common idea being that it was important for them to keep up with the technology of the times. Most of them, however, were also apprehensive and nervous, mainly because they didn't know what to expect. This was particularly a problem in organizations where there were no word-processors in use, as no information was available about the capabilities of the technology. A considerable range of worries and concerns was expressed by the secretaries, with only three suggesting that they had no worries at all. The major worry was about actually using the technology and their own personal competence. For older women in particular, this was a concern:

> Girls are learning it at college now, so I have to be able to say I have the ability to be able to learn just as well as they do. I think I've got to prove that, for when I get judged, it's always with the younger girls.

Concerns outside of the individual ranged from job loss, loss of skills, and loss of social contact to health hazards in using the technology. There was a consensus that organizations would need fewer secretarial staff in the future as a result of new technology and therefore jobs would disappear. However, none of the interviewees felt that *her* job was threatened. One person for example suggested that the secretary's job will always be safe:

> I don't think we'll ever lose the personal secretary touch or the shorthand. That will not die out completely because there will always be some men who like to have a secretary about. I don't think it will ever die out.

It is interesting that the social relations on which secretarial work is based are seen as crucial in defending women's jobs from the negative consequences of advancing technology.

In terms of job and promotion opportunities, most of those interviewed felt that being able to use a word-processor would have no impact on their prospects. Although word-processing skills were viewed as necessary when looking for new jobs, most of them believed that there wasn't much chance of promotion within their present job anyway. As one pointed out: 'What can you get promoted to? A bigger word-processor?' There was a variety of views, though, about how their status might change. Half the sample thought that it would remain the same: as one said 'You're still just a secretary'. Some, however, felt that the status of office work would increase. As one woman said about the men for whom she worked:

> I suppose they do hold you in higher regard when they see you can operate this machinery because half of them are really baffled by it. It's like anything that you see being done that you can't actually do yourself.

Therefore this new skill that nobody else understood would give secretarial staff more control over their work. One of the women in the sample who was already using a word-processor made the following comment:

> The bosses are really thick about it, they have no idea how these systems work. At . . . they had a system similar to ours and for quite a long time the secretaries said they couldn't do letters on it and of course they could. But the bosses didn't have any idea at all.

It is easy to see how in this context a secretary who understands the technology could acquire more status and control within her role. Some interviewees however had equally strong views that the status of secretaries would decrease considerably. The title 'word-processor operator' was an anathema to this group. The phrase was seen as conjuring up the image of a robot pressing keys:

> My husband for example, he seems to think that a word-processor operator is a lot less intelligent than someone who's still a secretary. You've learnt a new skill but it's like everything will be the same, there'll be no individuality throughout.

In reviewing the worries and concerns of these women, it is noteworthy that the majority of those concerns related to intrapersonal competence and confidence. These concerns outweighed those external to the individual such as job loss and health hazards. This is perhaps a reflection of the underlying relationship between gender and technology. The implications of 'using machinery', as it was described, arose a number of times:

> Looking at a computer I go 'good grief', my mind just isn't into that whereas some people are really into that – they'll love it. I'm the sort of person that's not very mechanically minded.

A number of women in the sample suggested that being worried about technology had something to do with gender:

> I think perhaps for women it's a bit more frightening than for men because men are more into machinery and that sort of stuff. I think there's that initial barrier that is often worse for women.

This view emerged particularly when the secretaries were asked about how they thought their colleagues would react to using word-processors. Technology was viewed as threatening to women collectively, and older women in particular. It is important to point out, however, that most agreed that this fear of 'machinery' could be easily overcome when the necessary training or experience had occurred:

> I did type for twenty odd years, I started out with a manual typewriter and I've literally come through it all, going on to electric, then the golfball and now a more sophisticated one so it's never worried me. I always thought I'd never manage this, but you do. I won't let machinery worry or defeat me, though I get mad at it at times and swear at it.

In practice, it seems that women's exclusion from technology, reflected in the view that they are not 'mechanically minded', raises particular issues for women who are about to use technology in the office for the first time. Lack of access and experience feeds the worries and concerns about competence and ability with regard to its use. However, this explanation in itself is not enough to give an understanding of the interviewee's reactions to the introduction of the technology. Rather we must go back to the stereotypes held about female office workers.

Management policies to implement change without adequate consultation are reinforced by the stereotypes of women office workers as passive people with other priorities. The expectation is that change will be passively accepted. This lack of information and consultation during organizational change, coupled with the implications of women's general exclusion from technology, means that women workers are understandably concerned about their capabilities as technology users. Women are clearly capable in any technological field when, as with men, sufficient access and information is made available. The attitudes of the women in the sample who had started to use word-processors are a testament to this.

All of this group preferred using word-processors to typewriters. Six of them felt that their work had become easier, and five found the work more interesting. In contradiction to the research that suggests that word-processors can de-skill office workers and lead to the fragmentation of their work, this group of women felt that their working lives had been improved. Clearly caution needs to be expressed in generalizing these results to other groups of women workers. Apart from the small size of the sample, it must be noted that this group performed the same tasks after the introduction of word-processors as they had done before. Essentially the content of their work remained the same. Management, in introducing word-processors, had expected them to be used in the same way as typewriters, rather than as a tool for reorganizing work. This was the case in all four organizations.

Where next?

Within this chapter I have raised a number of issues about investigating women's experience of work, with particular reference to women and IT. A clear recommendation is that consultation about the introduction of new IT systems into offices will enable women workers to be active in the change process. There are a number of ways in which this consultation could be achieved. Involving secretaries in discussions about the purchasing of equipment and about the tasks that are most appropriate for computerization is a start. However, consultation can extend beyond this to include participation within the systems design process. In this approach the eventual users of a system participate in the overall design of that system with systems designers and other people whose roles are affected (Clegg and Symon 1989). User participation within the systems design process has been recommended by a number of authors (e.g. Hirschheim 1985; Ehn *et al.* 1983; Mumford 1983). As well as improving the information available to users and allowing their experience to be used in the design of the system, user participation can also lead to improved commitment to change from the workers involved (Hirschheim 1985).

Recently research is beginning to emerge about how women clerical workers can become more involved in the systems design process. An exciting project in this area is reported by Green *et al.* (1989). The authors describe an intervention within a local authority department designed to enable women clerical workers to become active in the systems development process. The researchers adopted a 'study circle' method as developed by researchers in Scandinavia (e.g. Vehvilainen 1986). The study circle is a regular group where women clerical workers have discussions about the new computer system and particular issues that they perceive as important such as training, health and safety and job design. The authors suggest that the study circle method takes into account

> the women's need for 'confidence-building', but at the same time acknowledges the potential strength of their contribution to the systems development process.
>
> (Green *et al.* 1989: 12)

Participation within the study circle is on a voluntary basis and the programme is adapted according to the perceived needs of the group. Each group has seven two-hour meetings about once a fortnight and is facilitated by a researcher and someone who has been a participant in a previous study circle. At the end of each study circle the group compiles its own summary report. This focuses on the particular concerns and issues that group members feel emerged the most strongly from the meetings. These reports are then circulated around the department and submitted for discussion to the systems design team. Green *et al.* suggest that the influence of this particular initiative can be seen in three areas. First, the women workers can now take their own initiatives around the technology instead of responding to the ideas of other people. Second, their skills and experience are now recognized in the context of the systems design process. Finally the authors argue that this experience has helped to demonstrate the importance of the links between the technical and non-technical aspects of the systems design process.

The authors argue that

> the Study Circles have provided a basis for the women clerical workers to play an active role in the process of office systems design. They have done so because they have been based on an understanding of clerical workers' experience of technology, and of the support and learning needs of women.
>
> (Green *et al.* 1989: 12)

Such innovative strategies present an alternative approach to the introduction of technology and organizational change. In this approach women are actively involved in the change process. Clearly for this to be the case education, communication and participation are crucial, together with the recognition that women office workers have skills and experience to contribute to discussions and decisions about organizational change. The concerns of women office workers should not be perceived as a problem for those women themselves. Rather there is a collective responsibility to recognize the origins of such concerns and attempt to deal with them in a non-sexist manner.

Conclusions

This collective responsibility of understanding women's everyday experience of work extends to researchers. It is all too easy to forget the experiences of women in sex-stereotypical jobs. It is far more exciting, perhaps, to consider the experiences of women battling away in a high-powered male environment, aiming for the elusive top jobs, rather than focusing on women who work in jobs that are considered appropriate to their sex. In describing the social relations of office work I have argued that its roots can be found in the view of women as passive, unambitious people there to cater for the needs of their bosses. The introduction of IT systems into the office environment without consultation or participation in the change process reinforces this view. Therefore in understanding any form of work organization, the social construction of gender must be viewed as a crucial organizing process. It is only from this perspective that women's work experience can be detailed and, above all, understood.

References

Barker, J. and Downing, H. (1980) Word processing and the transformation of the patriarchal relations of control in the office, *Capital and Class*, 10: 64–99.

Bird, E. (1980) *Information Technology in the Office: The Impact on Women's Jobs*, Manchester: Equal Opportunities Commission.

Buchannan, D. A. and Boddy, D. (1982) Advanced technology and the quality of working life: the effects of word processing on video typists, *Journal of Occupational Psychology*, 55: 1–11.

Butterriss, M. and Clark, A. (1977) Giving word processing a new meaning, *Personnel Management*, 9: 31–3, 39.

Cecil, P. B. (1980) *Word Processing in the Modern Office*, 2nd edn, New York: Benjamin/Cummings.

Clegg, C. and Symon, G. (1989) A review of human-centred manufacturing technology and a framework for its design and evaluation, SAPU memo no 1036, available from MRC/ESRC Social and Applied Psychology Unit, University of Sheffield.

Cockburn, C. (1987) *Two-Track Training: Sex Inequalities and the YTS*, London: Macmillan Education.

Coyle, A. (1988) Continuity and change: women in paid work, in A. Coyle and J. Skinner (eds) *Women at Work*, London: Macmillan Education.

Crompton, R., Jones, G. and Reid, S. (1982) Contemporary clerical work: a case study of local government, in J. West (ed.) *Work, Women and the Labour Market*, London: Routledge & Kegan Paul.

Davies, M. (1974) Woman's place is at the typewriter: the feminization of the clerical labour force, in Z. Eisenstein (ed.) (1979) *Capitalist Patriarchy and the Case for Socialist Feminism*, New York and London: Monthly Review Press.

Davy, T. (1986) 'A cissy job for men; a nice job for girls'; women shorthand typists in London 1900–39, in L. Davidoff and B. Westover (eds) *Our Work, Our Lives, Our Words: Women's History and Women's Work*, London: Macmillan Education.

Downing, H. (1980) Word processors and the oppression of women, in T. Forester (ed.) *The Microelectronics Revolution*, Oxford: Basil Blackwell.

Ehn, P., Kyng, M. and Sundblad, Y. (1983) The Utopia project, in V. Briefs, C. Ciborra and L. Schneider (eds) *Systems Design for, with and by the Users*, Amsterdam: North-Holland.

Game, A. and Pringle, R. (1984) *Gender at Work*, London: Pluto.

Green, E., Owen, J., Pain, D. and Stone, I. (1989) Human-centred systems . . . woman-centred systems? Gender divisions and office computer systems design, Paper presented to the BSA Annual Conference, Plymouth Polytechnic, 20–23 March.

Griffin, C. (1985) *Typical Girls? Young Women from School to the Job Market*, London: Routledge & Kegan Paul.

Griffiths, D. (1985) The exclusion of women from technology, in W. Faulkner and E. Arnold (eds) *Smothered by Invention: Technology in Women's Lives*, London: Pluto.

Hirschheim, R. (1985) *Office Implementation: A Social and Organizational Perspective*, Chichester: John Wiley.

Huws, U. (1982) *Your Job in the Eighties: A Woman's Guide to New Technology*, London: Pluto.

Lockwood, D. (1958) *The Blackcoated Worker*, London: Allen & Unwin.

McNally, F. (1979) *Women for Hire: A Study of the Female Office Worker*, London: Macmillan.

Morgall, J. (1983) Typing our way to freedom, is it true that new office technology can liberate women?, *Behaviour and Information Technology* 2, 3: 215–26.

Mumford, E. (1983) *Designing Human Systems*, Manchester: Manchester Business School Publications.

Mumford, E. and Banks, O. (1967) *The Computer and the Clerk*, London: Routledge & Kegan Paul.

Oakley, A. (1982) Interviewing women: a contradiction in terms, in H. Roberts (ed.) *Doing Feminist Research*, London: Routledge & Kegan Paul.

Pullman, C. and Szymanski, S. (1988) The Impact of Office Technology on Clerical Worker Skills, in the Banking, Insurance and Legal Industries in New York City: Implications for Training, *Proceedings of the 3rd IFIP Conference on Women, Work and Computerization*, Amsterdam, 27–29 April.

Sherrat, N. (1983) Girls, jobs and glamour, *Feminist Review*, 15, winter: 47–62.

Softley, E. (1985) Word processing: new opportunities for women office workers?, in W. Faulkner and E. Arnold (eds) *Smothered by Invention*: Technology in Women's Lives, London: Pluto.

Vehvilainen, M. (1986) A Study Circle approach as a method for women to develop their work and computer systems, Paper presented to the IFIP conference 'Women, Work and Computerization', Dublin, August.

Webster, J. (1988) Influencing the content of women's work in automated offices, *Proceedings of the 3rd IFIP Conference on Women, Work and Computerization*, Amsterdam, 27–29 April.

West, J. (1982) *Work, Women and the Labour Market*, London: Routledge & Kegan Paul.

14 | Women and politics
Louise Ricklander

I am a Swedish woman who has worked for thirteen years in local politics. I am educated as a psychologist. This chapter is about thoughts and feelings on the world of work from a middle-aged woman with experience from local politics and an addiction to analyse. The very last part is the only one that is based on a study. Perhaps my own difficulties and successes can throw some light on the problems described in more formal studies and previous chapters.

Historically the external world has been the business of men. Women took care of the internal world. Politics traditionally is external, but not necessarily the business of all men – often only of the few. It is only this last century that all men in the western world have gradually been able to vote. The voting rights of women followed decades later. In Switzerland, for example, it was not until the 1970s that women had equal voting rights with men.

To be able to vote is the first step towards the possibility of getting a public commission. Nowadays women also have access to these possibilities. But where there is real power, few women have yet appeared. Just now the world has four or five top female politicians: certainly fewer than 1 per cent of the possible leading positions. Incidentally we do not have even 0.1 per cent of the leading positions in the world of finance, which some would see as even more important in terms of power.

In the town of Lidingö, where I live, there are about 40,000 people and we have a town council of 51 elected members. They are from seven different parties – the same parties that make up our National Parliament, plus a local party. We have the town government consisting of eleven members from the same parties. The group leaders of the biggest parties in this government are the only professional politicians in the town. Two come from the majority and one from the opposition.

Of these professional politicians, the leader of the biggest party is the most powerful. In Sweden we have around 290 such politicians; 10 per cent of them are women. This proportion has not changed over the last elections. But in the town councils and on all the boards and committees the number of women has been steadily increasing and is now around 30 per cent, with a higher percentage in the cities and biggest towns.

I started my political activity in 1977 as a deputy member of a school board. Three years later I became a member of the town council and the leader for my party of the committee. During this time I also worked as an educational psychologist. From 1985 to 1989 I was leader of my party in the town government and the leader of the opposition, that is a professional politician. I left office early in 1989, but stayed on the town council, and spent time writing a book on my experience as a woman within the political process. Now I write and work as a psychologist on a freelance basis.

I was born in the 1930s into an upper-class family, which naturally has coloured my way of seeing things. Women were not supposed to take initiative except inside the home. The prime duty of a woman was to find a man with a good career. It certainly was not to make a career herself – this would be a threat to her husband. My father was a politician on the national level and my mother a housewife. My brother, who is two years younger than me, started his political career ten years before me and is now a member of Parliament, a Conservative like my father. I am a Social Democrat, a party comparable to the Labour Party in Britain.

When I started my own political work at the age of 43, I did not believe that there was any difference in the possibilities for women to have political careers compared to the possibilities for men. I thought it was just a question of will: if a woman wanted a political career, she was as capable as a man. It took me quite a time to see that wanting was not enough. The whole political world was built up in a male way. I and my 'sisters' had to stumble around a lot before we found our feet. Our way of looking at things and our priorities were not mirrored in the political world. Added to that we did not automatically have the code to this male way of seeing things.

The beginning

With children of my own and working as a school psychologist I became more and more interested in the organization of society. I joined a political party and was soon invited to my first annual meeting. I did not know anyone and I felt lost and shy in the big group. I seated myself at the back of the room and listened with interest to the speeches. Everybody seemed so clever – especially some of the men. I admired. Naturally I did not say a word. I was afraid of making a fool of myself. I noticed a few men who seemed new like myself, but they were not silent – and they did make fools of themselves once in a while. I judged them silently inside myself.

Some meetings later they were not making fools of themselves any longer, but I had still not said one word. Nobody knew anything about me.

It had to be a small group before I felt able to speak. Once I was in a study group organized by the party, I was quickly established as a reasonably intelligent and trustworthy person. Half a year later I was known by people and given a commission on the school board as a deputy member. I was surprised to get this appointment as I judged myself inferior to the others. I was very thankful and I felt full of my own importance.

Women do stay in the background in big groups. They are often afraid to be seen and afraid to make fools of themselves. They wait for someone to notice their good behaviour.

The above differences are unfortunately not only relevant for women born in the 1930s and 1940s. You can see the same in the schools of today. Girls are much more silent than boys. Boys do sometimes make fools of themselves. When I worked in schools I did not see that they thereby trained themselves for future careers. But I gave them, as school workers do, much more attention than I gave the well-behaved girls – in spite of the fact that girls are more clever and get better marks during the first ten years of school.

To be surprised, grateful and proud of oneself is a female way of receiving a new position of trust. Men take their appointments as their natural rights and, if they were astonished at anything, it was the fact that it had taken so long.

On the school board

As an elected member of the board I discovered new ways of communicating. We politicians and some of the leading civil servants met once a month in a very formal way. The meeting was preceded by pages and pages of written material in stiff old-fashioned language which I had real difficulties in understanding, despite my education.

The spoken language in the meetings was just as formal and there were many rules about when and how you should say things, not to mention the complexity of the decision-making. I had worked ten years as an educational psychologist and thought I knew about schools, but these rules silenced me again.

And I wanted to influence school. For me it was an important political question how we educated our children. But I soon understood that the answer to that question in reality was for the civil servants. Politicians decide about the resources. For instance we decide how many school psychologists to have but not how they should work.

The written and the spoken languages are designed to minimize mistakes. The rules are many. Men seemed to understand the words and know the rules quickly. They even seem to like them. Women are hindered by them and impatient with them. They try to get at the contents of things. But tradition and the civil servants hinder them. Of course, the tradition is male, and the question which remains unanswered is whether women should join the tradition and learn the language, or fight for change.

You see these differences between women and men early in life. In every school playground young boys are playing all sorts of complicated games with many names and rules, while girls walk along two by two and talk and talk. Girls are training in relationships and human communication. Later they take to horses and baby caring while boys start playing football or ice-hockey or data-games with even more complicated rules. Women have difficulties in understanding the meaning of all these rules. They generally find the issue in question of more importance. The formalities for them are merely an aid in managing whatever the content in question is. If they are not helpful they may be ignored. Women do make more formal mistakes than men. For men rules are significant and they get suspicious of women who try to skip them.

Recently we had a very clever female Minister of Law in Sweden. She was involved with some people who thought they had a good inkling of who had murdered Olaf Palme, our late Prime Minister. She gave one of them an official letter of introduction which she did not register. That a Minister of Law could make an error like that was unbelievable for most people. Another error was her personal involvement. Personal involvement is not allowed. It seems to be a myth among men that you can act without it, even in dramatic situations. Men often deny that their personal feelings influence their official decisions in any way.

In spite of the fact that this minister had done any amount of good work she had to leave her position. She had made a couple of very 'feminine' mistakes.

The town council

Gradually I got used to being a deputy on the school board. In the next election I was elected a member of the town council. This time I appeared on the voting ballot of my party. I had been put there by influential people without my knowing how that happened. For the first time I confronted the public and the press. I was again very surprised by the fact that people really seemed to want me and very pleased at the same time. The men on the ballot took it as a matter of course.

In the town council I met the political language in full. The language we politicians use is designed to impress each other and the public. We all talk well of our politics and of our own party and we criticize everything in the politics of other parties. We are the angels and they are the devils. When people use such language in ordinary life it is judged as childish, splitting and in bad taste. People outside politics suspect that politicians never see their own mistakes, but we do have discussions internally in the party group. When the group has taken a majority decision, everyone follows that.

But it is a language that makes the differences between the parties clear for whoever listens. In a principal way the positive as well as the negative sides of different political views get taken care of.

I found this language very difficult. I could talk well of my own politics – that was easy – but I could not criticize the others. I got frightened just thinking about it. And I was even more afraid of being criticized by them. I could not understand the men who counted every attack on themselves as a victory. Men easily took to this language and they seemed to like to argue. I even heard people being really abusive to each other and still go out for a drink afterwards like the best of friends.

Women generally have difficulties with this. We are trained not to hurt other people, and besides we hate getting hurt ourselves. We compensate by being clever and by being very well prepared when we speak. And we gradually learn.

Women and men differ when they deal with guilt. Women tend to take guilt on themselves and males tend to project it on to others. The political language – and that may well apply also to the politics of work – is projecting all guilt on to other parties: I am right and you are wrong. It is difficult to take for women who are raised in the belief that they have to take whatever guilt happens to be around.

Unfortunately it is more fun to listen to a debate where people abuse each other. The members of the town council who get most press are the attacking ones. And to be written about is important for politicians. As a matter of fact it is better to get bad reviews than no reviews at all: Oscar Wilde was right.

Behind the scenes

There is a lot of political work that has to be done between meetings. There are plans to be made, reports to be written, minutes to be taken and study groups and internal meetings to be run. I was asked to do a good amount of that and I tended always to accept. Very quickly my two political commissions took me about twenty hours a week and I could not keep my ordinary full-time job. I seemed to be eternally occupied and I was often annoyed with some of the men who did not take their part of the internal work.

Most of the routine work behind the curtain is done by women. Often we mutter and complain, but nevertheless we do the job. It is difficult for us to say 'No'. We say 'Yes' even when we do not want to do something. We easily get angry with whoever asked it of us. Women obey people, while men obey rules and laws. The tradition that women should live through men is still around to quite a large extent.

The leading politician

The female way of conducting yourself can lead to power, but it takes a longer time. I made myself dependent on my superiors and did a good job. People liked me. After nine years in politics I was number one on the voting ballot and became group leader for the opposition in the town government. I still had not learnt to be a good debater in the town council but I knew what I talked about and I was reliable. I worked hard on the unpaid behind-the-scenes jobs. Because of being a psychologist I also helped many people in personal matters. I was some sort of mother for the group. I was practically never free. In those first years I loved the job.

And in Lidingö it happened to be three women who made the preliminary decisions in all important issues. We were unique in Sweden. Despite being on opposing political sides, we met with the leading civil servants and discussed the budget or the buildings, the schools or the roads. Our meetings were open and informal. We laughed a lot. We could easily tell each other our personal views and sometimes state to meetings that we had to ask the others before we took our final stand in the town government. We also influenced each other and acknowledged that. One can say that we could put our respective cards openly on the table and discuss them.

The civil servants were able to compare our way of behaving with that of the earlier male group. The men had made the meetings much more formal. It never happened that one of them said that he might change his mind after talking to his group. To have his personal opinion overruled by his group would have been a token of weakness. They also denied being influenced by each other.

Women take their time to see the power struggle and to understand it. We concentrate on being clever and good while waiting for somebody to notice us and give us our due reward. So we get dependent on the powerful people while we play our obedient waiting game. We do dislike forward men who overtake us, and even more we dislike the few forward women who join the men in taking their own initiative. For women it is allowed to use the female way to get power – but not the male way. Female chiefs who have used the male way, with initiative, aggressiveness and demands, are sure to get some trouble, especially with their subordinate sisters. Men love to talk about how mean women can be in such a situation. They are right, but they do not see how most women generally hold themselves back because they have learned to do so, and, as I have said, they have also learned to live through men. Other ways of operating by women are often difficult for them to understand.

A democratic society like ours is supposed to be ruled by all the representatives of the people – not by the top politicians. If you have to judge the using of groups as a token of weakness you are apt to be autocratic – and naturally you find many women weak. This is another difficulty when women compete with men. Women do work more democratically which in fact makes many men distrust them.

A man is educated in the expectation that he will be judged by his position in society. For a woman, her position in her working-life is interesting and important but until recently has not usually been a necessity. Women tend to combine their different roles, and they are sensitive in all of them. For instance, the politician and the mother and the school psychologist and the sexual woman are one and the same. Attacks on any of the roles are taken personally and affect the other roles. People in politics and outside also discuss all the female roles together. Comments on how a female politician handles her other roles are common when she is being judged as a politician. When you judge a male politician, that is unusual. For instance, you do not talk of his role as a father; if he does not take any part in the education of his children that is no minus.

And men themselves do not mingle their different roles. If attacked on roles other than the political, they tend not to understand or to project the guilt on to others. They take away their private persons, which is quite consistent with the fact that men see themselves as doing things on behalf of their groups. You can talk on behalf of people even if you do not listen to them.

Leaving politics

I left my position as the leader of the opposition after four years. One of the reasons was that I did not get enough power to influence the things I found important. For instance, I got tired of writing reservations all the time when it came to buildings and child-care. Another reason was that I felt eaten up by my diary and I tended to have all my evenings and weekends taken over by political work.

Men seem to tolerate having all their time absorbed by work. Besides, they are better than women at saying no to things. Women leave political commissions more often than men do.

Study on local politicians

Finally, I shall discuss a study we did on politicians in our town in 1985. I proposed in a motion in the town council that we all should have a look at our feelings and attitudes to political work. Not only women but also men are worried by the fact that young people seem to avoid politics and that people elected to commissions often leave their positions after a very short time. So all parties in the town council agreed that the results of a questionnaire would be interesting. Another reason for my suggestion was the uncomfortable fact that people outside politics tend to be contemptuous of us. Being a woman with an urge to be liked I had to tackle this universal distrust.

Anonymously 187 of 220 politicians answered the questionnaire: 111 men and 76 women. Some of the questions concerned feelings. When asked about positive feelings there were not significant differences between the answers of the men compared to the women. When asked 'Do you often in your political work feel powerless, angry, insecure, or do you have a bad conscience?' there was quite a difference between men and women. The women felt more powerless (54 to 29 per cent), more angry (56 to 15 per cent), more insecure (52 to 14 per cent) and they suffered more from conscience (48 to 33 per cent). This in spite of the fact that Lidingo by that time was the only Swedish local government with a female majority in the town government.

We were also asked how we estimated outside opinions. There we agreed – men and women – that we were judged negatively as a group. People do not seem to trust politicians.

This study cannot be generalized but it gave a good indication that my feelings were shared by others. We all agreed in the town council that it was important to start talking of the feelings and the behaviours of politicians. Every party group had its own discussion on the findings.

One way to start a discussion on the political process is to tell about your own feelings and thoughts as a politician. That is what I have done in my book (Ricklander 1990) and in this chapter. Probably it is much easier for a woman to start such a talk than it is for a man. Since powerless and angry women are dangerous and denying men are apt to get heart attacks, it seems to be time to start talking.

Reference

Ricklander, L. (1990) *Bakom Politikerkollen*, Stockholm: Wahlstrom o Widstrand.

15 Women at work: reflections and perspectives

Jenny Firth-Cozens and Michael A. West

This chapter was to be our joint reflections on the themes of the book and the ways forward, but each of us found it particularly difficult to write on behalf of the other. This might have happened if we were both men or both women, but it feels to us as if it reflects our inevitably different experiences within the world of work. For this reason we are writing separately and then ending with a joint piece commenting on what's gone before. In this way we may understand one more strand of the processes and differences involved.

Speaking as a woman: Jenny Firth-Cozens

What is shocking, reading through the chapters again, is how little has changed for women in the last twenty years. Despite the consciousness raising of the early 1970s, the equal opportunities legislation, the changes made in something so fundamental as our language, in most countries our position in the world of work has barely altered at all (see the Appendices in *Women: A World Report* 1985 and the *Report of the Hansard Commission on Women at the Top* 1990).

The chapters and other writing and experience show us that there are three reasons why the changes are failing to occur. The first is that economic forces have not necessitated change. The second is that men – the vast proportion of the work-force with any power – do not want things to change. And the third is that women themselves are reluctant, or at least ambivalent, about helping change to come about.

Economic forces are a powerful vehicle of change. For example the ending of slavery in Britain was as much to do with the economic collapse of the sugar industry as it was with the power of a change agent like Wilberforce. It meant that keeping a slave work-force had become an unnecessary expense – better to let them be free when there was no work, even though many would starve as a result. We need-to remember such historic lessons over the next few years when an increasingly magnanimous attitude to women in the workplace is already beginning to take place due to the forecast shortage of workers.

If real advantage can be taken of the demographic changes that are anticipated this decade, then it may well be that some real improvements in women's position within the work-place can take place. There have been such improvements in the past, however. We have all read about women's ascendancy in the world of work during both world wars, as well as the almost instantaneous return to traditional roles once their labour was no longer needed: the power of economic forces strikes again! Having seen it happen twice this century, we can be sure that the next shortage of workers will have the same result if then there is a glut. We need therefore to pull together some of our personal and professional experience and research, as demonstrated within the chapters, to ensure that any gains made in the 1990s are maintained in the next millennium.

One of the primary needs is to change the power position of men and to make them feel that women in the work-place, at all levels, are no longer a frightening or disturbing concept – or, less strongly, a problem. One of the places that this should begin is with the conception of a couple's first child. Many of the chapters are concerned with the interface between work and home and the difficulties this poses for women. The literature they discuss makes it clear that society's norms still place the burden and the guilt of child-care very firmly upon the woman's shoulders: the problems faced when both parents work are seen as the responsibility of the mother and never of the father. This perception is almost universal – which means it is shared by both women and men.

This is one of the areas in which fundamental change is essential. Back in 1976 Dorothy Dinnerstein wrote in *The Rocking of the Cradle* that the key to future equality lay in creating equality of child-care. This is radically different from the movement of women demanding better crèche facilities: what it would mean instead would be that both women *and* men demand crèches; both women and men are 'returners' and job sharers and have special needs. Once this happens then women shed their role of being problematic and demanding within the work-place. Various schemes for those returning to work pay lip-service to 'parental leave', but the reality within the organization, from my experience, refers only to ways of retaining mothers.

I have no doubt that crèches will be provided when the economic need really arises. In India, for example, women work on building sites for 10 hours a day for 12 rupees (just enough to sustain life), but they have crèches (French 1985). It's all a matter of economics, and it seems vital that we do not become lured by such easy mechanistic approaches to change.

Equal parenting, it has been proposed by a number of feminist psychoanalysts (e.g. Chodorow 1979), would have more radical results than women ceasing to be labelled as problem workers. It would, it is argued, mean that the mother/women-in-general would no longer be despised by their sons and daughters for their dependency and weakness; nor would the defensive split between these characteristics and fathers' strength and power be so easy to make. With equal parenting daughters could see their mothers as having both strength and dependency in common with fathers while also able to separate out the attributes which make them different. For women who achieve this relinquishing of splitting – and it happens in psychotherapy (see the case of Jane in Firth 1985) – they no longer have to be either their father *or* their mother: they are enabled to be both nurturing *and* strong, to be sexual *and* business-like. Ending the defence of splitting (Lawrence 1985) can, I suspect, come about only by ending the dominance of the power within the home which is acted out day after day in the work-place. In this way the misogyny of the shopfloor, the boardroom – and even the women's room – should decline.

The other area which pervades the work-place and keeps woman as an object rather than a subject is sex. Janet Stockdale in Chapter 5 talks about blatant and subtle forms of sexual harassment, but also the female reproductive system (discussed by Jacqueline Bates Gaston in Chapter 6) is itself the subject of ridicule within the work-place: 'It must be the hormones' is a phrase levelled at women without a corresponding phrase applied to men, for example, 'It must be the alopetia'.

But also within any group of people sexuality exists and, to some extent, it is its denial that creates the problems. When sexuality is recognized rather than turned into sexiness and/or abuse then men and women can act as adults. This important point is discussed by Hirschhorn (1988) where he points out how, in western cultures, 'men fight each for the prizes of money and sex, whereas the competition among women is suppressed'. The shame this makes men feel, he suggests, is handled 'by developing their own locker room culture through which they degrade women' (1988: 138). Women, on the other hand, hide their competitiveness in a sisterhood but this and the locker-room are lost when women reach senior management: then both groups have to confront each other as sexual adults. It's a relief to be an adult, but difficult too. The fears that this brings about in both sexes can, in times of change, cause a reversion to an even stronger form of the old system: 'Men may parade in front of women with their tools, and women may regress to the status of dependents. The old balance is lost' (Hirschhorn 1988: 139). An up-market version of the locker-room is the Masons, and the effects that such powerful movements might have in maintaining men in top positions have never been investigated in terms of discrimination against women.

These are all large-scale society changes, but we know from the happenings in Eastern Europe in 1989 that they can take place when the need really arises and those who are demanding change act together with one voice. Women represent more than half the world's population, so what is it that stops them acting for their benefit? In this volume Louise Ricklander in Chapter 14 makes a number of points in terms of their lack of assertiveness, their guilt, and the very different ways they have in tackling work issues. She also writes about the differences in the way women and men approach meetings and the language used at them. Language is all we have to think with and to plan, and the words we use can limit or enable a different future (Spender 1980). Changing the language of work must therefore help to change perceptions for both men and women; we still have seemingly entrenched phrases propping up the image of an exclusively male working world, for example we have 'the right man for the job', 'man-power', we 'man the post', and we work 'man hours'.

How can women change in order to achieve what they want in the work-place? One area of relevant research is Matina Horner's work (e.g. Horner 1972) which suggests strongly that women fear success. Despite a number of papers from other authors which have failed to uphold her original findings, the controversy remains on the boil perhaps because of an intuitive feeling that women do have a motive to avoid success (Hyde 1985) which certainly shows itself within those presenting for psychotherapy (Kanefield 1985). This ambivalence may come from society's view of what it means to be successful; for example Mead's (1949) statement – 'Each step forward as a successful American regardless of sex means a step back as a woman' – is still applicable today. It may also come from the rarely mentioned fact that women do to some extent have a choice which is not available to men: many of them *can* choose not to have a career but to be a full- or part-time mother, and choice is bound to create ambivalance because career paths are hard. Again, equal parenting will give both men and women the choice.

This ambivalence may also be one reason why women themselves also choose to keep their myths, as Jacqueline Bates Gaston points out they do in relation to the pre-menstrual syndrome. Eichenbaum and Orbach (1983), in *What Do Women Want?*, discuss this ambivalence in terms of the urge for dependency.

So what should women do? Looking at what they really want seems an important first step. Learning cognitive strategies – for example, to deal with guilt and with their attributional style of blaming themselves when things go wrong, and naming others when they have a success (Ickes and Layden 1978) – would also be useful. Keeping abreast of media trends and influencing the media at every opportunity is also vital: the return to the house which took place in the 1950s was very much a media-induced activity which made much of women being once more 'feminine' and domesticated.

In addition we need to become much more powerful in influencing the world of education and the training of teachers. Peggy Newton's Chapter 11 on the huge fall of women within the computing world is a sad reflection of how important schools can be in changing the posssibilities which are open.

But a question which underlies many of the chapters is whether, to bring about change, women should become more like men. Bem's work on adrogeny (Bem 1974) appeared to encourage this, as well as encouraging men to adopt certain feminine traits. However, this tends to support the idea that there are female and male traits and this is the basis for sexual stereotyping. Bem has therefore more recently changed her thesis (Bem 1985) to argue that these traits come from a belief system which organizes our world into the feminine and the masculine.

In terms of women's aiming for masculinity rather than adrogyny, as many women have tried to do, especially in the world of business, this may still be seen as deviant by colleagues. This no-win situation was described by a young graduate management trainee in Cooper and Davidson:

> I tried to be more like the men I worked with but that didn't really work as they wouldn't accept me anyway, regardless of what role I played.
>
> (Cooper and Davidson 1982: 75)

Perhaps change will come when, alongside the strategies discussed above, men also begin to welcome less narrow career paths, and there are many signs that this is starting to happen, even within fields such as medicine, as I showed in Chapter 10. As values and the criteria for success change, as the forecasts suggest they will, then many aspects of women's lives – the part-time work, job-sharing, home-working, career change – will begin to be welcomed by men, thus providing the possibility of new opportunities for women. It is clear that there is no one strategy for change: women are vastly different from each other, and some might argue that their lives and resources differ far more than they as a group differ from men. For this reason attempts at change should take place on every front – individual, group and societal.

Speaking as a man: Michael West

Writing my reflections on the contents of the book is a difficult task for two reasons. It is difficult primarily because of the emotional reactions they create in me, and secondly because the enormity of the changes required in the world of work are dauntingly great.

Perhaps the most important of the two to consider is my emotional reactions since they are likely to be similar to those felt by many men when confronted by the demand to change their behaviour and expectations at work. The range of emotional reactions that I have to the contents of the book is dominated by guilt. As a man my reaction is to plead guilty as charged. Moreover, I am guilty of other crimes which should be taken into consideration and a great number of which I am not even aware. The motivation arising from such guilt may well be an intent to change behaviour and to learn how to interact with women at work in ways which do not discriminate or abuse, however subtly.

There are feelings of anger too towards those who overtly abuse and harass women; those who publicly ridicule, patronize and privately despise; those who through their humour portray an aggressive emotional intent paralleled physically only in the viciousness of rape. But there is fear too of the anger of women who may react without discrimination against all men. And fear of the anger of those who do discriminate, but who may catch me in the act of another sexist comment or practice, no matter how careful I have tried to be. There is also anxiety that for all I might change my language and dutifully champion the causes of equal opportunities and anti-sexism, in truth, these changes, like those that have occurred in the 1970s and 1980s in organizations, are skin deep. It may only be a conscience-salving treatment rather than a fundamental realignment of my world view, which remains privately comfortable with things as they are.

Related to this is the feeling that espousing the causes of women in the world of work has disturbing echoes of wanting to please the mother. These echoes produce resistance and unwillingness to play the appeasing child to the angry mother; resentment of the source of the anger and a shifting of blame to others or back to the mother herself. Dominant though is a feeling of sadness at the pain, waste, dishonesty and loss of real relationships which attitudes of men towards women at work have caused – and this is perhaps the other peak in the range.

Contrition is no match for the economic and political forces which sustain men's attitudes and behaviours towards women and the preceding chapters indicate that change, where it has occurred, in the world of work, has been surface rather than deep. In the occupational psychology research unit within which I work, the director, research team leaders and tenured staff are all men. The short-term contract research staff include a minority of women while part-time, support, secretarial and cleaning staff are all women. Yet some 80 per cent of the trainee occupational psychologists are women. How little has changed in recruitment, selection and promotion practices when even an informed institution which studies the world of work, itself perpetuates the inequalities and ineffectiveness it seeks to identify. At the organizational as well as at the individual level, it is easier for men to do nothing about these issues.

One step suggested by Colwill and Vinnicombe in Chapter 4 is for women-only training but this idea might well be extended to men-only training focusing on the topic 'Working with Women'. In such training men could safely make explicit and discuss the kinds of feelings I have described above as well as other concerns about apparent threats to job security, promotion and status. The deeper issues about men's resistance to women bosses and how they behave towards women colleagues could also be examined.

It seems clear however that as long as men and women continue to work for change at the individual level of behaviour, success will be only on the surface. Structural and cultural change is required for organizations not to perpetuate past practice, and this is likely to be achieved only by determined political action within the organization. Men-only groups might examine what policy changes are required in the organization, and more importantly how they might be brought about.

Janet Stockdale's Chapter 5 on sexual harassment at work makes for disturbing reading and it seems an area where conflict and defensiveness are most likely to arise in discussion. Whenever I have raised the issue within organizations in mixed or men-only groups, the ensuing discussions have tended to begin with polite concern and end in vituperative disagreement, with a sharp gender divide. This may well be because most men feel some guilt about the issue and most women have been victims in some subtle or blatant form. Moreover, as Jenny Firth-Cozens points out, denying adult sexuality simply compounds the problem. The challenge remains as to how clear guidelines and disciplinary procedures can be implemented and, again, it requires men to actively participate in the process of their introduction. Organizations concerned with recruitment problems in the next decade could make their cultures less threatening to women by incorporating sessions on policies for preventing and managing sexual harassment in all management training and development programmes. At the same time it must be clear that disciplinary action will be taken against those who harass, so that the stated policies do not come to be seen as simply a sop to the feminist movement.

Jenny Firth-Cozens has argued strongly for equal parenting and there are many advantages for men in such a proposal. First, they are enabled to take on more fully the role of parent and experience the attendant depth of feelings of parenting. For most men such feelings are only transient because their contact with their children is not sustained. Such experience enables men to develop as human beings through exploring their parenthood more fully and integrating that aspect of themselves into their lives.

I have argued elsewhere (West 1990) that the qualities of parenting are required in healthy organizations and could well be nurtured and rewarded in enlightened organizations of the future. We need to learn how to protect, develop and train those within the organization (and within society) who have not yet acquired the knowledge or skills to function effectively, in order that they become fully functioning, effective and contributing members of the organization (and society). This also means encouraging people to think independently and to be prepared to exercise political power for change within organizations. At the very least, if men were to take on their parenting role fully it would provide a powerful antidote to the careerist and workaholic additions which damage so many people's lives.

Again, it requires men to be actively and separately involved in agitating for long paternity leave without career jeopardy. Women's demands are often dismissed by organizational power brokers but the concerted action of minority groups of men arguing for such a change could have important impacts. Such action could raise consciousness about gender issues generally as well as alerting organizations to the justification for long paternity (as well as maternity) leave of up to (say) five years.

In summary, it seems that change will occur in organizations only if change agents acknowledge that the issues are to do with politics and power. Creditable and necessary as individual action is, men and women have to act at the organizational level if deep change is to be effected. This means forming active, consistent, coherent, persistent minority groups within organizations, which are prepared for conflict and willing to accept unpopularity. The work of Moscovici *et al.* (1985) has demonstrated that such groups, through intelligent and consistent argument, and a sensitivity to the concerns of those they seek to affect, can be effective in changing culture. Powerful economic and social forces have contributed to change in Eastern Europe in 1989 and 1990 even against great resistance, and it might be argued that similar forces are behind change in relation to women at work. But men and women do not yet represent a cohesive social force with shared goals in this issue – nor yet do women alone. The resisting economic and social forces are also powerful. Organizations and men collectively have strong reasons for not changing. However, there are some signs which may be a cause for optimism.

The Green movement of the 1980s has begun to change the way that people think about their environment. This may force us to consider not just what we can get from the environment but how we should care for it as well. It may be that the transformation of the next millenium will be one in which nurturant views of the planet and people come to dominate; wresting from nature is transformed to working with nature; the traditional roles of women become valued for all; the stereotypical pathology of the aggressive grasping man is healed; and more holistic understandings of ourselves as men and as women are developed.

If organizations are to attract employees, they too must demonstrate a concern about and sensitivity to environmental and human social issues. However, as long as these changes are located at the individual level and do not translate through organized group action into organizational policies, change will continue to be surface rather than deep. Deep change will require a dramatic shift of cultures at work from those where relationships are subordinated to success and in which the currency of interactions is measured by task effectiveness to the exclusion of value expression. The signs are increasingly that the planet itself demands such a shift and this imperative ironically may be what finally produces deep changes in gender relations in society and the world of work.

Conclusion

We are pleased to see together within these chapters such an unexpectedly large body of research developing on women and work, but we are also aware of the very areas that are unrepresented. While the first two parts of the book cover themes and issues common to all women, the chapters of the third part refer to predominantly middle-class careers. There are within them glaring omissions such as nurses, teachers and housekeepers and they cover western, largely British, experience. The discipline used to study them is predominantly psychology, although both sociology and anthropology have equally useful tools to explore such important areas of human life. Finally, the research methods used in the majority of studies are still largely traditionally positivist, despite many arguments from feminists against this being the most useful method for studying experience.

Nevertheless the unusual amount of qualitative data contained in the chapters in the form of women's words suggests that female researchers are asking and receiving real accounts of experiences to enrich the quantitative data they collect.

We hope that the book will be a platform for future studies, perhaps from a variety of disciplines using a number of methodologies, and attending to the experiences of working women around the world.

References

Bem, S. L. (1974) The measurement of psychological androgyny, *Journal of Consulting and Clinical Psychology*, 42: 155–62.

——(1985) Androgyny and gender scheme theory: a conceptual and empirical integration. In T. B. Sonderegger (ed.) *Nebraska Symposium on Motivation, 1984; The Psychology of Gender, Current Theory and Research in Motivation*, 32: 179–226, Lincoln: University of Nebraska Press.

Chodorow, N. (1979) Feminism and difference: gender relation and difference in psychoanalytic perspective, *Socialist Review*, 46: 42–64.

Cooper, C. and Davidson, M. (1982) *High Pressure: Working Lives of Women Managers*, London: Fontana.

Dinnerstein, D. (1976) *The Rocking of the Cradle, The Ruling of the World*, London: Souvenir Press.

Eichenbaum, L. and Orbach, S. (1983) *What Do Women Want?*, London: Fontana.

Firth, J. (1985) Personal meanings of occupational stress, *Journal of Occupational Psychology*, 58: 139–48.

French, M. (1985) Women and work: India, in *Women: A World Report*, London: Methuen.

Hirschhorn, L. (1988), *The Workplace Within*, London: MIT Press.

Horner, M. (1972) Toward an understanding of achievement-related conflicts in women, *Journal of Social Issues*, 28: 157–76.

Hyde, J. (1985) *Half the Human Experience: The Psychology of Women*, Lexington, Mass: D. C. Heath.

Ickes, W. and Layden, M. A. (1978) Attributional styles, in J. H. Harvey, W. Ickes and R. F. Kidd (eds) *New Directions in Attribution Research*, vol. 2, Hillsdale, NJ: Erlbaum.

Kanefield, L. A. (1985) Psychoanalytic constructions of female development and women's conflicts about achievement, pts 1–2, *Journal of the American Academy of Psychoanalysis*, 13: 229–46, 347–66.

Lawrence, W. G. (1985) Religious transformations, *Changes*, 3: 45–9.

Mead, M. (1949) *Male and Female*, New York: Morrow.

Moscovici, A, Mugny, G. and Avermaet, E. U. (1985) *Perspectives in Minority Influences*, Cambridge: Cambridge University Press.

Report of the Hansard Society Commission on Women at the Top (1990) London: Hansard Society for Parliamentary Government.

Spender, D. (1980) *Man Made Language*, London: Routledge.

West, M. A. (1990) The world of work, in R. Brown (ed.) *You and the Community: Living in Groups*, Oxford: Andromeda Press.

Women: A World Report (1985) London: Methuen.

Author Index

Subject Index